MOVING
FOR
MARRIAGE

SUNY series, Genders in the Global South

———————

Debra A. Castillo and Shelley Feldman, editors

MOVING
FOR
MARRIAGE

Inequalities, Intimacy, and
Women's Lives in Rural North India

Shruti Chaudhry

Published by State University of New York Press, Albany

Printed in the United States of America

For information, contact State University of New York Press, Albany, NY
www.sunypress.edu

Library of Congress Cataloging-in-Publication Data

Name: Chaudhry, Shruti, 1982– author.
Title: Moving for marriage : inequalities, intimacy, and women's lives in
    rural North India / Shruti Chaudhry.
Description: Albany : State University of New York Press, [2021] | Series:
    SUNY series, Genders in the Global South | Includes bibliographical
    references and index.
Identifiers: LCCN 2021028918 (print) | LCCN 2021028919 (ebook) | ISBN
    9781438485577 (hardcover : alk. paper) | ISBN 9781438485584 (pbk. : alk.
    paper) | ISBN 9781438485591 (ebook)
Subjects: LCSH: Marriage—India—Uttar Pradesh—Case studies. | Married
    women—India—Uttar Pradesh—Social conditions—Case studies. | Uttar
    Pradesh (India)—Rural conditions—Case studies. | Uttar Pradesh
    (India)—Regional disparities—Case studies.
Classification: LCC HQ670.15.U8 C43 2021 (print) | LCC HQ670.15.U8
    (ebook) | DDC 306.810954/2—dc23
LC record available at https://lccn.loc.gov/2021028918
LC ebook record available at https://lccn.loc.gov/2021028919

10 9 8 7 6 5 4 3 2 1

*For the women of Barampur, who let me into their lives
and shared their stories with me*

Contents

Illustrations

Maps

Tables

Acknowledgments

This book is based on my doctoral research, which was supported by the University of Edinburgh College Research Studentship and Edinburgh Global Overseas Research Scholarship. I would like to start by thanking my doctoral supervisors, Patricia Jeffery and Mary Holmes. My work has been enriched immensely by Patricia Jeffery's experience of four decades of work in Uttar Pradesh, her insightful comments, and her meticulous attention to detail. Since the completion of my PhD, she has continued to be an informal academic mentor. I constantly turn to her for advice and she has always provided reassurance and support, for which I shall always be grateful. Thanks to Mary Holmes for her optimism and for always having something nice to say. Thanks too for nudging me in the direction of family sociology; it has been a fruitful journey. A special thank-you to Kaveri Qureshi, who has always been so generous with her time. Thanks, Kaveri, for helping me to conceive of a doctoral thesis as a book, for reading drafts, and for directing me to things to read. Most of all, thank you for your friendship. Lynn Jamieson's work on intimacy has provided much inspiration for this book. I feel very lucky to have her as a postdoctoral mentor. I am grateful to several other people who have helped and supported me since I first moved to Edinburgh: Crispin Bates, Hugo Gorringe, Liliana Riga, Lotte Hoek, Michael Rosie, Ross Bond, Steven Sutcliffe, Sumeet Jain, and Wilfried Swenden.

In India, a big thank-you to Indrani Mazumdar and Rajni Palriwala. I am particularly thankful for your support and advice during what was very challenging fieldwork. The idea of this research was planted while working on a project on gender and migration in India. Thanks, Indrani, for giving me the opportunity to work with you on this project. More so, thanks for the many conversations on the personal and the political. Your insights always make me think more deeply about things. The numerous discussions I have had with Rajni Palriwala since my time as a masters student in Delhi have profoundly shaped this work. Thank you for your time, for continuing to read drafts, and for providing feedback. Our conversations, when I was completing work on this manuscript, helped me to sharpen the arguments of this book. I hope this book will live up to your expectations. Thanks, too, to Ravinder Kaur for her interest in my work and for her encouragement and suggestions, which have been valuable.

I am greatly indebted to the women of Barampur who welcomed me into their homes and shared their lived experiences with me. Without them, this book would not have been possible. Thanks are also due to the family whose home I stayed in for the duration of the fieldwork and several others who helped with entry and access in the field.

Thank you to Carl Denig, Ceren Şengül, Daniel Cetrà, Eirik Magnus Fuglestad, Konstantinos Kostagiannis, and Neşe Kınıkoğlu, for being such wonderful friends. Thanks to Taneesha Devi Mohan for being my companion during the migration project, for pushing me to apply for a PhD, and for helping out with maps and census data. For decades of friendship and unending support, thank you to Reet Lamba and Taniya O'Connor.

I am very thankful for the support of my siblings, Anirudh, Priyanka and Smriti and I owe a special thanks to my parents. Thanks ma, for your enormous strength and for always letting me make my own choices. My father had been looking forward to seeing this book published but he passed away before he could see it. He would have read it with great interest.

Sunita Masi, thank you for always being there. Thanks, too, to my mother-in-law, Liz, for being so thoughtful and for being my family in Edinburgh. Daniel, thank you so much for all the small and large acts of kindness, for your patience, your love, and most of all your humor. Thanks for supporting me as I completed the PhD and this book. I have enjoyed sharing it all with you.

Lastly, I would like to acknowledge the publishers that allowed me to rework material from previously published articles. The introduction and chapters 1, 3, and 4 contain excepts from "'Flexible' caste boundaries: Cross-regional marriage as mixed marriage in rural north India," published in *Contempory South Asia* in 2019, reprinted by permission of the publisher, Taylor & Francis Ltd. Earlier versions of sections that appear in chapter 2 were originally published in the book chapter "'Now it is difficult to get married': Contextualizing cross-regional marriage and bachelorhood in a north Indian village in 2018," reprinted by permission from Springer Nature.

Chapter 7 derives in part from an article published in *Modern Asian Studies* in 2019 titled " 'For how long can your *Piharwāle* intervene?': Accessing natal kin support in rural north India," reprinted with permission of the copyright holder, Cambridge University Press. Thanks, too, to Rebecca Colesworthy at SUNY Press for her enthusiasm and for her prompt replies to all the queries I sent her way.

Introduction

> In my next life, I hope I am not born a woman and if I am, I will not get married.
>
> —Sarla, 48

> *Shādī bakwās hai* [marriage is rubbish]. No one should get married . . . but marriage is *zarūrī* [compulsory] . . . since I got married, I have never felt *kī sahī hai* [that it is correct/right] . . . *par nibhānā partā hai* [but it is a relationship you have to keep].
>
> —Jaya, 45

Both Jaya and Sarla had moved to Barampur village,[1] in the north India state of Uttar Pradesh, following marriage. Sarla had moved from a nearby district, while for Jaya, this move had entailed traveling over 1200 kilometers from her native state of West Bengal, crossing multiple boundaries—of region, state, language and caste—to become a wife in what I term a "cross-regional marriage," in contrast to a "regional marriage." Since the early 2000s, cross-regional marriages have become the subject of much media speculation in India and internationally (e.g., Agal 2006; DHNS 2019; Huggler 2009; Masoodi 2014; Siwach 2010; Bajwa 2019; Bedi 2003; Raghavan 2015). These reports condemned the "buying" and "trafficking" of "poor" women from the southern, eastern, and non-eastern states of the country to men in India's bride-deficit northern and northwestern states—Gujarat, Haryana, Rajasthan, Punjab, and Uttar Pradesh. The reports provided descriptions of "hundreds of thousands of women and girls forced into sexual and domestic slavery" (del Estal 2018), being "sold like cows and goats" and "treated as commodities" that could be "recycled and resold" (Gooch & Jolley 2016).

1

What also appeared were reports of NGOs involved in the "rescue and rehabilitation" of "trafficked" women "coerced into marriage."[2] In the midst of this, the issue also became the subject of academic work that described these as "across-region," "bride-import," "cross-border," "cross-region," and "long-distance" marriages (Ahlawat 2009, 2016; Blanchet 2008; Chaudhry & Mohan 2011; Ibrahim 2018; Kaur 2004, 2010a, 2012; Kukreja 2018a, 2018b; Kukreja & Kumar 2013; Mishra 2016; Mukherjee 2013). These studies note the bringing of brides not only from other regions but also across the border from Bangladesh and Nepal.

This research stemmed from an interest in interrogating the moral panic around the status of "trafficked" women who became brides in geographically distant and culturally distinct rural communities. Unlike existing studies on the topic, however, it not only makes cross-regional marriage the subject of analysis but incorporates a focus on regional marriage as well. This book is, thus, about the post-marital experiences of women, like both Sarla and Jaya, who *migrate for marriage* to this rural context. The central argument of the book is that in everyday contexts, many of the difficulties that cross-regional brides face are in fact shared by women married regionally. By distinguishing where distance and regional origins make a difference, I will aim to address the undue attention to supposedly "problematic" or "foreign" wives, who are brought from far away. I begin with a discussion of some of the key issues that have emerged in the literature on cross-regional marriages in India.

Cross-regional marriages have been described as a "new" phenomenon (Kukreja & Kumar 2013, p. 5), "hitherto undocumented," "unusual," or "unconventional" (Kaur 2004, pp. 2595–2596), even though several studies suggest that such marriages have a long history in the northern region.[3] Writing on Punjab in 1925, Malcolm Darling, for instance, described "a regular traffic of women . . . imported from the hills of Kangra, the plains of the Ganges and the deserts of Bikaner" ([1928] 1977, pp. 49–50). More recent ethnographic studies also describe cases of the "buying of wives" in the 1970s and 1980s in villages of north India (Jeffery & Jeffery 1996, pp. 75–77; Raheja 1988, p. 236; Sharma 1980, p. 141). Studies suggest that while such marriages have existed historically, they are no longer exceptional (Chaudhry & Mohan 2011), with men of almost every caste bringing cross-regional brides (Kaur 2004) and the influx of brides into the north Indian states increasing over the years (Mishra 2016).[4] Ravinder Kaur contends that long-distance, cross-region marriage is becoming "a socially, if not numerically, significant category of marriage migration in India" (2012, p. 79).

In the academic writing, three significant issues have highlighted how cross-regional marriages represent a "new" and undocumented type of marriage pattern. First, these marriages have been explained as resulting from compulsions in both bride-sending and bride-receiving regions. In the former, the inability to provide a dowry for daughters due to poverty has been identified as the primary explanation. Other factors identified include being "socially over age by local standards" (Mishra 2016, p. 223), failed previous marriage, "girl not attractive," family violence, or lack of interest on the part of fathers in arranging a marriage (Blanchet 2008, p. 172; Kaur 2012, p. 80). Scholars have also explained long-distance marriage migration in terms of a desire to move from poorer to more desirable regions (Kaur 2004, 2010a): what William Lavely (1991), in the Chinese context, describes as "spatial hypergamy." In the bride-receiving regions, bride shortages due to masculine sex ratios combined with other forms of "disadvantage": unemployment, landlessness or marginal landownership, hard labor occupations, physical disability, lack of education, "older" age or prior marital status (these may be secondary marriages for men), and "flawed" reputation (Blanchet 2008; Chaudhry & Mohan 2011; Chowdhry 2005; Kaur 2004; Mishra 2016) have been understood as the primary explanation for men seeking brides from other states.

Masculine sex ratios had been identified as a long-term trend in India by the 1960s and '70s (CSWI 1974). There is a large body of literature that has discussed not only pronounced son-preference (Agarwal & Unisa 2007; Arnold et al. 1998; Bhat & Sharma 2006; Das Gupta 1987; ICRW 2014; Miller 1997) but also "daughter aversion"—the growing unwantedness of daughters and the idea that they can be "dispensed with" (John et al. 2009, p. 18)—as explanations. The northwestern region of India—Punjab, Haryana, Rajasthan, Maharashtra, Madhya Pradesh, Gujarat, parts of Uttar Pradesh, as well as the capital city of Delhi—has highly imbalanced sex ratios, while the southern and eastern states (barring a few pockets) have comparatively better sex ratios (Kaur 2020). Pronounced son-preference has been a longstanding component of the "northern demographic regime" (Dyson & Moore 1983) related to patrilineal systems of descent, inheritance, and patterns of post-marital residence and dowry (Das Gupta 1987; John et al. 2009; Miller 1981, 1997). Son preferences is linked to such behaviors as bias in intra-household distribution of food and nutritive elements and poor medical care during illness of girl children (Agnihotri 2001, 2003; Bhat & Sharma 2006), what Barbara Miller (1997) describes as "sex selective child care."

Until the 1980s, masculine child sex ratios reflected differential care of girls and boys that led to higher rates of infant and child mortality among girls. Since the mid-1980s, new technologies (first amniocentesis and later ultrasound) became widely available in India. Initially developed to aid the detection of fetal abnormalities, they came to be increasingly used to determine the sex of the fetus and were then followed by sex-selective abortion (Jeffery 2014). Pre-natal sex determination and selection has continued unabated (George 2002; Patel 2007) despite legislation that made pre-natal sex determination illegal. In 1994, the Government of India formulated the Pre-Natal Diagnostic Techniques (Regulation and Prevention of Misuse) Act, which came into force in 1996 and has been amended twice since—in 1996 and then in 2003.

Furthermore, northern India has witnessed a fertility decline that has been accompanied by couples' increasing efforts to affect the gender balance of their children (Guilmoto 2008; Guilmoto and Attané 2007) contributing to the persisting gender imbalance.[5] Family planning policies such as the "two-child norm" have also contributed to reinforcing the rationale for sex selection and the devaluation of daughters (Kaur 2020). A consequence of the sex ratio imbalance has been a "mismatch in the marriageable population," what demographers describe as a "marriage squeeze" (Guilmoto 2012; Kaur 2016), that is already unfolding in the northern states, with cross-regional marriages being one response to it. This parallels other Asian contexts (China, South Korea, Japan, and Taiwan) where demographic and social changes have rendered some men similarly "disadvantaged" and "unmarriageable" within local contexts, resulting in bride import (Bossen 2007; Davin 2008; Fan & Huang 1998; Freeman 2005; Kim 2010; Lee 2012; Lu 2008; Min & Eades 1995).

A second key issue that emerged in the literature on cross-regional marriage is that such marriages "deviate" from north Indian marriage norms: parentally arranged, endogamous (within the caste and religious group), following norms of *gotrā* (clan/lineage) and territorial or village exogamy (outside the clan, village, and neighboring villages) with a limited marriage distance between a woman's place of birth and marriage (outside the village, but usually within the district or in a neighbouring district). Patri-virilocality is the predominant pattern of post-marital residence, with dowry being the accepted and honorable form of marriage payment. These norms give a particular color to marriage as a continuing "strategy" for social reproduction (Bourdieu 1976, 1977). Marriage is thus regulated and breaches are not tolerated. Indeed, they are often punished with violence termed "honour" crimes or killings (Chakravarti 2005; Chowdhry 2007; Mody 2008). I use the term "regional marriage" to describe all marriages that conform to the aforementioned norms.[6]

By contrast, cross-regional marriages cross regional and even international boundaries and so entail very long-distance migration for marriage, being inter-caste and sometimes inter-religious. Studies argue that such marriages are "accepted" in a context where breaches in caste and marriage norms are otherwise not tolerated (Chowdhry 2005; Kaur 2004; Mishra 2016). These marriages are not self-arranged "love" marriages in defiance of parental authority and caste and community norms. In most cases, they are initiated by the grooms and "accepted" by their families and their caste and village communities despite being inter-caste or inter-religious. Janaki Abraham describes this coexistence of "honour" killings and cross-regional marriages in the north as an "endogamy paradox" (2014, p. 57). Further, these are dowryless marriages: the groom meets the marriage expenses, and the "go-between" who mediates the arrangement often receives a payment. This has resulted in the categorization of cross-regional marriages as "bride-buying" and "trafficking" (Blanchet 2008; Chaudhry & Mohan 2011; Kaur 2004). The writing on cross-border marriages, especially the so called "mail-order brides," has also noted a similar tendency to label all women in such marriages as "commodities" and "trafficked" women (Constable 2005, 2009; Nakamatsu 2003).[7]

The third issue highlighted in the scholarly writing is that the spouses in cross-regional marriages belong to different cultural and linguistic backgrounds and the incoming bride faces a difficult process of adjustment. A question that has generated much interest relates to the incorporation of cross-regional brides, of uncertain origins, in the receiving communities. As with the journalistic accounts, some academic work has supported a "victim" narrative focusing on the "harsh lives and the low status" of such brides (Blanchet 2008, p. 177). Prem Chowdhry writes, "Not more than bonded labor they are subjected to extensive exploitation of all kinds" (2005, p. 5195). Likewise, Reena Kukreja argues that there exists "caste discrimination, ethnoracist prejudice, forcible cultural assimilation, and religious othering on a daily basis" (2018b, p. 383; see also 2018a and Kukreja & Kumar 2013). Other studies have attempted to counter this "victim" narrative. Paro Mishra (2016), for instance, argues that such marriages have become the norm in Haryana. Ravinder Kaur maintains, "Not all marriages are a failure and not all brides are unhappy after the initial adjustment. . . . It would be an incomplete representation of the truth to argue that companionate conjugality fails to develop in all such marriages" (2012, pp. 83, 85). Furthermore, some of these studies explore the post-marital experiences of cross-regional brides, at times drawing parallels and contrasts with "local brides" but making only cross-regional marriages the subject of analysis.

The existing academic studies on cross-regional marriage, thus, provide conflicting depictions, either supporting accounts of widespread discrimination and victimization of brides in receiving communities, or arguing that discrimination is exceptional and brides are accepted in tradition-bound rural communities. My research tells a more complicated story about women's location within patrilineal, patri-virilocal marriage. It aims to highlight variations in women's lived experiences shaped not only by their regional origins, but also by their stage in the life-course and their embeddedness in relations of caste, religion, class, and gender. This book adopts a comparative approach. It not only assumes cross-regional marriages as problematic but it problematizes "normal" or regional marriages as well. I situate the book in recent debates about "the trouble with marriage" in India (Basu 2015; Basu and Ramberg 2015) and similar discussions on the (also) troublesome nature of couple relationships in the West (Jamieson 1998, 1999, 2011). The book will integrate and engage with these two forms of critique to provide an empirically informed approach to the gendering of intimacy in a Global South arranged marriage context.

The Trouble with Marriage Is Marriage

Srimati Basu writes that marriage is "at the core of gender trouble" (2015, p. 216). The troubled institution of heterosexual marriage has long been the subject of critique for Western feminists who have addressed women's economic dependency and violence within marriage (Barrett & Mcintosh 1982; Delphy & Leonard 1992; Dobash & Dobash 1980; Pateman 1988). In more recent sociological writing in the West, much of the discussion on couple relationships has followed Anthony Giddens's (1992) claims that processes of social change characteristic of late modernity have resulted in the weakening of traditional social structures such as the family. No longer bound by tradition or external constraints, individuals thus have greater choice and agency to develop and maintain relationships for their "own sake." He argues that what distinguishes present-day relationships from past decades is the emergence of "the pure relationship" and "confluent love" in which equality results from "mutual self-disclosure" (p. 6). He postulates that a "transformation of intimacy" is underway (p. 3) and states that a pure relationship

> refers to a situation where a social relation is entered for its own sake, for what can be derived by each person from a sustained association with another; and which is continued only in so far as it is thought by both parties to deliver enough satisfaction for each individual to stay in it. . . . Marriage—for many, but by no means all groups in the population—has veered increasingly towards the form of a pure relationship. (p. 58)

Giddens argues that romantic love has for long affected women's aspirations more than men's. He distinguishes "confluent love" from romantic love, arguing that the latter has been replaced by the former: "confluent love is active, contingent love, and therefore jars with the 'fore-ever,' 'one-and-only' qualities of the romantic love complex" (p. 61). While romantic love is "imbalanced in gender terms," "confluent love presumes equality." He writes, "Love here only develops to the degree to which intimacy does, to the degree to which each partner is prepared to reveal concerns and needs to the other" (p. 62). For him, intimacy leads to democracy (p. 188). At the same time, he sees problems with heterosexual relationships, as they are intrinsically imbalanced. He contends that "men's anger against women" in some substantial part is a reaction against women's claims for equality in their relationships that drives the pure relationship (p. 149).

The idea that couple relationships have become more equal has been widely debated (Jamieson 1998, 1999). Based on a review of empirical studies on marriage and couple relationships in Euro-American contexts, Lynn Jamieson points to "persistent inequalities" (1998, p. 138). She draws attention to the asymmetrical compromises that women make, at times muting discontent and even rationalizing inequality, whether around the household division of work, parenting, sex, or their partner's emotional absence or lack of participation in the relationship, in order to sustain marriage (see more recently Carter 2012; Twamley & Faircloth 2015). Jamieson considers the "pure relationship" to be a "near impossibility" for domestic partnerships that are embroiled in material and financial concerns over and above the relationship (1999, p. 490). Furthermore, she argues that while for Giddens, mutual self-disclosure is the key to the "pure relationship," empirical evidence suggests that it is neither the sole nor necessarily the ascendant type of intimacy between couples (p. 485). Giddens offers an approving view of women's claims for gender equality in personal relationships but does little to engage with the body of earlier feminist work that has long addressed these issues.

In the Indian context, too, some scholars have engaged with Giddens's thesis. Jonathan Parry writes approvingly of a nascent trend toward companionate marriage. He sees companionate marriage differently from Giddens, for whom it is "a kind of attenuation of the pure relationship" (Parry 2001, p. 788). Like Giddens, he argues that there has been a "new ideological stress on the couple" yet differs from him with regard to his claims around the possibilities for "de-coupling" (p. 816). He supports Giddens's argument that intimacy leads to equality. Caroline Osella (2012) critiques both Giddens and Parry and expresses dismay that academics are so deeply "embedded within their own modernist liberal expectations of a pure love" that they evaluate so negatively "sacrifice, compromise, the little touch of pragmatic adjustment and realism, the love enmeshed in the everyday messiness of domestic duties and hidden bargainings" (2012, p. 242). Other scholars have explored questions of equality in discussions of companionate marriage that has emerged as an ideal in some Indian settings (Gilbertson 2014; Reddy 2006; Twamley 2012) and that has been described by Jennifer S. Hirsch and Holly Wardlow as representing a "global shift in marital ideals" (2006, p. 2). These scholars explore the primacy given to emotional intimacy, desire, and love not only in the making of marriage but also in the ways in which companionate ideals frame marriage itself as an affective project. In keeping with the findings from other contexts, they conclude that despite the shifts in marital expectations, couple relationships remain inegalitarian.

Another stand of scholarship points to the normalizing and marginalizing function of marriage. Over two decades ago, John Borneman wrote on anthropology's failure to subject marriage to a "rigorous critique." He stressed the need to understand marriage as a "privilege" that operates through "exclusionary means . . . a series of foreclosures and abjections, through the creation of an 'outside'" (1996, p. 216). Marriage, thus, "circumscribes the realm of the legitimate" (Biswas 2011, p. 425) and thereby marginalizes those "who fall outside its parameters or never enter it"—the unmarried, celibate, the divorced, the homosexual, and the widowed (Palriwala & Kaur 2014, p. 5). Since Borneman's contention, the writing on India has included several queer critiques of marriage. Rekha Pappu, for instance, points to the failure of the Indian feminist movement to create alternatives to marriage. She argues that the efforts have mostly focused on democratizing the institution rather than abolishing it (2011, p. 376).

Ashley Tellis (2014) finds the disciplines of sociology and anthropology in India responsible for "leaving the foundations of institutions like marriage and family unquestioned" (p. 345). He describes marriage as "the most burdensome model on same-sex loving people in India," yet he contends that marriage continued to constitute the imaginary of his queer informants (p. 344). He asserts that what we need is the creation of spaces "outside marriage within which same-sex subjects can breathe and imagine their lives the way they want" (p. 346). Likewise, Nithin Manayath (2015) expresses his dissatisfaction with LGBT activists' demands around sexual citizenship that have been framed within a global "rights" discourse with many calling for the legal right of same-sex couples to marry.[8] This, he argues, is detached from the desires and lived reality of certain erotic/intimate bondings. He asks, should non-heterosexual intimacies only be imaginable within the frame of marriage to gain legitimacy?

A key issue that emerges in this literature is how in India, marriage becomes the focal institution through which intimacy is policed by the state. The legal framework not only privileges marriage and monogamous married women within it, but it also sets "the boundaries of deviance" denying the benefits of marriage—rights, entitlements, and social legitimacy—to those "outside" it (PLD 2010, p. 41; Basu 2015).[9] Srimati Basu and Lucinda Ramberg (2015) argue that there is thus a need to "trouble" the normalizing conception of marriage (monogamous, patrilineal, and heterosexual). They assert that while the pursuit of marriage as a means for same-sex relationships to gain legitimacy before the state and to procure rights may ameliorate the position of married same-sex couples, it threatens to further marginalize those persons (single) or relationships (friends, siblings, lovers but not domestic partners) who cannot or do not wish to access their rights as citizens through marriage. They ask, "Is it possible to reclaim marriage in the pursuit of recognition for non-normative forms of love, intimacy and sexual practice?" (pp. 6, 10).

What these Western and Indian studies imply is that marriage is an inherently inegalitarian and exclusionary institution. In this book, I build on these critiques of marriage through an exploration of the post-marital lived experiences of women in a rural north Indian context where compulsory heterosexual marriage is the norm. I detail the factors that make for women's continued dependence on marriage to show how all women (whether regional or cross-regional) "are made vulnerable by marriage itself" (Okin 1989, cited in Basu 2015, p. 16).

Moving for Marriage

As Lucy Williams observes, exogamy is considered to be the most common global marriage pattern, so cross-border marriage of brides can be seen as an example of the long tradition of women leaving their natal homes to join their husband's family (2010, p. 55). There is now a very large body of literature on cross-border marriage migration (see Bélanger & Flynn 2018; Brettell 2017; and Williams 2010 for a review). The existing literature encompasses, first, studies that describe transnational "within community marriages," such as those between spouses from a South Asian country and the South Asian diaspora (Charsley 2008; Qureshi 2016; Qureshi & Rogaly 2018; Abraham 2008; Mand 2008); second, marriages between spouses belonging to different Asian countries—Japan, Taiwan, Vietnam, Thailand, Malaysia, Philippines and Pakistan (see Ishi 2016; Freeman 2005; Lu 2008; Nakamatsu 2003; Suzuki 2005; Yeoh et al. 2014); third, marriages of women from Global South countries with men in the Global North (Constable 2005; Del Rosario 2008; Lauser 2008; Pananakhonsab 2016). There is also a relatively smaller but growing literature on marriages within national borders, notably cross-regional marriages in India and inter-provincial marriages in China that also involve long distances between the bride's natal and marital homes (Davin 2008; Fan & Huang 1998; Fan & Li 2002; Gilmartin & Tan 2002; Liu et al. 2014; Min & Eades 1995).This literature outlines multiple factors and diverse motivations to explain marriage across borders, seeing the increase in cross-border marriages as largely tied to processes of globalization.

In much of Asia, however, marriage migration has long existed where certain kinship rules of post-marital residence (patri-virilocality) and exogamy (not just outside a kin group such as a clan or patrilineage but also territorial exogamy) have involved territorial dislocation, at times over a considerable distance, for young women. The institution of *marriage itself* has thus entailed women's migration (Palriwala & Uberoi 2008, pp. 24, 28). In India, for instance, 46 percent of the total migrants cited marriage as their reason for migration, and of this, 97.4 percent were women (Krishnan 2019). This migration for marriage is more than simply a shift in place of residence and has significant implications for women's rights and status within marriage. Rajni Palriwala and Patricia Uberoi argue that the gendered implications become sharper when the rule of patri-virilocal residence combines with kinship rules of patrilineal descent, inheritance, and succession, as is the case in much of South Asia (Palriwala & Uberoi 2008, p. 29; Palriwala 1994). The move following marriage, thus, implies the transfer of labor, rights, and maintenance from the natal to the marital home. Residence, then, as Leela Dube notes, "is a material as well as an ideological expression of principles of kinship" (1997, p. 93).

Palriwala and Uberoi outline three implications of these kinship rules for women's autonomy and bargaining power within marriage. The first relates to women's inheritance rights as daughters, especially with respect to immoveable property (e.g., agricultural land). Even when granted by the state (as in India), patri-virilocal marriage means that a married daughter moves away on marriage. This makes it difficult for women to establish claims to property, often resulting in them forgoing their rights. Second, an in-marrying woman's say within her marital family is weakened by her unfamiliarity with the local customs and family traditions of her husband's family. Further, she is treated with suspicion in the home to which she has migrated and her rights, especially to property, are curtailed. A married woman's primary rights to support are as a wife, yet she has few rights to and limited ability to lay claims to matrimonial property. Third, the security or vulnerability of women post-marriage and the constraints or possibilities of their agency are related to their ability to access support, particularly natal kin support, and proximity is crucial (Palriwala & Uberoi 2008, pp. 29–30). Indeed, this third issue has been the subject of several early studies that contrasted the kinship systems of north and south India to explore the implications of different forms of marriage alliance for gender relations. It was argued that in north India, rules of village exogamy and the prohibition on marriage with near kin, along with the preference for distant marriages with strangers, alienate women from their natal kin and limit their autonomy. By contrast, in south India, the preference for close kin marriages results in the marriage of daughters to families not too far from their natal homes, placing them in a relatively more favourable position (Dyson & Moore 1983; Karve 1994; Trautmann 1981).

In this book, I consider the implications of geographic distance by extending this north–south contrast to explore the contrast between the regional and cross-regional bride, with the marriage distance for the latter being multiplied manifold compared to the also exogamously marrying regional bride. Further, by drawing on the discussions in the wider literature on marriage migration, I trace commonalities in the experiences of cross-regional brides and women in cross-border (international) marriages, as both traverse large distances, often marrying in contexts that are culturally alien to them. At the same time, while highlighting the specificity of the experiences of cross-regional brides, I will show that all women, whether they move for marriage across a village border, district border, or state border, are as a consequence uprooted from their homes and families. I aim to shed light on how this territorial dislocation is experienced to argue that to differing degrees, marriage migration places all women in vulnerable positions.

Intimacy

Holly Wardlow and Jennifer S. Hirsch argue that to study gendered relationships it is necessary to attend both to the socially, politically, and economically structured inequalities within which couples negotiate and to the possibilities for tenderness, pleasure, and cooperation that exist in spite of these inequalities (2006, p. 3). In this book, I set such an agenda in motion by studying marriage not only as a relationship "fused with trouble and strife" (Basu 2015, p. 3) but also as one where there is space for intimacy to develop and exist within relations of inequality.

Love is not "new" to South Asia, as discussed by Francesca Orsini (2006), who traces the historical trajectory of discourses of love. She discusses several literary repertoires—the devotional song, folk stories about famous lovers, and Indian film—that have shaped imaginations of love in the South Asian context. Orsini sums up: "The spaces for love in Indian society still lie mostly in the literary or filmic imagination. In the interstices of ordinary life, when no one is looking or in the interval between the dreams and expectations about the future spouse and the epiphany of reality at the wedding" (p. 37). Yet love has received insufficient attention in the writing on conjugal relationships. This in part may have to do with the assumption that love is unique to Western modernity (Khandelwal 2009). In the Indian context, studies note how discussions of love have centered on "love" marriages and elopements that transgress marital norms (Mody 2008). Writing primarily on urban contexts, some others explore how love and desire play out in pre-marital courtship practices that may or may not culminate in marriage (Bhandari 2017; Chakraborty 2012; Donner 2016; Fuller & Narasimhan 2008; Nisbett 2006; Twamley 2014). From these studies, we learn about pre-marital, romantic love. Yet, as Wardlow and Hirsch point out, conjugal love is not the same as romantic love and is often difficult to sustain once a couple is married. They explain, "For one, parents, siblings and other kin may dispute the centrality of the marital bond, insisting on the equal or greater value of their own economic and emotional claims making love both a practice through which kin ties are constructed and at times are in tension with those same ties" (2006, p. 3), as is the case in India.

Anthropological studies have, thus, long drawn attention to conjugal practices that are kept "hidden" (Das 1976; Trawick 1990). Married couples are expected to avoid the slightest familiarity or displays of affection in the presence of others, as intimacy between spouses is viewed as threatening the unity of the joint family. Ann G. Gold notes that a woman's affinal kin may stand in the way of conjugal bliss, yet they never totally stifle it. True love between couples is, thus, predicated on "private intimacy" (2006, p. 321). Gold focuses on women's songs in rural Rajasthan to provide insights on women's desires for conjugal intimacy. Through songs, women create an alternative world to one where family life is centered on the patrilineal extended household and a man's ties to his own kin are expected to be prioritized over the conjugal bond. In some songs, women abuse their husbands and praise lovers, while others allude to sexual pleasure with husbands. She notes a disjuncture between song and practice: "Those who spoke of sex at all portrayed it as something accomplished as rapidly as possible during that rare moment of privacy that couples in a joint-family household must await" (Raheja & Gold 1994, p. 40).

Unlike in the West, where the couple relationship is at the center of personal life (Jamieson 1998), in India what we find is the centering of the institution of marriage but not of the conjugal relationship. This is perhaps what led Jacqui Gabb and Janet Fink to conclude that for South Asians, the couple may be a meaningless unit of analysis for understanding intimacy. Writing about an Indian couple in Britain, they argue that the presumption of intimacy and the intimate dyadic couple is called into question and represents the wrong starting point for analysis, as the couple relationship is steeped in cultural expectations of intergenerational extended family care (2015, pp. 92–93). Should a focus on the couple then be abandoned? The South Asian couple no doubt is embedded in wider kinship relationships, yet I argue that there is a need to bring it into focus, for we know little about the texture of conjugal relationships or the nature of the "private intimacy" that scholars have written about. This may in part have to do with the difficulties in researching love and intimacy in a cultural context where it is neither celebrated nor vocalized. In her work on a Tamil family, for instance, Margaret Trawick (1990, p. 93) writes,

In the ordinary course of affairs, people did not often talk about love. They talked about what was to be cooked for dinner, or what one of the children had done that day. . . . Occasional indirect references were made to love. Even more occasionally, words for love and words of love were used. Yet acts of love,

including acts done in words, were as common, and as wrapped
in cultural significations, as eating. . . . Discovering the meaning
of love to this family was rendered difficult by the fact that for
them, love was by nature and by right hidden.

Given the urban location and caste-class trajectories of her informants,
Shalini Grover (2011) describes a different experience in her work on
marriage among working-class women in a neighborhood in Delhi: "In the
low-income neighbourhood I studied, marriage is by no means a private
matter . . . most people in my field conversed about marriage and love with
surprising ease and frankness." She adds, "While there were few barriers
in conversing about marriage, it was still a challenging subject to capture
analytically. In a setting where people are candid about their relationships,
deciphering emotions is still not an easy task" (p. 17).

In the Indian context, where so much of the writing has focused on
love in the making of marriage, Grover's work has been extremely significant
in shifting the focus onto the "post-wedding phase" (p. 6). By examining
how marital relationships are lived and experienced between spouses and
among sets of kin, her ethnographic study provides valuable insights into
"the dynamics of conjugality" (p. 2). My work contributes to this focus
on women's lived experiences of marriage. While for Grover, questions of
conjugal stability and asymmetry have been central, I not only interrogate
how inequalities shape conjugality but also set out to explore the intimate
and affective dimensions of conjugal relationships. As Rajni Palriwala and
Ravinder Kaur note, "Though the negativities of contemporary marriage for
women have been a focus in earlier work, there has been little work on
conjugality itself, on the dimensions of emotion, support and care which
the fact of marriage is taken to frame" (2014, p. 7).

Perveez Mody notes that intimacy is a "latecomer" to anthropology. She
asks, "why bother with intimacy, if other analytics (for instance, "kinship,"
"relatedness," "love") can do the same work using different categories." The
answer to this, she argues, lies in "the way in which intimacy describes the
quality of relationships" (2019, p. 258). It is precisely for this reason that
I employ the analytic of intimacy in this book taking inspiration from
Lynn Jamieson's (1998, 2011) influential work in sociology. For Jamieson,
"intimacy refers to the quality of close connection between people and the
process of building this quality" and intimate relationships are "a type of
personal relationships that are subjectively experienced and may also be
socially recognised as close" (2011, p. 1). Jamieson develops the concept

of "practices of intimacy" and demonstrates its value for the analysis of personal relationships across cultures. She defines practices of intimacy as "practices which enable, generate and sustain a subjective sense of closeness" (p. 1). She broadens the definition of intimacy by seeing intimacy as a multi-dimensional concept.[10] She argues (2011, p. 3),

> Intimacy is not solely or perhaps even primarily practiced through self-disclosure . . . but that it relates to a wider repertoire of practices. The component practices—giving to, sharing with, spending time with, knowing, practically caring for, feeling attachment to, expressing affection for—are not exclusively about intimacy. That is, each practice tends to produce intimacy but is not a sufficient condition.

In this book, I will draw on Jamieson's conceptualizations of intimacy, intimate relationships, practices of intimacy, and dimensions of intimacy. I will pay heed to Jamieson's (2011) call to move away from "Euro-North-American ethnocentrism" and explore how intimacy is understood across cultures. This book substantiates two of Jamieson's arguments: first, practices of intimacy are present in all cultures, even where they may not be culturally celebrated and relationships are emotionally constrained; second, gender inequalities can exist alongside intimacy.

Relationality

Lynn Jamieson et al. point out that "grasping the meaning and significance of any specific personal relationship requires an understanding of the whole constellation of personal ties within which people are embedded" (2006, p. 1). An understanding of conjugality, thus, demands an inquiry into the multiple relations within which it is embedded. In the writing on India, there have long existed discussions of the relational person. In some early anthropological accounts, such as those of McKim Marriott (1976), the Indian person was described as a "dividual" in contrast to the Western person—the "individual." In his formulation, the latter were defined as bounded and self-contained and Indian persons as open and unbound, constituted through their transactions with other persons (through sex, living together, feeding, etc.), places, and things. Sarah Lamb (1997) nuanced the understanding of relational personhood by attending to both gender and life-course, aspects

ignored in earlier anthropological accounts. She demonstrated ethnograph-
ically how in India, where persons are constituted through networks of
"substantial emotional ties," women's experiences differed significantly from
men's in the ways in which their ties were created but also "unmade" over
the life-course. Lamb takes issue with the dichotomized view that associated the East with the "relational" person and the West with "individuals"
(see also Dumont 1970). She asserted, "there is no simple or single model
of selfhood in either the contemporary Western or contemporary Indian
cultural system" (p. 297).[11]

Within Western sociology, relationality has a long history, but there
has been a renewed interest in the concept among scholars of the family,
intimacy, and personal life (Duncan 2015; Holmes 2014; Jamieson 1998;
Smart 2007). There are three ideas in this sociological writing on relationality that are particularly relevant for my work. First, people are not
isolated; rather, they are inherently connected to others—networks of kin
and friends. Second, individuals make important life choices with significant
others in mind. I will draw on Ian Burkitt's (2016) and Simon Duncan's
(2015) discussions of "relational agency," which sees agency as not individual but rather interdependent and realized through "joint actions" and in
relation to "other individuals and collective agents." Third, relationality is an
important concept because it transcends the limitations of kinship, however
redefined. Carol Smart writes, "The word itself clearly acknowledges that
people *relate* to others who are not necessarily kin by 'blood' or marriage,
thus allowing for considerable flexibility in approach" (2007, p. 48). She
points to the importance of conceiving not of kinship but of "personal life"
as a more inclusive term: "A term now increasingly applied to include not
only families as conventionally conceived, but also newer family forms and
relationships, reconfigured kinship networks, and friendships" (p. 27). In the
writing on India too, some studies (e.g., on friendship) are reflecting this
shift away from analyzing relationships within the frame of kinship (Desai
2010; Dyson 2010; Froerer 2010).

Sasha Roseneil and Shelley Budgeon assert that while sociology has
expanded the scope of the term "family," it continues to marginalize the
study of love, intimacy, care, and sociality beyond the family (2004, p.
137). They call for "decentering the family" and the (heterosexual) couple
with a view to recognizing the "the extra-familial" relationships of significance in individuals' lives. Focusing on the relational lives of adults living
without a partner in Britain, they argue that there is a strong emphasis on
friendship and a "deliberate de-emphasizing of the importance of the couple

relationship" or a "clear prioritizing of friendship over and above sexual partnerships" (pp. 146, 150).

In this book, I will build on the aforementioned arguments developed within sociology and anthropology to address how women's relationships with their husbands, natal kin, children, and other (kin and non-kin) women are lived out and transformed over time. As detailed above, my ethnographic argument is that in the Indian context, the couple should not be treated as meaningless for understanding intimacy (or "decentered"), but in fact needs foregrounding to aid our understanding of its inner dynamics. At the same time, I make a case for also exploring women's relational lives beyond the couple. I will demonstrate that women's relationships with their children, natal kin, and affinal women and female friends, like the conjugal relationship, may be conflict-ridden, but they also serve as vital structures of support and care. Indeed, I see these other intimate relationships in women's lives as *enabling* conjugality, by providing an important outlet for the tensions and strife of the conjugal relationship.

A Return to the Rural

Over the last two decades, there has been a remarkable expansion in writing on marriage and intimate relationships in India, with numerous studies covering new ground and enriching the existing body of work. Studies have analyzed lived experiences not only within marriage, but also "outside" it, thus documenting experiences of widowhood and remarriage, marital breakdown, same-sex relationships, alternative living arrangements, and singlehood (see the volumes by Basu & Ramberg 2015; Kaur & Palriwala 2014; and Sen et al. 2011). What appears to be a glaring gap in this literature, however, is studies on marriage in rural India.

In the mid-1970s, 1980s, and early 1990s, several ethnographic studies provided insights on rural married women's lives (Jeffery et al. 1989; Jeffery & Jeffery 1996; Kolenda 1984; Minturn 1993; Narayan 1986; Raheja & Gold 1994; Palriwala 1991; Sharma 1980; Wadley 1994, 1995). In the recent writing, however, there has been little interest in researching marriage in rural contexts, despite this being the setting in which the demographic majority of Indian women actually live. Recent academic work on marriage and intimate relationships has been drawn toward the "new"—the middle class, the internet, urban spaces (slums, neighbourhoods, cybercafés) or state institutions (such as courts) (Bhandari 2017; Chakraborty 2012; Donner

2016; Grover 2011; Kaur & Dhanda 2014; Mody 2008; Nisbett 2006; Twamley 2012). As with studies on Western contexts, the focus has been on how modernity, economic processes and democratic shifts are impacting familial relationships (De Neve 2016; Osella 2012; Palriwala & Kaur 2014). Greater agency in entering and leaving relationships and a shift toward a desire for a "companionate marriage" has been noted among middle-class and diasporic Indians. Comparisons are made with earlier ethnographies of rural India that take for granted the situation in rural contexts today rather than carrying out new fieldwork. By contrast, this study returns to rural India and reassesses the situation today while adopting similar analytics: modernity, globalization, and economic transformations. It presents a picture of an India—although located at a distance of only 60 kilometers from India's capital city—where the contours of change have been different. I ask: how is marriage, as process and practice, changing or being reiterated in contemporary times in rural north India?

The Setting: Barampur

This book draws on ethnographic fieldwork conducted over an eleven-month period from September 2012 to August 2013 in a village in Baghpat district of the north Indian state of Uttar Pradesh (Map 1). With a population of 199.58 million, Uttar Pradesh (UP) is India's most populous state, accounting for 16.5 percent of the country's population (Census of India 2011b). UP lags behind other Indian states on almost all development parameters and large disparities are visible between different regions in the state (Mamgain 2019; Srivastava & Ranjan 2016). Western UP is distinct from the rest of the state because it is comparatively more prosperous, as is evident in its higher levels of industrialization, and by its concentration on sugar cane and wheat agriculture (Jeffrey 2010, p. 42). Its agrarian structure and infrastructure made western UP the "springboard of the green revolution in UP" (Srivastava & Ranjan 2016, p. 35).

Located in the western part of the state, Baghpat was created in 1997. Until then it was a *tehsil* (administrative division) of Meerut district. Baghpat is one of the 75 districts of UP. Its western boundary is the bank of the Yamuna river. The total area of the district is 1321 km². It is divided into three *tehsils* (Baraut, Baghpat, and Khekra). According to the 2011 Census, the total population of the district is about 1.3 million, with 78.9 percent of the population being rural. UP is one of the Indian states with a significant

Muslim population (19.23 percent) and a large proportion of Scheduled Castes (SCs) (20.5 percent).[12] Muslims constitute 27.98 percent and SCs 11.4 percent of the population of Baghpat district. For 97.3 percent, Hindi is their first language.

Uttar Pradesh is part of the "northern demographic regime" (Dyson and Moore 1983) that is characterized by higher levels of fertility compared to the southern states, even though fertility has been declining rapidly in the state since the 1990s. The total fertility rate (TFR) in UP declined from 4.36 in 2001 to 3.59 in 2011; the TFR figures for Baghpat district were 3.9 and 3.5 in 2001 and 2011 respectively. The TFRs for UP and Baghpat are still higher than those for India as a whole, which were 3.16 and 2.66 in 2001 and 2011 respectively (Guilmoto & Rajan 2013). UP also has some of the most masculine sex ratios in the country. "Normal" sex ratios (number of females per thousand males) without gender bias are around 950 or so. According to the 2011 Census, India has an overall sex ratio of 940. The sex ratio for Baghpat district is 861, which is lower than the state average of 912, which is also skewed. The sex ratio in the

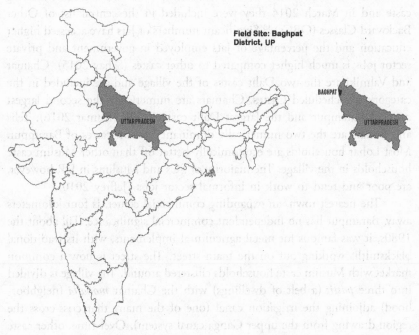

Map I.1. Field site: Baghpat District, UP.

0–6 age group for Baghpat is 841, again lower than that for the state as a whole, which is 902. The sex ratio for rural Baghpat is 856 and for rural UP as a whole is 918. Baghpat has a literacy rate of 72 percent, which is higher than the average for UP but lower than that for the country as a whole (Census of India 2011a). The female literacy rate lags far behind the male literacy rate for the district as a whole (82.4 percent for males and 60 percent for females) as well as for rural Baghpat (male and female literacy rates are 82.7 percent and 58.9 percent respectively).

Barampur village is located on the State Highway that connects Delhi to Saharanpur district. The village is regarded as one of the largest villages of UP. It comprises over 1500 households and has a population of almost 10,000, with an overall sex ratio of 824. The sex ratio in the 0–6 age group is 849. The Scheduled Caste population of the village is 958 (9.7 percent of the total population), of which 496 are males and 462 females with a sex ratio of 931. Nearly 66 percent of the population is literate: 73.7 percent of males and 55.5 percent of females (Census of India 2011b).

Barampur has 22 caste groups: 17 Hindu and 5 Muslim (Appendix 1). Jats are the dominant caste of Barampur. They are dominant both numerically and in terms of land ownership. Jats are a middle-ranking caste and in March 2014 they were included in the central list of Other Backward Classes (OBCs).[13] Significant numbers of Jats have accessed higher education and the percentage of Jats employed in government and private sector jobs is much higher compared to other castes (Sahay 2015). Chamar and Valmiki are the two Dalit castes of the village and are included in the category of Scheduled Castes. Chamars are numerically the second largest caste of Barampur and the largest Dalit caste in UP (Kumar 2016). Telis and Lohars are the two numerically dominant Muslim castes of Barampur. Most Lohar households are economically better off than other Muslim caste households in the village. The majority of SCs and Muslims in UP, however, are poor and tend to work in informal sector jobs (Jeffrey 2010).

The nearest town, an expanding commercial center, is four kilometers away. Barampur has no independent commercial significance. Till about the 1980s, it was famous for metal agricultural implements, with its traditional blacksmiths working out on the main street. The street is now a common market with Muslim caste households clustered around. The village is divided into three *pattis* (a belt of dwellings) with the Chamar *mohallā* (neighborhood) adjoining the irrigation canal (one of the many that criss-cross the region drawing from the upper Ganga canal system). Over time, other caste households developed all around, with some Chamar and Valmiki families now clustered together behind the main village temple. Jat households are concentrated in two *pattis*. Most of the houses in Barampur are *puccā* (permanent house) or *kucchā-puccā* mixed (semi-permanent), with a handful of *kucchā* houses (temporary).

What Led Me to Barampur

In 2008 and again in 2010, I visited Barampur as part of a project on gender and migration. During these visits, respondents talked about the difficulties that men from the Chamar community in particular had been facing since the late 1990s in finding wives. This had led them to "buy" wives from other states. When I returned to India in July 2012 as a doctoral student to carry out fieldwork, I visited Barampur as a potential site for my research. At the time, Chamar informants said that the difficulties that young men in their 20s faced with regard to marriage had increased. I also heard of men of other castes, such as Jats, experiencing similar difficulties and of the presence of a significant proportion of bachelors among them. Western UP had so far not figured in work on cross-regional marriage, despite its sex ratios having been among the most masculine in the state. I gained access through the Chamar family who had helped during my earlier fieldwork, but I lived with a Jat family for the duration of my work. Given the power dynamics underpinning caste relations in rural India, only a Jat family could provide access to Jat and other caste informants and offer the protection that I needed while I was in the field. I was introduced to this family by the village headman, who was also a Jat.

The Research and Methods

For this ethnographic study, data were collected through a survey, interviews, and observation. The survey covered all 22 castes of the village. Given the large size of this village, one-fourth of the total households within each caste were surveyed. Every fourth household was selected from a house list provided by the secretary of the *panchāyat* (a local government institution; see the glossary for commonly used terms). The survey gathered information on caste, religion, *gotrā*, structure of household (joint/nuclear), property/assets, and the sex, age, education, marital status, occupation, and income of individual household members. It also collected data on migration details of household members and marriage details (age at marriage, marriage distance, etc.) of couples and out-married women (daughters/sisters) of the household (Appendix 2). The village survey provided basic information on important aspects of life in the village.

In Barampur, men of five castes—three Hindu (Jat, Chamar, Kumhar), and two Muslim (Teli and Lohar)—had brought cross-regional brides. For this reason, I focused on these five castes for this research. Using the survey as a means of introduction to relevant families, I then conducted semi-structured interviews with 38 key informants (19 regional brides and 19 cross-regional brides) belonging to the five castes (Appendix 3). I also conducted 25 structured interviews with a range of informants—affinal kin and husbands of brides, marriage intermediaries, never-married men, and others—which allowed me to compare testimonies of the lived experiences of marriage with local commentary on the subject (Appendix 4). However, the interviews with the 38 regional and cross-regional brides form the mainstay of my ethnography in this book.

I attempted to match the regional brides with the cross-regional brides in terms of years of marriage, marital status (married/widowed), and caste. As women's location in domestic structures is altered over time and women do not "experience their daily lives from the same vantage point" (Jeffery & Jeffery 1996, p. 19), I used years of marriage (less than 10, 20, 30, over 30) rather than age as criteria in identifying and selecting these key informants. Interviews with informants at different stages in their married lives also helped map intergenerational changes and continuities (e.g., regarding marriage patterns and gender roles and expectations). As far as class or economic status is concerned, most cross-regional brides were married to poor men (casual laborers, landless or with marginal holdings) and most regional bride informants selected were from similar backgrounds. This book, thus, discusses some of the key issues of experience in marriage for those in poverty. Some regional bride informants did belong to economically better-off families and were better educated. As factors of caste, class/poverty, religion, and life-course were factored in in the selection of respondents, this book thus provides insights on how, alongside regional origins, these were crucial in shaping women's lived experiences of marriage.

Given that Barampur is a large village, I found a significant number of cross-regional brides in this one village (approximately 45). Yet I also faced particular difficulties in gaining access to cross-regional bride informants, particularly among the Jats. Due to family status concerns, Jats denied that Jat men had brought cross-regional brides, or family members did not allow me to speak with them. The largest number of cross-regional brides (28) were married to Chamar men. Thus, the number of cross-regional brides interviewed among the Chamars was more than among the other castes. Among the Muslim Telis and Lohars, I found one cross-regional bride each, and I interviewed both. I also confronted difficulties in accessing regional brides. It was extremely difficult to talk to women who lived in joint households unless their mother-in-law consented. In nuclear households, some women said that they would talk to me only if I asked their husbands for permission. Some refused to talk because they were afraid that if their husbands or in-laws heard of what they had talked about they would be beaten up. Some people were suspicious of my motivations and refused to be interviewed.

I talked to key cross-regional and regional bride informants through repeat visits, where I conducted small topic-based interviews. Repeat visits were also vital, given that this research seeks to address questions that deal with informants' private lives and explores "sensitive" topics. The initial interviews covered less personal subjects and helped in establishing trust. I interviewed some women through the course of the 11 months I spent in Barampur. Some others lost interest in talking after my first or second visit: "you have already asked everything," they said. Some accounts are thus more elaborate than others. Several issues that this research seeks to address could not be understood through interviews alone. Ethnography enables researchers to access "naturally occurring" oral accounts that are not produced by informants in response to the ethnographer's questions but may be "unsolicited" (Hammersley & Atkinson 1983, p. 110). I spent extended periods in the women's households and at their work sites, observing their daily interactions and their performance of household and other tasks. This allowed me to delve much more deeply into the daily lives of both categories of wives, adding richness to the information elicited through interviews. Informal conversations with several people in the village, observation, gossip, and rumor all served as additional sources of information. Informal conversations with family members of key informants at times revealed "multifaceted, cross-cutting and even diverging perspectives on the same episodes" (Narayan 2004, p. 245). I also gauged a lot of what at times remained unsaid and implicit through observing interactions, gestures, and facial expressions. Gary Alan Fine writes, "It is through gossip and rumour that one can gain what is, in effect, a map of the social environment in which one lives and works" (Fine in Sassatelli 2010, p. 82). Gossip and rumor proved vital in providing insights into the normative tenor of gender, caste, and class relations in the village. It also became evident to me that there is some information that informants would not reveal about themselves. At times, contradictory accounts of the same event emerged in conversations with different informants.

Lila Abu-Lughod contends that "ethnographic representations" are "positioned truths" (1991, p. 142). My gender, age, marital status, caste, and urban background thus became considerations in whom I could gain access to and what information I could gather. This being a gender-segregated context, while my gender made it possible for me to enter the lives of women, something that a male researcher could not have done, my gender, age, and marital status made it impossible for me to talk to young men. I had access only to brief conversations with a few young men, which took place in the presence of older male and female informants. I could speak with older male informants, but that too only in the presence of other people, and there were certain questions that I could not ask. As public spaces were male spaces, I interviewed informants in their homes. I had conversations with male informants in their homes as well, as it was not appropriate for me to talk with men in the street or the *chaupāl* (courtyard).

Owing to my urban background, I could walk around the village, unlike unmarried village women. Yet my age and gender made it necessary for me to be chaperoned to ensure my safety. The gender and caste status of facilitators was also crucial with regard to acceptance by different groups within the village (see Berreman 1972, p. xix, and 2012). I started my work among the Chamars with Satender (55, Chamar), who had helped with access during my previous fieldwork in Barampur. He was one of the few men of his generation and caste with an undergraduate degree. As he was male, the advantage was that he stayed away while I talked with women due to *parda* restrictions. The fact that he was a man and I an unmarried woman did not create problems when I moved around among the Chamars, as he was well known and respected within his community. I conformed to what was regarded as appropriate in this context; I dressed "modestly" in traditional Indian clothes, wearing *salwar suit* with a *dupatta*, and always walked behind him, as men and women did not walk together.

Due to his caste (Dalit) status, Satender could not provide entry into other castes. Three months into the fieldwork, I was introduced to a Jat ASHA (accredited social health activist) by the Jat family I lived with, and she agreed to help me with the village survey.[14] In the course of carrying out the survey, however, some women told me that she had been telling women not to share anything with me about their private lives, which proved to be counterproductive. My Jat landlady then introduced me to Rani, also a Jat in her mid-30s, who agreed to chaperone me if I paid her an hourly wage. Rani's husband was suffering from an illness and was unable to work. She told me that in different circumstances she would not have left the house to work. As others in the village were aware of her situation, no one gossiped about her. Rani could not help me gain access to the Muslim castes, however. It was only six months into my fieldwork that I was introduced to Muslim families by Kavita (41, Jat), an *anganwādi* worker (government appointed health worker). In the initial months of fieldwork, questions were also raised about my caste status. I succeeded in avoiding the question on most occasions. Chamar informants in particular were confused: "She lives in a Jat household but she eats with Chamars." Some people remained hostile. One woman, for instance, remarked, "She cannot be trusted, she does not say what her caste is." Despite the difficulties confronted, with the help of these multiple facilitators, I was able to gain access to enough informants for my research.

I recorded the data gathered through interviews, observation, and informal conversations through note-taking in field diaries as well as through the use of a digital recorder, where my informants agreed. I conversed with respondents in Hindi but took notes in English, noting only colloquial phrases and terms in Hindi. I transcribed the recorded interviews and translated them into English. For recorded interviews, I also made notes of my observations in my field diary after I returned from the interview. I attempted to transcribe interviews the same day or week, as further questions emerged in listening to the recordings that I pursued in my next visit with informants. For the village survey, I used printed questionnaires that I filled out.

Throughout this book, I use narratives to give "voice" to my informants (see Jeffery & Jeffery 1996). Some of the voices that I choose to highlight are unique in some ways and highlight variations in women's experiences, while some others bring to the fore more general concerns that emerged in conversations with other informants as well. I introduce key (regional bride and cross-regional bride) informants interviewed in the text by providing their names, details of their regional and caste identity and age: for example, Sarla (RB, 47, Jat). For cross-regional marriages that are inter-caste, I provide the caste of the husband—for example, Varsha (CRB, 28, Jat)—as their own caste origins are obscure and they take on the caste status of their husbands. I introduce other women informants by providing their name, age, caste, and gender: Kavita (41, Jat, F). Likewise, for male informants, I provide their name, age, caste and gender: Rampal (87, Jat, M).

Outline of the Book

This book is in two parts. The three chapters that make up part 1 locate cross-regional marriages within the wider context of marriage arrangement and changes unfolding in north India. Chapter 1 describes the "norms" observed in negotiating a regional marriage. I demonstrate that regional marriages include a range of marital forms, with some regarded as ideal and prestigious and others as lower forms of marriage. I discuss the intermediaries or matchmakers involved in negotiating regional marriages and the changes with regard to modes of marriage arrangement over time. I address the question of "choice" available to young men and women in decisions concerning when and whom to marry. Finally, I detail marriage payments, especially dowry, which is the dominant form of marriage payment across castes.

Chapter 2 takes the universality and compulsory nature of marriage as a starting point to contextualize cross-regional marriage and bachelorhood. First, I focus on Barampur and explain the difficulties encountered by some men in finding wives within the local region. The *Census of India* data on sex ratios show that masculine sex ratios have a long history in this region, which I contextualize within my field data to provide insights on the persisting sex ratio imbalance. Beyond the demographic explanations, I examine why some men of the five castes (Jat, Chamar, Kumhar, Lohar, and Teli) fail to meet the idealized norms of marriage outlined in chapter 1 and I look at the strategies they adopt in response to this situation. I then move to outline the factors that explain why women migrate over long distances for marriage. I discuss the five factors that are crucial to understanding the reasons for why women became cross-regional brides in Uttar Pradesh: (1) economic constraints (poverty and the inability to provide a dowry); (2) "spatial hypergamy"; (3) family circumstances; (4) "individual attributes"; and (5) deception. I integrate a discussion on "choice" and "coercion" in decisions around marriage migration.

Chapter 3 discusses the process of negotiation entailed in cross-regional marriages. I begin by examining the role of "go-betweens" in cross-regional marriages. I show that distance makes it impossible to rely on caste and kin networks in such marriages, and thus new kinds of intermediaries enter the negotiation process. I then move on to address whether cross-regional marriages can be categorized as cases of "bride-price," "bride-buying," or "trafficking." I draw on the anthropological literature on gift and exchange and on commercially mediated marriages to show that regional and cross-regional marriages alike always entail material transactions, but any payment made by the groom to the bride's family (instead of dowry) is construed as the "sale" of a bride. Finally, I address what makes a marriage a mar-riage, by focusing on rituals and practices regarded as necessary within the regional context to provide social legitimization to a marriage. In view of this, I examine whether, in local perception, alliances arranged over long distances and across regions are recognized as "legitimate" marriages. This has implications for the in-marrying brides that I explore in part 2 of the book (chapters 4 to 7).

The chapters in part 2 of this book focus on women's post-marital lived experiences. In chapter 4, I discuss how marriage marks a critical life-transition for women as their ties with their natal homes are ruptured and "unmade" (Lamb 1997). I compare what the process of adjustment in the marital home means for regional and cross-regional brides alike, who leave their natal kin and homes to live at their marital home when married. I show that while marriage for all women entails territorial dis-location, this transition was more difficult for cross-regional brides. For them, marriage meant not only movement over a very large distance but adjustment in a culturally and linguistically alien context. I then focus on women's work as a crucial aspect of their day-to-day lives in their marital villages. I discuss the work that women do alone and with men, but I focus primarily on the work that women share with other women and highlight how decisions around work for regional and cross-regional brides alike are shaped by factors such as stage in the life-course, poverty, composition of the household, and widowhood. Finally, I explore questions of belonging and incorporation for married women, highlighting specificities in the experiences of cross-regional brides.

Chapter 5 focuses on women's relationships with their husbands. I begin by outlining and locating my work within the key arguments that have emerged in the literature around questions of democratization in cou-ple relationships in the Indian context. I highlight the inequalities of the marital relationship through a discussion of marital violence that includes coerced sex, wife-beating and verbal abuse, and various forms of controlling behaviors such as control over reproductive decisions. Finally, I attempt to provide insights into the nature of conjugal intimacy in rural north India by developing Lynn Jamieson's argument that intimacy does not necessarily need to be culturally extolled to exist. I unpack the meanings of marriage and support to highlight the possibilities for intimacy despite inequality (Jamieson 1998, 2011).

Chapter 6 is the first of two chapters where I explore relations of support for women beyond the conjugal relationship. I further develop on Jamieson's (2011) argument that just because forms of love and intimacy might not be spoken about at length or culturally extolled, it does not imply that they do not exist. First I explore women's relationships with their young and adult children. As for young children, I discuss how "practices of intimacy" (Jamieson 2011) are useful in understanding the mother–child relationship in a context where love for a child remains unspoken. I show that women continue to value their ties with their adult daughters even after they are married, while they often feel unsupported by adult sons. In the second part of this chapter, I discuss women's relationships with other women both kin (through marriage) and non-kin. I demonstrate that household hierarchies make it difficult for women to forge supportive ties with other affinal women, yet as women advance in their marital lives, they have opportunities to establish friendships with women beyond their households.

In chapter 7, I explore women's relationships with their natal kin. Here I attend to the differences in regional and cross-regional brides' lived experiences of marriage by considering the implications of geographic distance separating their natal and conjugal homes. For regional and cross-regional brides alike, I begin by discussing visits to the natal home and the significance of gift-giving in sustaining women's relationships with their kin. In the last section, I outline the factors that determine a married woman's access to natal kin support. Focusing on moments of "crisis" (marital violence, breakdown, and widowhood), I draw on conceptualizations of relational agency (Burkitt 2016; Duncan 2015) to highlight the significance of natal kin support for a married woman and the implications of its absence.

In the conclusion, I tie together the arguments of each chapter to return to the question: In what ways does an ethnography of rural north Indian marriage advance our thinking on marriage and its gendered implications in a non-Western arranged marriage context?

PART 1

CONTEXTUALIZING MARRIAGE IN RURAL NORTH INDIA

Chapter 1

Making a Regional Marriage

In Barampur, there existed several forms of marriage. Some were regarded as desired, prestigious, or normatively correct within this regional context, while others were considered lesser ways of marrying. In this chapter, I begin by discussing the "rules" observed in the negotiation of marriage and the intermediaries or matchmakers involved. I then explore whether there has been a change over time with regard to choice on the part of young men and women in decisions concerning their marriages. Finally, I discuss marriage payments, with a focus on dowry as the honorable form and its role in establishing and maintaining affinal relations between two social groups. Additionally, I describe other practices such as dowryless marriages and payments to the parents of the bride that exist alongside the practice of dowry, although locally regarded as negatively affecting the status of those involved.

The "Rules" of Marriage

As per north Indian marriage norms, marriages among Hindus in Barampur were arranged within the caste (were endogamous) and followed norms of *gotrā* (clan/descendants from a common ancestor) exogamy. In the past, most castes observed the four-*gotrā* rule that prohibited marriage between a man and woman who shared any of the *gotrās* of their father, mother, father's mother, or mother's mother. During my fieldwork, however, informants said that this rule was now relaxed, with only the father's and mother's *gotrā* being excluded for the purpose of marriage. They did not specify when exactly this shift took place but spoke of it as a response to the difficulties confronted by men with regard to finding brides (chapter 2).

The norm of *gotrā* exogamy was extended to the village or *guwand* (neighboring villages or those under a *khāp*—clan territory). Those born within the same village were regarded as "brothers" and "sisters" having to observe norms of brotherhood or *bhaichārā* (see also Madsen 1991; Pradhan 1966). A violation of *gotrā* and village norms was, thus, considered to be a violation of the rule of incest. In north India, incest is a wide category that includes all inhabitants of a village as well as inhabitants of those villages that share a boundary with it, and all *gotrās* represented in the village that may be located anywhere, by creating a fictive brother–sister relationship between them (Chowdhry 2007, p. 123). Marriages that transgressed these norms of caste endogamy and *gotrā* exogamy were punished, often through the use of violence (see Chowdhry 2007; Kaur 2010b; Mody 2008). Rampal (87, Jat, M) told me about an intra-village elopement among the Jats in the early 1990s: "The faces of the fathers of the couple were blackened and they were made to sit on donkeys and taken around the village (a common means of public shaming). The girl was later brought back and married off to someone else." During my fieldwork, I heard rumors about a few young women in inter-caste relationships who had "committed suicide" or "died of an illness" under unexplained circumstances. Babli (19, Chamar, F) commented on one case in 2009: "It is known to everyone in the village that the girl was murdered by her father." Distinct from the observation made for Haryana (Chowdhry 2007), caste *panchāyats* were not involved in these instances, nor was there any talk of seeking their intervention in meting out punishments for transgressive behavior.

As a form of "group closure" (Kalmijn 1998, p. 396), endogamy enables a caste group to reproduce itself in terms of status and control over property and to maintain the "purity of blood" by preventing "outsiders" from intruding into the group. As women are regarded as "gateways"—literally points of entrance into the caste system (Das 1976, p. 135)—alliances that evoke the most violent responses are those between upper-caste women and Dalit men. The control of marriage and women's sexuality is thus essential to the reproduction of caste and patriarchy (Chakravarti 2003; Dube 2003; Rege 2003). Inter-religious, especially Hindu–Muslim marriages were also violently contested.

Rampal (87, Jat, M) emphasized that *gotrā*, *gāon* (village), and *guwand* (neighboring villages) had to be excluded for the purpose of marriage:

All Jats in Barampur belong to the Tomar *gotrā*. There are 84 Tomar villages that are placed under one *khāp* [clan territory] in the Meerut, Muzzafarnagar [neighboring districts], and Baghpat region. Marriage cannot be arranged in any of these villages. Those of the Balyan *gotrā* cannot marry in 84 Balyan villages but we can marry there. We can also marry in the 54 Malik villages. There are some bordering villages where the *gotrā* is different yet we cannot marry there as they fall under the *guwand*. Although now marriages are being arranged in some of these villages. My wife's *gotrā* is Dhakha. There are five Dhakha villages so my children can neither marry in these five villages nor in the 84 Tomar villages.

Marriages were thus arranged between "strangers," with marriages being oriented to the expansions of affinal networks (Palriwala 1994). For Muslims in Barampur, marriages were also caste endogamous. They did not, however, have *gotrā* and marriage was permitted with consanguineal relatives, as also noted by other studies on Muslims in South Asia (Donnan 1988; Jeffery 1979; Jeffery et al. 1989; Vatuk 2014). "*Mā kā dūdh bachnā chāhiye*," informants told me, indicating that marriage was only prohibited between those having the same mother or those who had shared the milk of any woman and became milk-siblings. Close-kin marriage, however, was not the norm among Muslims in Barampur and some informants stated that marriages with outsiders were preferred by their families. Muslims, like Hindus, observed the norm of village exogamy. Muneera (RB, 32, Lohar) explained, "If my *pīhar* was also in Barampur, my parents would hear everything that happened in my *sasurāl*." Patricia Jeffery (1979) noted that intra-village marriages were favoured among Muslims in Nizamuddin, but in Bijnor, UP, they found that intra-village marriages were less common and not preferred by men and women alike (Jeffery et al. 1989), just as in Barampur.

Post-marital residence across castes was patri-virilocal, with the woman leaving her natal home and village to live at her husband's/in-law's home. For Hindus and Muslims alike, while norms of village/territorial exogamy were followed, marriages were arranged within a limited geographical region—within the district or in another (neighboring) district but within the state of UP, with some exceptions. According to my village survey data on 638 married couples, daughters/sisters were married into, and wives came from, villages within Baghpat or in the districts of Muzaffarnagar, Meerut, Shamli, Saharanpur, Ghaziabad, Baghpat, Hapur, and Bijnor (Map 1.1). Daughters were also married into districts in Haryana, but informants said that they were married into families that had migrated from villages in western UP districts. Based on village studies, scholars show that marriages are generally arranged within a 25-kilometer radius (Agarwal 1994, pp. 379–389; Libbee 1980), with the exception of the upper castes such as the Brahmins and Rajputs, who typically marry over longer distances (Gould 1960; Parry 1979; Plunkett 1973). More recent studies, however, note an expansion of marriage distance and an increase in village exogamous marriages (Mazumdar et al. 2013). According to my village survey, the marriage distance for women in regional marriages varied between 3 and 70 kilometers, with a handful married over relatively larger distances (within a radius of 150 kilometers).

Scholars note a tendency towards hypergamy among castes in north India (Dumont 1970; Karve 1994). In this pattern, the daughter "marries up," with there being a slight inferiority of the wife's family in relation to the husband's, but this in no way contravenes caste endogamy. This pattern corresponds with the Brahmanical-classical and universal ideology of *kanyādān*—a girl's marriage being a "gift of a maiden/virgin" with no payment received in return. Louis Dumont writes (1970, p. 117),

> The gift in general is an extremely meritorious action . . . "gift of a maiden" is a special form of gift, and it is meritorious on condition that no payment is received for the girl; here the girl is, on the whole, assimilated to a material good, and the giving of her is in fact accompanied by material gifts.

Studies on north India note hypergamy among ranked clans (Parry 1979) or economic status and *gotrā* operating as conflicting components of hypergamy within the caste (Khare 1960) or directional hypergamy with brides being given in a northerly or westerly direction (Marriott 1955). In Barampur, only the Jats observed hypergamy. There was no hierarchy among Jat clans, as Dipankar Gupta noted: "Jats prize the ethic of equality above all else, it is not possible to pull rank among them" (1997, p. 42; see also Madsen 1991). Thus, marriages were hypergamous in the sense that women married into families of higher economic status. Unlike the Jats, Chamar, Kumhar, Teli, and Lohar informants pointed out that daughters were married into families of more or less equal status—they were isogamous. "Marrying up" meant high demands for dowry. While families negotiated isogamous marriages, the giving of dowry and gifts in one direction from wife-givers to wife-takers made the relationship asymmetrical. Sylvia Vatuk explains: "The existence of the marital alliance itself establishes the superiority of the bride-takers . . . independent of the relative position of the two families in terms of economic assets, prestige, and local reputation" (1975, p. 159).

Map 1.1. Districts within which regional marriages are arranged.

Exchange marriages involving the exchange of spouses between two or more families are regarded as conflicting with the ideal of *kanyādān*, as the "gift of a maiden" is a religious gift that does not obligate a material gift in return. It also conflicts with the norm of hypergamous marriage (Milner

1988). Ethnographic accounts noted how exchange marriage was differently viewed by different castes. The high castes generally did not approve of this form of marriage, while it was considered an acceptable form of marriage among the lower castes (Das 1975). The Gujars of western UP avoided exchange marriage, as it implied "taking a bride for a price" (Raheja 1988, p. 120), while the Brahmins (though an upper caste) in parts of Gujarat practiced a form of exchange marriage (Van Der Veen 1973; see also Madan 2002 on reciprocal marriages among the Pandits of Kashmir). In Barampur, forms of exchange marriage were practiced by the Chamars and Kumhars. Although acceptable, as they conformed to caste and community norms and entailed dowry, these marriages were not *nirol* (the ideal form of marriage) but lesser forms of marriages and became vital in evaluating status.

According to the 2001 Census data for Baghpat district (rural) (Census of India 2001b), the mean age at marriage for men was 20.25 and for women 17.6 (C—Series: Social and Cultural Tables). During my fieldwork, informants talked of a rise in the age at marriage, with there being a change from the earlier practice of *shādī* (wedding) at an early age and *gaunā* (cohabitation) a few years later. In Barampur, the gap between wedding and *gaunā* no longer existed. It is difficult to establish when this change took place, as some informants married for less than 10 years said that they came to Barampur at *gaunā*. Informants said that daughters were generally married between 18 and 22 years. Among the Jats, as women were pursuing higher education, some were getting married in their mid-20s. Men were usually married in their early to mid-20s. An unmarried man below the age of 30 years was referred to as *kuwārā* (marriageable). Once he reached 35 years, he was considered to have passed the "appropriate" age for marriage and the term *randwā* was used to indicate his never-married status.[1]

For all the Hindu castes, the wedding ceremony was conducted by a Brahmin priest, apart from the two Scheduled Castes in the village—Valmikis and Chamars—who relied on a caste member. The wedding rituals entailed filling vermilion in the parting of the bride's hair and an exchange of garlands. The *pherā* (the rite of seven steps that involves circling the sacred fire), which makes a Hindu marriage "legally binding" (McGee 2004), was regarded as the most important ritual in the ceremony. It was described as essential for a marriage to be legitimized as a marriage by the caste and village community. Other rituals such as worshiping the *kul devtā* (clan god) that followed the wedding were a prerequisite to consummating the marriage. Among Muslims, a religious specialist was called in to conduct the *nikāh* (Muslim marriage ceremony). Both the boy and girl were asked if they consented to the union and a *nikāhnāmā* (marriage contract) was produced as evidence.

The Process of Arrangement: The Matchmaker or *Bīcholiā*

In their work in Bijnor, Patricia Jeffery et al. (1989) noted that among Muslims it was the groom's parents who approached a prospective bride's family with a marriage proposal (see also Jeffery 1979). In Barampur, however, across castes (Hindu and Muslim alike) it was the accepted practice for the woman's family to approach a prospective groom's family with a marriage proposal. First a woman's father and/or male relatives visited the prospective groom's household to see him. Up until about three decades ago, the bride was not shown to the prospective groom's relatives. The new practice was that following a visit from the bride's relatives, the groom's relatives visited the prospective bride's family. At these visits, various assessments were made. For instance, the prospective bride's parents judged if the prospective groom's household had enough space (e.g., a separate bedroom) to accommodate the new bride. For women, attempts were made to gauge the ability of the bride's family to provide her with a "good" dowry. The young woman's attractiveness was judged, with skin tone being an important consideration.[2] If the boy and girl were found to satisfy the desired criteria, the match was formalized with *roknā*: the bride's father giving cash to the groom. This used to be a token payment, as Rampal (87, Jat, M) explained: "*Ek rupayā kī shādī*" (formalized with the payment of one rupee). The time period between *roknā* and wedding varied between informants, depending mainly on the family's financial situation, from a few days to months up to a year. During my fieldwork, I observed that the *roknā* was followed by a *sagāī* (engagement), with the bride's father giving cash and gifts to the groom and the groom's kin to the bride, with those given by the bride's family exceeding those given by the groom's.

In north India, marriages were mediated through networks of kin and affines, "for people do not make a marriage with families about which they know nothing and the information runs along kinship channels" (Mayer 1960, p. 4). The more recent writing on India notes a decline in the role of traditional matchmakers (Majumdar 2004), a weakening of caste and kin networks in marriage negotiation (Shukla and Kapadia 2007), and the emergence of a range of new modes of arrangements that families have come to rely on when seeking a spouse for their offspring. These include marriage fairs (Pache 1998) and newspaper- and internet-based matrimonial websites (Chauhan 2007; Kaur and Dhanda 2014; Sharangpani 2010; Titzmann 2013). In Barampur, Satender (55, Chamar, M) mentioned that he had visited a marriage bureau in the nearest town to arrange a second marriage for his daughter. He added that he decided not to go ahead with using this service, as they charged a fee of ₹5,000. This marriage bureau shut down during the course of my fieldwork. Similarly, Muneera (RB, 32, Lohar) talked about the difficulties they were encountering in finding an equally educated spouse for her *nanad* (husband's sister), a post-graduate in her early 30s, and said that they would have to seek the help of a professional matchmaker to arrange a marriage for her. It is interesting that in rural areas too, professional matchmakers/bureaus have cropped up, yet they did not appear to be relied upon much, except in some cases when finding a spouse presented difficulties (for women).

In the village, the term *bicholiā* was used for matchmakers or intermediaries that negotiated regional marriages. Elderly Jat informants (over 65 years) talked about marriages of their fathers' and grandfathers' generations being arranged by the family *nāi* (barber) and Brahmin (see also Pradhan 1966). Harpal (70, Jat, M) said that families stopped relying on the *nāi* and Brahmin because they started arranging "*be-mel shādis*" (unsuitable matches)—for example, the groom had a physical disability or the age gap between spouses was too large. He added that the *nāi* and Brahmin were given grain by Jat farmers for their services and some started demanding cash payments for arranging marriages. For these reasons, families started calling on kin networks to arrange marriages. Most marriages in Barampur continued to be negotiated through caste and kin networks. According to my village survey data on 606 couples in regional marriages, 14.5 percent of marriages were arranged by parents, siblings, or spouse of a sibling, 71.1 percent through extended family members, 10.9 percent by a caste member, and 3.5 percent by a member of a different caste.

Ethnographic studies on the rural north noted the important role that women play in arranging marriages by bringing "suitable" girls (such as their sisters or their brother's daughters) to the attention of their husband's kin (Jeffery et al. 1989, p. 25; Minturn 1993, p. 48; Sharma 1980, pp. 144–147). Ursula Sharma (1980) suggests that by bringing a sister or niece to marry a kinsman of her husband, a married woman hopes for an ally or friend in her marital village. More recent studies note the role of mobile phones in increasing and aiding rural women's role in negotiating marriages. For rural West Bengal, for instance, Sirpa Tenhunen writes, "Phones are also used to discuss marriage arrangements. People inform one another about arranged marriages, ask information about potential brides and grooms, ask advice about marriage offers, and deliver news of the acceptance or rejection of marriage proposals" (2008, p. 165). Likewise, in Barampur, mobile phones enabled women to make enquiries from extended family kin about prospective brides and grooms for their children. Men also often acted as mediators, bringing in their wives' sisters as spouses for male kin or fellow caste members. Chamar and Kumhar informants talked about how, with migration for brick-kiln work, marriages were also being arranged (though in small numbers) through other brick-kiln workers who drew on their networks in their source villages. Labor migration, thus, helped widen the marriage circle among these castes.

Informants across castes stressed that in the "past," marriages were arranged based on trust in the *bicholiā* but this was no longer the case, as they were known to lie, exaggerate, and withhold information. I witnessed this myself on one occasion when a *bicholiā* brought over to my landlady's house the father of a prospective bride for her son. I watched the *bicholiā* point at the neighbor's cattleshed and tell him that it also belonged to my landlady's family. Women talked about their families being deceived with regard to their husbands' employment, age, a previous marriage, size of landholdings, etc. On account of this, Shakuntala (37, Jat, F) explained that at present the role of the *bicholiā* ended once a match had been suggested. Families made enquiries through relatives or acquaintances in the prospective spouse's village. Amarpal (65, Jat, M) told me, "A woman's father may come to the man's village, for instance, on the pretext of buying a buffalo and then he will get information about the man and his family from the neighbors. Some go as far as traveling to the prospective groom's place of work to confirm that he does in fact work as claimed."

Kumhar informants said that it was common to give the *bicholiā* a gift (e.g., a set of clothes) for negotiating the marriage. The same was the practice among the Chamars, although my informants pointed out that families had started giving a bottle of alcohol or cash in addition to sets of clothing. Jagdish (38, Chamar, M), among others, said that *bicholiās* had started demanding gold rings and mobile phones for arranging marriages. When I asked Harpal (70, Jat, M) if something was given by Jats to the *bīcholīā* for arranging the marriage, he remarked, "We are not Chamars," distancing his caste and looking down upon such a practice. Muslim informants also said that *bīcholīās* were not given anything for negotiating marriages.

"Choice" in Marital Decisions

In contrast to western marriages, where love and choice are the basis on which two individuals enter a marriage, in India, as in much of South Asia, the selection of spouses for one's offspring is the sole responsibility of family elders and parents. Ravinder Kaur and Priti Dhanda describe the arrangement of marriage for one's adult children as a "peculiarly South Asian inter-generational contract" based on a sense of mutual obligation between the generations (2014, p. 271). Perveez Mody (2008, pp. 7–8) explains:

> Marriage . . . is not concerned with whether or not the couple are "in love"—in fact, in the case of Hindus, it is geared around the assumption that ideally the girl and the boy are strangers to each other and that it is their obligation to their parents that makes them sometimes reluctant, though consenting, parties to the marriage. For Muslims, where marriage can be between close kin such as first cousins, the kinship proximity does not translate into social familiarity, and the boy and girl nonetheless behave as strangers on the day of the marriage. Hence, the construction of the relationship between love and marriage is that love should never precede marriage.

Madhurima Mukhopadhyay described this lack of choice in decision-making for participants in a marriage as a "hangover from the custom of infant marriage" (2011, p. 123). Writing on rural Himachal Pradesh, Ursula Sharma noted that parental arranged marriages were based on the rationale that the boy and girl were too immature to make the necessary judgments themselves. The bride was expected to be innocent of what is going on in conformity with the idea that an unmarried girl should have too much sexual modesty to take an interest in her own marriage (1980, p. 151). Similarly, in their work in rural Uttar Pradesh, Patricia Jeffery and Roger Jeffery found that young women neither were consulted nor made suggestions about how their parents should settle them in their marriage, as their families would be dishonored by their brazenness in doing so (1996, p. 2). More recent studies, primarily on urban South Asia, suggest that while there is greater choice available to young people and space for emotional compatibility and love to be factored in, in the making of marriage, parental approval remains key (Abeyasekera 2016; Bhandari 2017; Donner 2016; Fuller and Narasimhan 2008; Lietchy 2003; Twamley 2014) and there has not been a shift away from the system of arranged marriage (Vatuk 2014).

In Barampur, across castes, women were not consulted during decision-making on choice of spouse, reflecting little change from the observations made by earlier ethnographies on rural north India. Once parents saw that a daughter had become *jāwān* (mature) her marriage was arranged. Kripa (RB, 75, Jat) believed that women of her and her daughter's generation had no control over their marriages, but women of the present generation of marriageable ages, who were pursuing higher education, had some say in their marital decisions. This choice was limited to convincing their parents to delay the marriage for a year or two. There were some exceptions, however. Muneera (RB, 32, Lohar), for instance, told me that she had managed to convince her father to avoid settling her in a close-kin marriage. Likewise, Ritu (RB, 25, Jat) said that her father was not keen on marrying her in the same village as her older sister but he eventually agreed once she told him that it is what she wanted. Not all parents took their daughter's opinion into consideration. Family circumstances had a bearing on decisions around the timing of marriage. Abha (RB, 25, Chamar), for instance, was married at the age of 13. She told me that the daughter of her *tāū* (father's elder brother) was the same age and was still unmarried. She explained that her mother passed away and her father could not "keep an eye on a young unmarried daughter" and hence she was married off at a very young age. Similarly, Koyal (RB, 16, Chamar) said her mother gave her no option but to marry, saying that they had her four younger sisters to marry too.

Women talked about how it was regarded shameful for them to express their opinion to their parents. Shanti (RB, 24, Kumhar) told me, "When I saw my husband I thought he was *kālā* (literally black, but used to describe dark skin) and I am light-skinned yet I could not say to my parents that I didn't want to marry him." Babli (19, Chamar, F) was a second-year undergraduate (one of the few women in her caste to attend university). She talked to me about how she wanted to marry in her mid-20s and wished to marry an educated boy with a *naukrī* (regular/salaried job). She added that she could not tell her parents this and was aware that if her parents decided to marry her after a month to a brick-kiln worker, she would have no choice but to agree. Similarly, some unmarried Jat women shared their ideas on the kind of man they wanted to marry (e.g., with a government job), yet they stressed that the decision would be made by their parents. Omvati (65, Jat, F) explained the difference between young women of the present generation and those like her: "We did not think about such things (desired qualities in a spouse), whatever and wherever our parents decided." Like women, men were not usually consulted with regard to when and where they should be married, though some women informants stressed that men had more say on the matter than women. Sarla (RB, 47, Jat) remarked, "A man can refuse a proposal if he doesn't find the prospective bride beautiful, but a woman cannot do so." Satender (55, Chamar, M) talked about telling his father that he did not want to marry until he completed his graduation, yet his father fixed his marriage when the family was approached with a marriage proposal for him. He asserted that the final decision then and now rests with parents. Elderly informants (over 65 years) said that they had not seen their husbands until after the wedding. Some others, like Sarla (RB, 47, Jat), who had been married for over three decades when I first met her, said that her husband had come over to see her but she was not told that he was a prospective groom until much later. The common practice was to show the young man and woman a photograph of the future spouse once the marriage had been fixed by family elders.

Despite the enforcement of parentally arranged caste endogamous marriage, the desire for a "choice" or "love" marriage was expressed by some of my younger informants. I heard of several pre-marital relationships in the village. Pre-marital relationships have also been the subject of the writing on urban contexts that notes the role of new technologies in enabling courtship practices. In his work in urban Bangalore, Nicholas Nisbett noted how internet chatrooms "provide new forms of interaction between the sexes," enabling young men to make the kind of relationships that they found difficult to make elsewhere (2006, p. 133). Similarly, in her work in the urban slums of Kolkata, Kabita Chakraborty discusses young Muslim women's "self-directed romantic relationships." She argues that online relationships are a safe method to meet young men, as they reduce the physical risks of courtship in a community that disapproves of public interaction between unmarried men and women (2012, pp. 197–198). In the gender-segregated rural context described here, mobile phones served the same purpose, enabling young people to pursue love, desire, and sex in pre-marital relationships even though they were aware that these would not culminate in marriage.

In the early months of fieldwork, I noticed my landlady's neighbor's son on the phone night after night visibly upset and crying on some occasions. When I asked my landlady what the matter was, she said, laughing, "He's pining after his *girlfriend* [she used the English word]. Her marriage has been arranged with another boy." Kriti (22, Jat, F) told me that at night she jumped over the wall after her mother fell asleep to meet her "boyfriend." She explained, "I give him a missed call to let him know it's time" and laughed. I asked her if she worried about getting caught, to which she replied, "If I do, what will they do . . . just get me married off the next day." There have also been other changes that have widened opportunities for young people to form relationships. These include an increase in the number of young people, especially women, in higher education that requires them to travel to nearby towns. Babli (19, Chamar, F), for instance, met Anmol while she was a student at the college in the nearest town. She told me that she was aware that they could not be seen together in public, so they arranged to meet at particular times to catch the same bus back and "tried to exchange glances from a distance." She would catch hold of her mother's mobile phone whenever she could to message Anmol. *"Hum dono ke beech pyār hai"* (there is love between us), she told me as she broke into a song from a popular Bollywood film.[3] She explained that if she asserted her choice and married a man without parental consent, even if he was a Chamar, her parents would sever ties with her.[4] These aforementioned cases were all intra-caste relationships, but I learned of others that crossed caste boundaries.[5] The point is that both kinds would fail to gain parental sanction for being self-initiated relationships prior to marriage.

In Barampur, mobile phones have not only facilitated pre-marital relationships but also made possible courtship practices between soon-to-be spouses. Three regional brides (married for less than 10 years) said that they talked to their husbands on the mobile phone during the period between *sagāī* (engagement) and wedding. Unlike the urban Indian context, where the period of engagement may become a "safe parent-sanctioned space for romantic courtship" (Gilbertson 2014, p. 230), in this rural context, such conversations had to be carried out in secret with the mobile phone becoming the medium (see also Doron 2012, pp. 427–429).

Marriage Prestations: Dowry

Across castes, older and younger informants alike said that there was no dowry when they got married. In their understanding, what was given to a daughter at her wedding were *sāmān* (goods) and this was a *rivāj* (custom) given *apnī marzī se* (willingly). This was not *dahej* (dowry) because it was not demanded. A few informants, though, believed that *sāmān* was also *dahej*, yet they insisted that this was not demanded but given *khushī se* (out of happiness, voluntarily). Apart from the *sāmān*, the wedding expenses that included a *dāwat* (feast) were also met by the bride's family. Studies have drawn attention to "dowry inflation" over the years (AIDWA 2003; Palriwala 2009; Rao 1993), a concern often expressed by my informants. Some said that their daughters were of marriageable ages yet they would delay their marriages, as they could not afford to meet wedding expenses. The necessity of dowry put an enormous strain on the poor, who often fell into debt. Even for those who were better off, it was not easy. Kripa (RB, 75, Jat) told me about her granddaughter's wedding in 2013: "My son's annual income from agriculture is ₹100,000. My husband receives a pension. We drew on his savings and borrowed some from a relative and that is how we spent ₹600,000 on the wedding."

In responding to questions about dowry escalation, informants stated that what had changed over time were the *sāmān* given to a daughter. Elderly informants said that when they got married they brought with them items such as a bed, utensils, sets of clothing for the bride and husband's kin, bicycle, and umbrella, but the *sāmān* that are given to daughters now constituted furniture, utensils, and clothes but also a range of consumer goods such as electrical appliances such as a television and refrigerator and even cash. As noted by earlier studies, they were in no sense the woman's own property but rather remained in control of the senior members of the groom's family. Dowry was not "women's wealth, but wealth that goes with women" (Sharma 2005: 21; Palriwala 1994). Rajni Palriwala (2009) contends that in a situation of increased desirability for consumer goods, families may see dowry as a way of obtaining them.

Informants married before the 1990s suggested that demand for dowry was a "new" phenomenon, although dowry demands are known to have a longer history (Aziz 1983; Sambrani & Sambrani 1983; Srinivas 1984). Khalida (RB, 45, Teli) stated, "People have become greedy. Last week they came to see my *devar's* daughter. They left saying the girl is dark-skinned. The *bicholiā* told us that after they learned that my *devar* has five daughters and is a rickshaw puller, they thought he would not be able to give much to his daughter. Her skin tone was just an excuse." I was told that only a man with a government job could demand a dowry and these demands were communicated through the *bicholiā*. Ashok (39, Jat, M) explained:

> A man with a government job will be given a motorcycle, cash, and a gold ring and chain. This the bride's family will give on

their own. An engineer's or bank job is considered better than a job in the Police. Employment in the Delhi Police is considered better than in the UP Police because it means living in the city. So a boy in the Delhi Police will get a car in dowry and the wedding will take place in the town and a man in the UP Police will get less. When a boy in the Delhi Police, for instance, is approached his family will first ask how much the woman's family is willing to spend and the family willing to spend the most will be chosen. It is like *a system of bidding* [emphasis mine].

What Ashok alludes to is that the amount of dowry is proportional to a man's position within the occupational hierarchy or his "eligibility." Also, that a family hoping to secure an "eligible" groom is aware that they will have to provide a large dowry due to competition for the few eligible grooms (chapter 2). Rita Sambrani and Shreekant Sambrani describe this as the "virtual auction of the eligible men to the highest bidders" (1983, p. 602). Rampal (87, Jat, M), for instance, told me that his son-in-law works as a food inspector in the nearby town and that there were no demands from his family, yet in 2010 they gave him a car that cost ₹800,000. It was widely believed that such men deserved or had earned the dowry they were given by virtue of being successful. Kajri (RB, 35, Jat) remarked, "The parents of a man with a *sarkārī naukrī* [government job] think that they should be given a dowry as compensation for spending on their son's education." Abdul Aziz argues that the transition from "a voluntary gift" to "a compulsory payment agreed to by mutual bargaining" occurred when "the concept of groomhood underwent a drastic change from the normal eligible bachelor to a fancy product" (1983, p. 604), as seems to be the case in Barampur.

Kavita (41, Jat, F) told me, "A man in the Police receives a vehicle in dowry, then another, also a government employee starts having the same expectation and then it becomes an accepted practice." Yusuf (77, Lohar, M) similarly explained the practice of giving a motorcycle among Muslims in dowry as an imitation of the practices of "others"—Hindus, he clarified (see also Vatuk 2007). Among Muslims, Sylvia Vatuk noted that dowry called *jahez* takes the form of household goods, clothing, and jewelry rather than cash, but that it was taking on a form approaching that of Hindu groom-price, commonly known as dowry (Vatuk 1993). Among Hindus and Muslims alike, I often heard talk of *achī shādī* (a good marriage), which meant a marriage with a good dowry that reflected the status of both families. When a bride moved to live at her *sasurāl* (marital home, with her in-laws) after the wedding, a *mūh dikhāī* (face showing ceremony) took place that served as an occasion for the display of dowry and hence status.

Dowry has been seen as integral to hypergamy: the girl's family gives a daughter and goods to a family of superior status in exchange for the prestige that results from marriage with it (Dumont 1970, p. 117; Srinivas 1984). In Barampur, poor informants, across castes, stressed that they arranged isogamous marriages for their children as they could not fulfill the demands that came with marrying hypergamously to a man with a *naukrī*. In an isogamous marriage, there were no demands; they gave as per their means. It was believed that a daughter could not be sent to her *sasurāl khālī hāth* (empty handed). It was essential to give *thorā bahut* (a small amount) for the sake of one's *izzat* (honor). Muslim informants said that even when marriages were arranged with close kin, the woman's parents had to give her *sāmān*.

A daughter was given *sāmān* so that when she set up her own household she would have everything she needed. People in Barampur said that even if the groom's family made no demands at the stage of negotiation, it was not possible to give only a daughter in marriage, as her in-laws would taunt her: "What did you bring from your parent's home?" Thus, while they insisted that they gave willingly, they pointed out that there were expectations on the part of the groom's family that had to be met. Parents had to give to ensure the happiness of their daughter in her *sasurāl* and so that she could secure her position in her *sasurāl*. Thus, as noted in earlier work, the voluntary character of gifts has disappeared and dowry has become a coercive practice (Aziz 1983; Palriwala 1989; Srinivas 1984; Srinivasan 2005; Srinivasan and Bedi 2007). In this context, in their work in Bijnor, Patricia Jeffery and Roger Jeffery noted that people talked about a married daughter as a potential "hostage" and the "looting" perpetrated by families with sons (1996, p. 70).

Across castes, women shared their experience of being taunted by their in-laws for not bringing enough dowry or bringing less than other in-married women of the household. Koyal (RB, 16, Chamar) pointed out to me all the things that her parents gave, which included almost all the furniture in her household. She said that her father did not give a refrigerator and an air cooler and her *sās* (mother-in-law) taunted her saying that her parents gave her nothing. Ritu (RB, 25, Jat) declared proudly that she had brought a much larger dowry than her two *jethānīs* (husband's elder brother's wives) and was favored by her *sās*. Rajni Palriwala argues that while in the past "gifts cemented and reaffirmed alliances, affinal ties now ensure gifts and wealth. If the demands are not met, the tie is endangered" (1994, p. 88). Harassment for dowry has long been reported for north India (Dube 1997). During my fieldwork, I heard about the daughter of a Chamar family who had died following an "accident" at her *sasurāl*. When I asked how, I was told "electrocution." The rumors suggested that she had been murdered by her in-laws because it was well known that her parents were finding it difficult to meet her in-laws' continued demands. "They were after a refrigerator," a Chamar woman told me. "*Denā partā hai*" (you have to give) is what most informants across castes said to explain why the birth of a daughter brought sadness. More so, the gifts given to a daughter did not end at wedding but were given to her through the course of her married life (chapter 7).

Some believed that a daughter was not given a share in her parental property so dowry served as her share; as scholars describe it, it was seen as "pre-mortem inheritance" (Goody 1973). Srimati Basu explains that property is represented as a son's compensation for care in old age and ritual respon-sibilities and as parallel to a daughter's dowry being pre-mortem inheritance irrespective of whether a daughter receives a dowry and a son takes on eldercare (2019, pp. 285–286). Unlike among Hindus, where dowry has a strong religious sanction (Dube 1997, p. 137), among Muslims, Yusuf (77, Lohar, M) explained, dowry is not sanctioned by the Shariah and it is the duty of the bridegroom to pay *mehr* to the bride. *Mehr* or marriage settle-ment is meant to provide for a woman in difficult times (Jeffery 1979, p. 57). The amount is supposed to be negotiated at the time of the *nikāh* and written in the *nikāhnāmā* (marriage contract). Women informants pointed out that a marriage should not be consummated without the payment of *mehr*, yet it was rarely paid in practice, as noted by earlier studies on Muslims in South Asia (Donnan 1988; Jeffery 1979, 2001; Vatuk 1993). Muslim women said that they had either *māf kīyā* (forgone the *mehr*) or that they would claim it in the event of divorce, even though most were unaware of what the amount owed to them was.

Dowryless Marriages

While dowry was the predominant and honorable form of marriage pay-ment in Barampur, Jat and Kumhar informants cited cases of marriages where men had taken women from poor families in marriage without a dowry. Such men were regarded as ineligible owing to factors such as a physical disability or previous marriage. Yet, as Kripa (RB, 75, Jat) pointed out, parents of daughters agreed to such marriages because these men were wealthy or landed and parents thought that their daughters would have comfortable lives. Kajri (RB, 35, Jat) told me that she got her oldest daughter married to a much older widower (also Jat) with three children because they did not have to give a dowry. I heard rumors of this not just being a dowryless marriage but one where the groom had paid a big sum of money to the father of the bride for the marriage. Chamar informants cited instances where fathers who were "alcoholics, gamblers, or those in debt" had "*paisay le kar*" (taken money) to get their daughters married to "ineligible" men within the caste. Satender (55, Chamar, M) referred to this as *bechnā* (selling) and added, "Everyone in the caste knows about this, *par iss bāt par pardā hai*" (but this is hidden).

Bride-price is known to have existed among the Chamars in the past (Briggs 1920, p. 36), even though Chamar informants suggested that they could not recall anything other than the giving of dowry ever being an accepted practice among them. Dowry has had an association with higher-status groups and bride-price with lower-status groups (CSWI 1974; Uberoi 1994; Unnithan 1992), yet a shift to dowry among communities that previously practiced bride-price has been noted (AIDWA 2003; CSWI 1974; Oldenburg 2002; Palriwala 2009; Sheel 1999), with "Sanskritisation" being one explanation (Srinivas 1984). Ethnographic accounts suggest that higher or non-bride-price-practicing castes speak of bride-price among the lower castes as sale of a daughter or woman (Das 1975: 78; Parry 1979; Unnithan 1992, p. 67). For the Pandits of rural Kashmir, T.N. Madan noted, "The idea of selling a child is very repugnant to the Pandits and a man who receives money for his daughter is regarded as one fallen very low." Thus, payments to the parents of the bride among the upper or dominant castes are infrequent and concealed (2002, p. 104; also Raheja 1988, p. 266).

Writing in the mid-1950s, Pauline Kolenda found that groom-price was a recent introduction among the Rajputs of north India. Yet she noted that widowed and poor men who struggled to find a wife had to pay a "bride-price," a practice that was fairly common among them in earlier decades (1984, p. 108). In Barampur, Chamar informants did not refer to the payments made by the groom's family to the bride's as "bride-price," and through the course of my fieldwork, I did not hear a term that in local usage connoted bride-price. In fact, Chamars themselves used *mol* (price) and *bechnā* (to sell) when talking about such payments. They said that such practices were "hidden," as among the upper castes, and they attempted to distance themselves from what was regarded as a demeaning practice—giving a daughter in marriage "without *dān dahej*" (without a dowry, negating the spirit of *kanyādān* marriage) (Raheja 1988, p. 236). What this points to is the idea that price or sale and not gift accompanies all marriage prestations made to the parents of the bride by the groom, even among groups where bride-price was a practice they had followed just a few decades ago.

Conclusion

In Barampur, a "proper" or "correct" marriage was one that conformed to norms of caste endogamy, *gotrā*, and village/territorial exogamy. While there has been an expansion in marriage distance, marriages continued to be arranged within the district or in a neighboring district and within the state of UP. Among Muslims, there was no *gotrā*, and kin marriages forbidden among Hindus were permitted even though they were not the norm. Forms of exchange marriage were not exceptional or "deviant" and "aberrant" practices as described in earlier ethnographies (Minturn 1993, p. 63; Pocock 1972, p. 152). Although not regarded as ideal or prestigious ways of marrying, they conformed to the aforementioned norms and had emerged as acceptable forms of marriage in response to the difficulties confronted by some men.

Some informants mentioned relying on intermediaries such as professional matchmakers, and others talked about "new" networks that labor migration created for facilitating marriages. Yet most regional marriages continued to be negotiated through networks of caste and kin. There has been a rise in age at marriage for both men and women and there is no longer an age gap between wedding and cohabitation. There had been little change, however, with regard to greater choice for rural young men and women in their marital decisions. The final decisions rest entirely in the hands of parents or family elders.

My findings suggest the persistence of dowry (described as *sāmān*, with *dahej* less commonly used) across castes and dowry escalation in hypergamous marriage. Cases of dowryless marriages appeared to be few, despite the difficulties confronted by men in finding brides. Given the ideology of *kanyādān* marriage with dowry as customary and honorable, all payments made by the groom to the bride's family were perceived as "sale" of a daughter/bride and hence regarded as a lower practice. Some men accepted lower and less prestigious marriages, yet some others failed to marry regionally, either remaining bachelors or bringing cross-regional brides. In the following chapter, I discuss the reasons *why* some men fail to marry according to the desired norms outlined in this chapter, and the strategies they adopt in response to the difficulties faced.

Chapter 2

A Compulsory Marriage?

Contextualizing Cross-Regional Marriage and Bachelorhood

Writing on Punjab in 1925, Malcolm Darling, a British official, stated, "The bachelor's life is not a happy one. . . . There is no one to look after his house, no one to bring the midday meal to the fields, no one to pick the cotton or to help in the weeding." He stressed that marriage was not only "a religious duty," but also an "economic necessity" in peasant societies ([1928] 1977, p. 58). In his work on the Pandits of rural Kashmir in the late 1950s, T.N. Madan noted that that begetting sons was not the only reason to seek a wife. "The gratification of sexual desire, the mutual love of spouses, and the joy and comfort of domestic life" also made marriage "a highly desired state of existence for a man." Bachelors were "pitied" in Pandit society, he wrote (2002, p. 89). In the Indian countryside, Ravinder Kaur writes that bachelors are marginalized and "referred to as *bechārā*" (one without food or resources) (2008, p. 113). What the above point to is the role of marriage in the social reproduction of families and communities, fulfillment of sexual needs, inheritance, rights and status, labor, and provision of care.

In India, as in most of South Asia, marriage as an institution holds "hegemonic sway." It thus "marginalises those who fall outside its parameters or never enter it" (Palriwala & Kaur 2014, p. 5), with non-marriage having implications for masculinities. In rural north India, hegemonic masculinity, i.e., "successful ways of being a man" (Connell 1995), entails earning and fulfilling provider roles for the family. Further, heterosexual marriage is seen as essential for a man (and woman) to transition into social adulthood. Successful masculinity is also tied to having a wife whose productive and sexual labor a man can command. The process of becoming a man is not regarded as complete until he gets married, has heterosexual relations, and proves his virility by producing an offspring, especially a son (Chowdhry 2011).

While these elements are common to understandings of what it means to be a man in this cultural context, masculinities are constructed differently across different socioeconomic groups within the same social context. As the experience of masculinities is about an entitlement to power, men have power vis-à-vis women but this entitlement to power is also dependent on men's location within systems of class, caste, and sexual orientation (Roy 2007) that place some in positions of domination while rendering other masculinities as "inadequate or inferior" and hence "subordinate" and "marginalised" (Connell 1995, p. 81; Cornwall & Lindisfarne 1994, p. 3). Furthermore, ideas of being a man are not "fixed" and there may be a change in defining components of masculinity over time.

In Barampur, the derogatory term *randwā* was used for the never-married, while the terms *malāng*, translated as "chronic bachelor," and *chharā* are used in Haryana and Punjab respectively. Likewise, in China, the stigmatizing term "bare branches" is used to connote a single man who failed to get married (Kaur 2015, p. 65; Mishra 2018, p. 34). Bachelorhood, however, is not "new," particularly in India's northern and northwestern states, with several earlier studies drawing attention to how the problem of bride shortages was resolved in the past. These included the practice of polyandry (Darling 1977; Hershman 1981; Pettigrew 1975), or involuntary bachelorhood (Kaur 2008), or marriage with women of inferior castes (Hershman 1981; Pocock 1972).

What appears to be "new" in the contemporary context is a moral panic around a "surplus" of bachelors. Much of this concern has been articulated in terms of bachelorhood being a consequence of the inability of some men to marry due to a "marriage squeeze," that is, a shortage of marriageable women resulting from highly masculine sex ratios at birth, with demographers predicting that in future an even more significant proportion of men will fail to marry. Christophe Guilmoto, for instance, postulates that the cumulative number of additional men remaining single during 2020–2080 could be closer to 40 million in India (2012, p. 92).

In this chapter, I discuss the growing concern around bachelorhood in this rural context. "*Ab shādī hone mein pareshānī hai*" (*Now* it is difficult to get married) was one of the most often repeated statements in Barampur. This chapter is divided into two parts—the first outlines why some men fail to marry within their caste and local region and hence seek wives from other states. I will outline the factors that make it difficult for some men to achieve normative ideals of masculinity, providing spaces for subordinate and marginalized masculinities to emerge (Cornwall & Lindisfarne 1994). In the last section of the first part, I analyze the implications that non-marriage has for masculinities. The second part of the chapter explains why women become cross-regional brides. As the growing concern in the north Indian states about the inability of some men to marry has been attributed largely to demographic factors, I begin by discussing sex ratios for the district. The sex ratios for the region have historically been and remain extremely masculine. I argue that while demographic factors are not insignificant, they alone cannot explain the difficulties faced by men with regard to marriage. Moreover, future projections made by demographers often overlook the *adaptive strategies* adopted by communities in response to the challenges confronted.

Barampur, Bride-Receiving Region

A SHORTAGE OF MARRIAGEABLE WOMEN? SEX RATIOS, SON PREFERENCE, AND "DAUGHTER AVERSION"

In India, sex ratios are reported as number of females per 1000 males. It is uncommon for sex ratios to be at parity; a sex ratio of 1000 would not be expected. Typically, different age groups have different profiles. Since more boys are born than girls, sex ratios at birth (SRB) and early ages display a surplus of males: sex ratios of around 950 would not be surprising for these age groups. In this region (Table 2.1), however, masculine sex ratios have been a matter of concern since the 19th century, when the British campaigned

Table 2.1. Overall Sex Ratios for Some Western UP Districts, 2001 and 2011

District	2001	2011
Uttar Pradesh	898	912
Baghpat	847	861
Bijnor	896	917
Ghaziabad	860	881
Meerut	872	886
Muzaffarnagar	871	889
Saharanpur	865	890

Source: Census of India 2001 & 2011.

against infanticide (Jeffery and Jeffery 1997, pp. 230–231; Miller 1997). Table 2.2 shows a pattern of highly masculine sex ratios in Baghpat district that have been consistently lower since 1901 than the sex ratios for the state of UP as a whole. These pre-date the spread of sex-selective technologies.

Insights from Barampur shed light on the persisting masculine sex ratios in the district. In the village, the necessity of a son was felt across castes. What existed was not only son preference but also "daughter aversion" reflected, for instance, in the words of Ompal (55, Kumhar, M): "You have to please god/s to ensure that you will get a son but daughters have a habit of arriving even when you do not request them." Son preference and "daughter aversion" were much stronger among the Jats than the other castes. Jats attributed growing bachelorhood to "*larki ki kami*" (a shortage of women) yet perceived bride shortages had not changed their attitude toward girl children. Jat informants admitted to going in for pre-natal sex selection even though they were aware of the PCPNDT Act, 2003, which banned pre-natal sex determination in India. They also cited instances of female neglect and lack of medical attention given to female infants and young girls in the past. Some talked about how infanticide was a common practice in Rajasthan and Bulandshahr (UP), but they could not recall any incidents of infanticide in this part of UP. Colonial records, however, suggest that the practice was found among several landowning castes such as

Table 2.2. Overall Sex Ratios, UP and Baghpat, 1901–2011

Year	UP	Baghpat
1901	938	877
1911	916	848
1921	908	851
1931	903	839
1941	907	848
1951	908	836
1961	907	847
1971	876	836
1981	882	832
1991	876	838
2001	898	847
2011	912	861

Source: District Census Handbook, Baghpat, 2011.

the Rajputs, Lewa Kanbis, and Patidars of Gujarat and Jats, Ahirs, Gujars, Khutris, and Moyal Brahmins in north India (Vishwanath 2004). Ethnographic accounts also show that infanticide was historically prevalent among the Jats of western UP (Jeffery and Jeffery 1997; Pradhan 1966). Saroj (35, Jat, F), an ASHA (Accredited social health activist), told me:

> Everyone here is aware that you can have pre-natal sex determination done. For the first child, people don't generally get ultrasounds because they have to pay a huge sum of money. It is done for the second child, if the first child is a girl. Over the last year, in my area [covering 150 Jat and a handful of Muslim households], 12 boys were born and only one girl. Till about a year ago, people got sex-selective abortions done through ASHA workers. I used to take women to private clinics at Shamli [40 km from Barampur]. The clinics would give us a commission for taking them. It can be done both at Baraut [the nearest town] and at Shamli. Earlier they took ₹1,500 and now ₹3,000–5,000. Now I no longer do this as I have understood that it has been banned by the government, that we may have to pay a fine and can even be jailed.

The ban on sex determination is over two decades old. Saroj did not explain when exactly she stopped and there was no way to confirm if she actually did. Table 2.3 shows caste-wise sex ratio data for the former United Provinces in which Barampur is located, last available for the 1931 Census. Of the five castes, sex ratios for the Jats are the most masculine and those for the Chamars most favorable.

Table 2.3. Caste-wise Sex Ratios, All Ages and 0–6, United Provinces, 1931

Caste	All Ages	0–6
Kumhar	928	1007
Chamar	957	1011
Teli	910	1013
Lohar	887	975
Jat	776	938

Source: Census of the United Province of Agra and Oudh 1933.

In 1920, G.W. Briggs wrote that female infanticide was not practiced by the Chamars, although female infants were neglected and were more subject to plague and malaria. Yet, drawing on the 1911 census figures, he states that the proportion of females to males was high (1920, p. 45). If we compare the sex ratios for Chamars in 1931 with those for the Scheduled Castes over a 50-year period (Table 2.4), it is clear that the sex ratios have become increasingly masculine and similar to those of other castes, as noted by other studies (Bhat & Zavier 2007; Siddhanta et al. 2009). Unlike Jat informants, Chamar informants claimed "check *nahī karwāte*" (did not get pre-natal sex determination done), but Teli, Lohar, and Kumhar informants said that even in their castes families had started using pre-natal sex selection. The sex ratios for Muslims (Table 2.5) are less masculine than those for Hindus, yet they are not favorable. Muslims are believed to practice less sex selection than other groups (Alagarajan & Kulkarni 2008; Bhat & Zavier 2007; Guilmoto 2008).

As has been well documented in the literature (e.g., John et al. 2009; Agarwal & Unisa 2007; Miller 1997), in Barampur too, the reasons for persisting son preference included old-age support and carrying forward the family name. A son was necessary to inherit the property, as a daughter was expected to get married and move away, and it was believed that it would be difficult to get a daughter married if she did not have a brother. After the parents passed away, a brother was necessary to sustain the affinal relationship—*len den* (taking and giving). Poor Chamar, Kumhar, and Teli informants stressed the desire for not one but two sons, as they feared that one son might not survive into adulthood. Informants across castes explained how the birth

Table 2.4. Scheduled Caste Sex Ratios,
All Ages, Meerut/Baghpat, 1961–2011

Year	Sex Ratio
Meerut	
1961	901
1971	863
1981	817
1991	842
Baghpat District	
2001	841
2011	865

Source: Census of India.

Table 2.5. Sex Ratios, Hindu and Muslim, All
Ages, Meerut/Baghpat, 1961–2011

Year	Muslim	Hindu
Meerut		
1961	873	836
1971	864	823
1981	877	826
1991	884	838
Baghpat district		
2001	897	829
2011	917	839

Source: Census of India.

of more than one daughter brought with it a feeling of sadness because of
dowry and gifts that had to be given through the course of her married life.
Saroj (35, Jat, F) explained, "No one desires a daughter because of increasing
expenses. You can neither educate them nor get them married. Boys will earn
and bring money into the family and then they will get married and their
wives will bring a dowry" (see also Jeffery et al. 1989, p. 182–188).

A look at the census data on marital status for the last 50 years (Table
2.6) for Meerut/Baghpat suggests that not much has changed with regard to
the percentage of never-married men in the district, with the exception of

Table 2.6. Percentage of Never-Married Men over
35 Years, Meerut/Baghpat, 1951–2011

Year	Never-Married Men (%)
Meerut	
1951	5.3
1961	7.9
1971	5.3
1981	5.4
1991	5.3
Baghpat district	
2001	5.7
2011	Not Available

Source: Census of India.

1961 (which saw a slight increase). Thus, the census data do not indicate inflated percentages of never-married men that would be expected to be the logical consequence of long-term sex ratio imbalances. Does this mean that the contemporary panic regarding increasing bachelorhood is exaggerated? If there has not been any significant shift in percentages of never-married men over a 50-year period, then why is the inability of men to marry spoken of as a situation peculiar to the present context?

I will argue that while demographic factors provide the context, there is a need to link marriageability to larger changes in political economy in this part of north India to understand the difficulties experienced by some men in the contemporary context with regard to marriage. As marriage is a "strategy" for social reproduction (Bourdieu 1976), I show that in the study context, men and families adopt various strategies in response to the difficulties faced and these strategies are tied to ideas of caste and necessities of livelihood. I thus provide a caste-wise description of the difficulties confronted by some men belonging to the five castes that are the subject of this research. Marriage strategies that worked in the past do not work in the present context. I propose that as men and communities have devised new strategies of marrying, percentages of never-married men have remained more or less unchanged despite the persisting female deficit.

UNABLE TO MARRY: THE UNEMPLOYED JAT MAN

One of the statements I heard most often from respondents across caste in Barampur was that in every Jat household there was at least one *randwā*. This, though exaggerated, highlights the apprehension regarding the inability of men to marry. When talking about *randwās*, informants distinguished between the "past" and the "present." Elderly informants (65–90) talked about how in their own and previous generations in every family one or two brothers were married and the remaining were left unmarried in order to prevent the fragmentation of land, given the system of partible inheritance. This has also been noted by earlier studies on the Jats (Chowdhry 2011; Jeffery and Jeffery 1997; Kaur 2008; Pradhan 1966). The last available data on caste-wise marital status (for 1931, United Provinces) show that a high percentage—18.6—of Jat men remained never-married (Census of India 1933). The fact that families did not strive to get all sons married in the past offers some insight on why the then-existing bride shortage and its consequences for marriageability were not recognized as concerns as they are in the contemporary context. By being left unmarried, such men were denied the possibility of fulfilling an essential element of hegemonic masculinity (that is, marriage) and filled subordinate masculine roles vis-à-vis the married.

Women, however, were not left unmarried. Marriage was in fact compulsory for them. Amarpal (65, Jat, M), a *randwā*, explained bachelor-hood in terms of the practice of *bithānā* (literally to cause to sit but refers to a levirate marriage), whereby a widowed woman was remarried with her generally unmarried *jeth* or *devar* (husband's elder or younger brother, respectively). Among the Jats of Punjab and Haryana, this leviratic marriage (described as *karewā*) was considered the most effective way to control a widow's right to inheritance and thereby retain property within the family (Chowdhry 1994). As joint living was the predominant pattern of residence, a bachelor was accommodated into the household of his married brother with his brother's wife cooking his meals. He worked with his brother on the land and his brother's children inherited his land. While families did not take into account individual desires to get married, even if to deny it, there were "arrangements" to fulfill the desires of the unmarried with a form of *de facto* fraternal polyandry whereby the unmarried brother had sexual access to his brother's wife, also noted by M.C. Pradhan (1966) in his study of the Jats of Meerut in the 1950s. Some respondents, however, denied that this was ever the case.

Jat informants stressed that while bachelorhood was not uncommon in the past, the situation faced by the present generation of young men was different. Rampal (87, Jat, M), a retired Jat school teacher, explained: "*Pehle karwāte nahī the, ab sab karwānā chāte hai shādī, par unkī hotī nahī*" (Earlier men were left unmarried, now they all want to get married but cannot). It became clear that over time several new considerations had emerged as significant in marriage negotiation. Among the Jats, size of landholdings had been the primary consideration in the arrangement of marriage. Informants married prior to 1980 explained that when their marriages were arranged, parents of daughters agreed to a marriage based on their assessment of the share of land that a man would inherit from his father.[1] Women married hypergamously, i.e., into families with larger landholdings.

In large parts of western UP, Jats have dominated landownership since at least the mid-19th century (Kumar 2016). While the construction of canals in the mid-19th century and agricultural developments such as the Green Revolution (1960s–1980s) made the Jats in this part of western UP prosperous, land ceiling legislations, population growth, and land frag-mentation over time made landholdings smaller. Moreover, from the late

1980s and early 1990s onwards, neoliberal economic policies, decline of state subsidies to agriculture, the rising cost of farming inputs, declining fertility of land, growing stagnation in farm production, and ecological precarity further weakened the position of Jat farmers (Jeffrey 2010, pp. 41–47; Kumar 2016). My survey of Jat households in Barampur shows that 31 percent of the households were either landless or had less than one acre of land; the majority—66 percent—had between one and five acres and only 3 percent had more than five acres of land. Anything less than three acres was considered too little to attract an offer of marriage.

The shrinking size of landholdings, the relatively poor returns from agriculture, and availability of employment opportunities in the non-farm sector meant that families were no longer being sustained through agriculture alone. In more than half (57 percent) of the Jat households, at least one male member was employed outside of agriculture. Informants said that Jats started moving into non-agricultural or salaried employment in the 1960s. Jats also started investing in their children's education (see Jeffrey 2010, pp. 63–69). According to my survey data on education levels of 150 adult Jat men, 16 were illiterate or had dropped out after class five, 16 had a middle-level education (class 6–8), and 118 had a class 10 or above education. Of them, 33 had an undergraduate degree and 11 a postgraduate one. Gaurang R. Sahay (2015), in his study of five villages in Baghpat, notes that a significantly greater proportion of Jats was represented in higher education than other castes.

The Jats of Barampur were employed in sugar mills, as school teachers, engineers, and factory workers, and in the railways, UP and Delhi police, Border Security Force, Central Reserve Police Force, and army. As Craig Jeffrey (2010) has also noted, it was rich Jats who were able to capitalize on education to secure government employment. Poorer Jat men tended to work as truck drivers, salespersons in shops, and security guards, and on UP Roadway buses. Many migrated out for work or were daily commuters to Delhi. As landholdings became smaller and non-agricultural employment increased, leaving men unmarried to prevent land fragmentation possibly ceased to be a meaningful strategy among the Jats.

Being educated and having a *naukrī*, preferably *sarkārī naukrī* (government job), came to define what it meant to be *kābil* (able) and *kāmyāb* (successful) and hence masculine and marriageable. In the "past," men in the army were not regarded as eligible, as the wife was left behind for long periods, but in the contemporary context, given the preference for government jobs, men in the army were highly eligible. As the criteria of eligibility changed, hypergamy came to operate in a different way. Alka (25, Jat, F), for instance, got married in 2006. She explained that her natal family owned four times the amount of land owned by her husband's family. Yet her marriage was hypergamous since her husband had a *naukrī* in the private sector while her father and brother were farmers. Vedpal (63, Jat, M) pointed out that even a man with more than 10 acres of land at times faced difficulties in getting married because he was not considered *kāmyāb*. Unmarried Jat women also talked about how they did not regard farmers as desirable spouses. Alice Tilche (2016) made a similar observation for the Patidars of Gujarat. Writing on Punjabi masculinity, Radhika Chopra (2004) notes that for men such as the Jats involved in agrarian work, "manliness" is tied to "work of the hand and body," to performing "hard labor" (pp. 43–47). In Barampur, a preference for salaried employment over agricultural work (that is, a masculinity associated with physical strength and the body) indicates a shift in one of the defining components of hegemonic masculinity.

This preference could be attributed, in part, to an increasing number of Jat women pursuing higher education. Brijpal (78, Jat, M), a retired college teacher, told me that most students at the university at present were women. The opposite was the case when he was an undergraduate in the 1950s. Education for women had emerged as a significant criterion in marriage negotiation. When I questioned Jat women in particular about their preference for daughters-in-law who had at least completed their schooling, they often responded saying "*naukrī thorī na karwānī hai*" (it is not because we will send her for salaried work). It was believed that an educated bride would be better placed to educate her children (see also Donner 2008, p. 32, on urban Kolkata). Informants agreed that women (unlike men) did not confront difficulties in finding spouses. Yet some informants shared how the search for a spouse for their daughters stretched over a few years, as eligible men were scarce. Kripa (RB, 75, Jat) was illiterate. She talked about her marriage in the early 1950s to her husband, a school teacher with a class 12 education. She compared herself with her postgraduate granddaughter, who was married at the age of 26 years, as they had struggled to find a "suitable" match for her—a man with an equal or higher level of education with a *sarkārī* or private *naukrī*. That Jat women had opportunities for higher education and were getting married at older ages reflects positive changes. The flipside is that *kāmyāb* men were few in number, so securing one for one's daughter meant competition for grooms and providing a large dowry for the marriage.

With regard to dowry, some scholars such as Monica Das Gupta and Shuzhuo Li suggested that "the surplus of men that could be expected from birth cohorts after 1980 means that there is hope that dowry inflation will taper off" (1999, p. 363). In their work in Haryana and Punjab, Mattias Larsen and Ravinder Kaur (2013) found that bride shortages had in fact resulted in reduced demands for dowry. In Barampur, some parents of men struggling to marry told me that they were willing to agree to a marriage without dowry. Yet there neither seemed to be a decline in dowry nor an increase in dowryless marriages. Sarla (RB, 47, Jat) explained, "Even an extremely poor Jat will borrow money from a moneylender to arrange a dowry for his daughter, but he will not get his daughter married to an unemployed man," pointing to the practice of hypergamous marriage and escalating dowry. Patricia Jeffery (2014) argues that the relation between marriage squeeze and decline in dowry is more complex than what "demographic determinism" can explain and what needs to be factored in is the existence of "multiple marriage markets." Such a "marriage squeeze" approach rests on assumptions of a "single perfectly competitive market in potential spouses," providing little insight into how marriages are arranged "on the ground" (pp. 178–179). She maintains that the complexity of marriage transactions and the presence of multiple marriage markets means that rather than withering, dowry is more likely to persist in the upper levels, while an increasing number of poor men must wait for several years to marry or remain unmarried (p. 182), as has been the case in Barampur.

For some men, even higher education had not helped them to secure employment. In his work on Meerut, Craig Jeffrey (2010) outlines various factors to explain educated unemployment. These included a reduction in the number of new positions created within government bureaucracies and economic liberalization that failed to generate private sector employment in UP at least till the early 2000s. While rising unemployment has been a challenge for young people across India (Joshi 2010), UP's level and pace of employment diversification is lower than that for India as a whole. According to the NSSO Employment and Unemployment round data for 2011–12, only 10.79 percent of workers in UP had a regular wage or salaried employment in any sector of the economy, compared to 18.45 percent of workers in the country. Further, the unemployment rate among tertiary educated young men was as high as 23.6 percent, compared to 19.2 percent for India as a whole (Srivastava & Ranjan 2016, p. 34). Yet elderly informants in Barampur were of the opinion that young men failed to find employment because they were not educated enough to secure the jobs they desired. Rampal (87, Jat, M) explained, "Many young men are unable to pass the entrance tests for recruitment in government services and if they manage because their families pay a bribe, they might still fail the physical test as they spend the entire day sitting at the Jat *chaupāl* [courtyard]."[2]

Rampal indicates that even though Jats had built networks with government officials, on which they could draw to get jobs for their children (cf. Jeffrey 2010; Sahay 2015), young men were still incapable of securing employment. Many unemployed Jat men neither did agricultural work (like men of the older generation) nor were willing to take up casual work (such as in construction), as they did not think it fit for someone of their caste status. I also heard exaggerated accounts of Dalit success that were presented to contrast to the dwindling prospects of young Jat men. Vedpal (63, Jat, M), for instance, told me, "There are no poor people in this village. The Chamars are in a better position than the Jats—they have jobs. They sit and drink alcohol every evening."[3]

In Barampur, across castes, it was the practice for the women's family to approach the prospective groom's family with a marriage proposal (chapter 1). I was told that neither did relatives of such (unemployed) men try to get them married nor were their families approached with proposals for them. Having failed to secure employment and hence the potential to fill provider roles, the unemployed were thus marginalized vis-à-vis the employed and hence marriageable Jat men.

JAT RESPONSES TO THE DIFFICULTIES FACED: BACHELORHOOD OR CROSS-REGIONAL MARRIAGE?

As marriage norms limit the circle from within which spouses can be selected, in Barampur, the difficulties in finding wives has resulted in the relaxation of certain norms of marriage, such as the four *gotrā* rule, which prohibited marriage between a man and a woman who shared any of the *gotrās* of their father, mother, father's mother, or mother's mother. Ashok (39, Jat, M) explained,

> My father's *gotrā* is Tomar. All Jats in this village belong to the Tomar *gotrā*. I cannot marry in the 84 Tomar villages. My *māmā*'s *gotrā* is Malik so I cannot also marry in the 84 Malik villages. My *dādī*'s [father's mother's] *gotrā* is Baliyan. If all the Baliyan villages had to be excluded as well, it would have become extremely difficult to get married since now additional criteria such as education and *naukrī* have become important. Now only the father's and mother's *gotrā* have to be avoided for the purpose of marriage.

Further, restrictions on marriage in some neighboring villages were also relaxed due to the difficulties encountered (see also Kaur 2014; Larsen & Kaur 2013). Another response to the difficulties faced by men has been cross-regional marriage. The village headman, a Jat, was of the opinion that cross-regional brides could be found among the "*nīchī jātī*" (lower castes) but not among the Jats. Some other Jat informants, however, acknowledged the presence of cross-regional brides among them, but stated that they were fewer in number as compared to other castes because *mol lānā* (buying a wife) from another state had an adverse effect on the *izzat* of the family. Jat informants insisted that they instead preferred to leave sons unmarried and stated that status concerns made bachelorhood preferable to a cross-regional marriage.

In the context of inter-caste marriages, Kusum (RB, 47, Chamar) told me about a Jat family with four bachelor sons: "They were telling me to bring them a wife from my natal village [in Muzaffarnagar, a neighboring district]. They said that they were even willing to take a Chuhra [Dalit, regarded by Chamars as even lower in status than them] woman in marriage." Whilst this statement indicates the desperation felt by some unmarried men, inter-caste marriages between Jat men and lower-caste women within the local region were not known to be taking place, with the exception of self-arranged marriages and elopements, which were resisted and often provoked violence.[4] Yet cross-regional marriages were tolerated and rationalized in terms of *majbūrī* (compulsion)—"for two cooked meals, to pass on the land and carry forward the family."

The first cross-regional bride among the Jats is believed to have come from Darjeeling (West Bengal) in the early 1960s. Jaya (CRB, 45, Jat) talked about the conversation she had with her husband when he first went to West Bengal to marry her in 1986: "I asked him, why have you come here to marry, are there no women in your village? Who are they marrying? Your sister must have married someone. After I came here, I understood that men go so far because they have some 'defect.' "[5] The commonly held opinion was that it was only "disadvantaged" men who brought cross-regional brides. Not all "disadvantaged" Jat men, however, brought cross-regional brides. The compulsion to marry was not experienced in the same way by all men; thus, some remained bachelors.

In Barampur, Jats considered it acceptable for a man to bring a cross-regional bride in two situations, both of which indicate that it was necessary for one man of each generation in a family to marry. One situation was that when it was evident that none of the men in a family would get married, one brother could then bring a cross-regional bride. Praveen (35, Jat, M) falls in this category. He was a landless truck driver with a class seven education. He had two younger brothers (30 and 32), also unmarried and drivers on private buses. Both had reputations of being alcoholics. Praveen brought Varsha (28) from West Bengal in 1992 when he was 25. His mother felt that it was sufficient that one son was married. She consented to a cross-regional marriage on the understanding that a regional marriage was not possible for her son. She added that before he went to West Bengal to marry, he secured the consent of her *jeth*, the senior-most male of the *kunbā* (extended family). Praveen's brothers lived with him and contributed their earnings to his household.

Alternatively, a cross-regional marriage was regarded as acceptable when a man was the only son and failed to get married within the local region. Vinod, for instance, brought Pushpa (late 30s) from Bihar in the early 1990s. Pushpa said that Vinod was "much older" than her. He had less than two acres of land. Additionally, he suffered from a physical disability and had previously been married to a cross-regional bride who "ran away." She talked about how it was necessary for Vinod to have a family of his own or else his sister's son would inherit his share of the land.

There were cases of men who did not fall in either of the above two categories. They were aware that a marriage in UP was not possible for them. Amar (52, Jat, M), for instance, was a drug addict. He owned less than an acre of land. His mother was the third wife of a Jat man from Barampur and though a UP woman, she was of unknown caste status. Amar was her son from a previous marriage. He brought Jaya (45) from West Bengal in 1986 without the consent of his family, prioritizing his desire to get married over necessity and familial approval. His mother said that she was extremely unhappy when her son had returned with a Bengali wife, as she was concerned that it would affect the marriage prospects of her younger educated employed son.

At the Bottom of the Eligibility Hierarchy: The Chamar Brick-Kiln Worker

Unlike the Jats, the difficulties that Chamar men faced in getting married were explained not in terms of unemployment but as linked to seasonal labor migration to the brick kilns. Informants said that parents who themselves worked in the brick kilns did not want to give their daughters in marriage to other brick-kiln workers because they did not want their daughters to have hard lives. Chamars were landless. They were traditionally leather-workers and agricultural laborers for Jat farmers. Migration to the brick kilns started from the 1960s and most Chamars had abandoned leather-work by the early 1980s. In the kilns, they worked as *patherās*—preparing the soil and molding it into raw bricks before they were shifted for firing in the kiln. *Patherās* require more than one person to manage all the tasks, and so the *jodī* (couple) or family unit is employed.

Satender (55, Chamar, M) talked about difficulties in getting married as a problem faced by men of his son's generation but not his own. I pointed out to him that it was largely men of his generation who had brought cross-regional brides. To this he replied, *"Hā, problem kāfī din se hai"* (Yes, there has been a problem for a long time). Jagmati (RB, early 60s, Chamar) told me that even when she got married in the mid-1960s, parents were unwilling to give daughters to brick-kiln workers. At the time, those who worked in the brick kilns were a minority. Satender believed that more men of marriageable ages of the present generation and in future would fail to marry, as labor migration to the brick kilns had increased over the years, with about 90 percent of Chamar households in Barampur employed in the brick kilns.

According to my village survey, 60 percent of the Chamar households (including women and children) migrated to the brick kilns (usually in other parts of the district or state, Punjab, and Haryana) for work for six to eight months in a year. During the remaining four to six months, most (men and women alike) were casual laborers for Jat farmers. The concentration of Chamars in brick-kiln work resulted from several factors that include decline in traditional leather-work (Varma & Kumar 2006) and lack of available employment throughout the year. Western UP lies in the Green Revolution belt, and mechanization meant that agricultural labor days declined, making the need for alternate employment essential for the landless poor. Unlike other artisan communities like weavers and potters, Chamars had limited opportunities for employment because of their caste status (Varma & Kumar 2006). A significant factor that explains the concentration of Chamars in brick-kiln work is that household income is more than that from other kinds of employment, since women's and other family members' (including children's) contributions make it more than a single wage.

SCs, such as Chamars, remain far behind upper castes and OBCs as far as access to education is concerned (Corbridge et al. 2013). The lack of or lower levels of education limited the possibilities for alternative employment for many Chamar men in Barampur. Moreover, migration to the brick kilns made it difficult for their children to acquire or continue their education: while some continued their schooling at the migration destination, many dropped out. My survey data on education levels of 130 Chamar adult men in Barampur show that 71 were illiterate or had dropped out after class five. Twenty-nine had studied to class 10 or above and only three had an undergraduate degree. Lack or lower levels of education also make it difficult to benefit from reservation in government jobs available to the Chamars due to their Scheduled Caste status. Only a small section among the Dalits have access to and benefit from reservation in public sector jobs (Corbridge et al. 2013). In their study in neighboring Bijnor district, Craig Jeffrey et al. (2008) note that Chamar men had failed to use formal education to gain secure employment. Young Chamar men attributed their failure to a lack of social networks and money needed to bribe recruitment officials or brokers for government jobs. Studies also show that even highly qualified Dalits encounter discrimination in the formal, urban labor market (Thorat & Newman 2007) and are less likely than non-Dalits to find jobs in the private sector (Deshpande & Newman 2007).

As marriage results in the transfer of a woman's labor to her husband's family, I argue that brick-kiln work makes marriage an "economic necessity" for men, since brick-making requires family labor, with the core unit usually comprising a husband and wife. On the other hand, it affects men's ability to get married by making them less eligible for marriage in relation to other men of the caste. In the hierarchy of eligibility, a *sarkārī naukar* (government servant) was at the top. According to informants, fewer than 5 percent of Chamar men in Barampur were in government employment—in the army, police, railways, or municipality. This was followed by men with a private *naukrī*: factory workers, caterers, and sales workers in shops were placed in this category, followed by barbers, tailors, masons, and transporters. Brick-kiln workers were at the bottom of the hierarchy. With the exception of brick-kiln workers, men could get married *nirol*. Being highly "eligible," a government employee could find the kind of spouse he desired, with beauty and education being considerations. Such a man also demanded a big dowry. Among Chamars, education in women was a desired attribute in marriage only for the eligible men and not for brick-kiln workers, "who married illiterate women." In Barampur, few young Chamar women were educated beyond class eight. Informants said that daughters were disinclined to study.

CHAMAR RESPONSES TO THE DIFFICULTIES FACED: LOWER FORMS OF MARRIAGE?

Failing to marry *nirol*, brick-kiln workers had to resort to other kinds of marriage arrangements. Some Chamar men got married after lying to the woman's family about their employment. It was common for a family working in the brick kiln to send their son to work elsewhere (as a tailor, in a barber's shop, or in a factory) and as soon as the marriage took place, he returned to brick-kiln work. There were rumors of men who had taken money from the groom's family (instead of dowry) to get their daughters married to brick-kiln workers. Respondents said that a woman, unlike a man, did not face any difficulties in getting married, unless she had a "defect" (e.g., she been previously married and had a child from that marriage). In such cases, she had no choice but to marry a brick-kiln worker who would otherwise find it difficult to find a local wife. Informants also told me that brick-kiln workers sometimes married the daughters of cross-regional brides, who were "less desirable" as spouses because of their mother's unknown caste origins (see Chaudhry 2019b, pp. 222–223).

There was also a system of *tigaddā* or *antā-santā* marriage, that is, an exchange marriage that took place between three families/villages. Direct exchange (A gives a bride to B and B reciprocates by giving a bride to A) was not regarded as acceptable but did occur in exceptional cases. Chamar informants were of the opinion that *tigaddā* had been in existence for more than a hundred years. Writing in 1920, G.W. Briggs noted exchange marriage ("*wattā sattā*," "*gurāwat*," "*adlā badlā*") among poor Chamars practiced to save marriage expenses (1920, p. 38). During my fieldwork, informants explained exchange marriage as a response to the difficulties confronted in getting married *nirol*. Sham (early 30s, Chamar, M) was of the opinion that the number of *nirol* and *tigaddā* marriages were almost equal in number. A brick-kiln worker, for instance, might give his daughter in marriage to another brick-kiln worker since he wanted a wife for his son who was also a brick-kiln worker and was facing trouble in getting married. Ajay (24, Chamar, M), an unmarried brick-kiln worker with a class 10 education, told me,

> There has not been a single proposal for me so far and I think that it is because I work in the brick kiln. Until I find alternative employment, it will be difficult for me to get married. I do not

want to have a *tigaddā* marriage even though I have three sisters because you can get any spouse; my sister might get a husband who is a drug addict. My elder sister has a class eight education and if she is married in *tigaddā*, she might get a husband who is illiterate. You do not get the kind of spouse you desire.

"Being a man" involves taking care of one's sisters and fulfilling duties toward them. Being a man also entails making a "good" marriage. In Ajay's case, this dilemma may rule out an exchange marriage. Men without sisters could not have a *tigaddā* marriage. Some with sisters, like Ajay, preferred not to have a *tigaddā* marriage. An exchange marriage, like a marriage involving a payment to the bride's parents, was considered an inferior form of marriage (chapter 1). In an exchange marriage, the in-married woman would belong to the same caste. It was, thus, considered preferable to a cross-regional marriage. Nevertheless, compared to the other caste groups in Barampur, I found the largest number of cross-regional brides among the Chamars (and hence a lower proportion of bachelors than the Jats). According to the 2001 Census, 3.25 percent of Scheduled Caste men over the age of 35 years remained never-married in (rural) Baghpat, compared with 6.7 percent of men of other (non-SC) castes (Census of India 2001a). In eastern UP too, Dalits form a large proportion of the men bringing brides from West Bengal and its neighboring states (Kaur 2012). Like the Jats, Chamar informants rationalized cross-regional marriage in terms of *majbūrī*.

Among the Chamars, the first cross-regional bride arrived in the early 1970s and brides have been coming in ever since, with the most recent bride arriving just a few days before I started fieldwork in September 2012. Informants, however, believed that cross-regional brides would decrease in future and hence a larger number of men would fail to marry as parents of (potential) cross-regional brides were unwilling to give daughters in marriage in UP. Satender (55, Chamar, M) explained that the parents "have understood that their daughters will be troubled here. Their husbands make false promises. They do not take them back to visit for several years." Jagmati (RB, early 60s, Chamar) shared her frustrations. She had approached three cross-regional brides to act as a go-between to arrange a marriage for her son. She was willing to pay the "expenses"—"*ab koi nahī karwātā*" (now no one agrees), she remarked. Data collected through the village survey for 22 men in cross-regional marriages shows that of them, 19 were brick-kiln workers. For majority of the men who brought cross-regional brides, factors such as a previous marriage, older age, physical disability, illiteracy, and a "flawed" reputation (due to gambling, drinking alcohol, consuming drugs) in addition to brick-kiln work had placed them at the bottom of the hierarchy of eligibility and accounted for their inability to get married within the local region. Such men, by managing to get married, had achieved successful masculinity vis-à-vis other Chamar men who remained bachelors. Yet, in failing to negotiate a "good" marriage (within the caste and region with a dowry), they fell short compared to Chamar men who had married *nirol*.

Six of 19 men in cross-regional marriage were above the age of 35 years when they went to bring a bride. Ratanpal (early 70s, Chamar, M), for instance, brought a cross-regional bride when he was over 50 years of age. "*Do rotī ke liye*" (for two cooked meals), he told me. Until then, he lived with his parents and worked in the brick-kiln with one of his married brothers. After their parents died, his relationship with his brothers was strained and they were unwilling to accommodate him in their households. The bride he brought "ran away" a few months later and Ratanpal was living alone during my fieldwork, ill and reliant on his neighbors for food. His case points to the necessity of marriage not just because solo living is unworkable for a brick-kiln worker but also because marriage ensures the provision of care and keeps "female tasks" (such as cooking) from having to be done by men. The brothers of two men in cross-regional marriages had also married cross-regional brides, while the brothers of four others remained never-married.

UNABLE TO MARRY *NIROL*: THE KUMHAR (CASUAL) LABORER

In comparison to the Jats and Chamars, among the Kumhars, concerns regarding the inability of men to marry were less articulated. That Kumhar men did confront difficulties in finding wives is supported by the fact that among their small number (inhabiting around 60–70 households in Barampur), 11 Kumhar men had brought cross-regional brides. Ramesh (50, Kumhar, M) explained that Kumhars were traditionally potters or traders of sugar and *gūr* (*jaggery* or unrefined sugar). In Barampur, only "two–three" young Kumhar men had government employment, with the majority being *mazdūrs* (casual laborers). Several Kumhar men from Barampur migrated to work in the brick kilns for six to eight months in a year, performing different tasks from Chamar brick-kiln workers, shifting sun-dried bricks to the kiln.

Marriage not only results in the transfer of a woman's labor to her husband's family but can also enable the out-migration of male members if women take over farming, household chores, and the care of children (Fan

& Li 2002). Unlike among the Chamars, only Kumhar men, not women and children, worked in brick kilns. For the remaining part of the year, they worked as potters or masons in the village or as salespersons in shops in the nearby town. Others, who did not migrate, worked as vegetable sellers or had small shops in the village. Some young Kumhar men migrated to Delhi to work as transporters or as factory employees. Ompal (55, Kumhar, M) explained that migration for brick-kiln work started with men of his father's generation, as men could no longer support families by working only as potters. He added,

> I started going to the brick kiln when I was 16 years old. I work as a potter for three months of the year and at times as a rickshaw puller or fruit and vegetable seller. Earlier I worked as a potter for 120 Jat families but that is now no longer the case. Before they needed *matkās* [mud pots] to fetch water from the well but now everyone has a submersible pump and refrigerator in their house. For that reason, I have to do other work for a large part of the year. Most young men of the caste do not know how to do this [potter] work because of education or they lack interest.

Under the *jajmānī* system (patron-client relations) that was common in this part of UP in the first half of the 20th century, Jats as the landowning caste (*jajmāns*) called on other castes to perform specific services for their households and land. For these services, they made payments in kind to the lower castes. The *jajmānī* system declined in northwestern UP in the 1960s and 1970s (Jeffrey 2010, p. 44), as suggested by Ompal above, who pointed out that the services previously rendered by castes such as his to the Jats were no longer required in the same way (as consumer goods became available) and hence they were forced to search for alternative sources of employment.[6] The commonly held opinion was that young Kumhar men were more educated than men of their fathers' generation. Yet many had failed to use education to secure salaried employment. My survey data on educational levels of 35 adult Kumhar men show that seven were illiterate or had dropped out after class five, 17 had a class eight education, and 11 had a class 10 or above education, with three (all in their 20s) being graduates. Informants explained how additional criteria had emerged over time in marriage negotiation. Jagbiri (RB, 71, Kumhar) explained that when she got married in the early 1960s, the only consideration was that the prospective groom came from an *izzatwālā parivār* (honorable family). Munesh

(RB, 38, Kumhar) said that when she got married in the early 1990s, the prospective groom's education was not considered significant. Parents looked for a man who could work and feed his family. She added that she was educating her daughter and when she gets her daughter married she will look for an educated boy (with at least a class 12 education), preferably with a private job. He should not have any "*burī ādat*" (bad habits) such as drinking alcohol, she added.

Kumhar Responses to the Difficulties Faced: *Badlā* or Cross-regional Marriage?

As most Kumhar men worked as casual laborers, informants considered they could not marry *nirol* and most were married in *badlā* (exchange), what the Chamars termed *tigaddā*. As among the Chamars, among the Kumhars a *badlā* usually took place between three families but could also be arranged between four or five families. Unlike with the Chamars, *badlā* did not necessarily involve exchange of women in the same generation; for instance, one informant explained that her brother was married in *badlā* for her eldest daughter. As with the Chamars, an *āmnā sāmnā badlā* (direct exchange) was regarded as *burrā* (bad) but Ramesh (50, Kumhar, M) explained that families resorted to a direct exchange in *pareshānī* (difficulty), when a marriage could not be arranged anywhere else. *Badlā* was regarded as *nīchā* (lower), yet parents gave daughters in *badlā* so that sons could get married. *Badlā* marriages took place between families of equal status, so there were no dowry demands in such marriages. Ompal (55, Kumhar, M) pointed to the lack of trust in *badlā* marriages:

> If I give my daughter in *badlā* to family [B], that gives their daughter to a third family [C], from where I should get a daughter-in-law for my son but a few years later since he is not yet of marriageable age, what happens in many cases is that in future, family [C] might refuse to give their daughter in marriage to my son.

He added that because it was common for families to do this, he was planning to get his son (20) married in *badlā* for his daughter (15). He said that the wedding would take place on the same day but he would send his daughter to live at her husband's home three to five years later. He explained that, by doing so, he would also be able to save on wedding expenses. The earlier practice was to get daughters married at younger ages (at times as young as 12) and they were sent to their husband's home when they became older at *gaunā/chālā*. This was explained in terms of the need to guard the sexuality of young girls. There was no longer a gap between wedding and cohabitation (chapter 1). Yet, as Ompal suggests due to the lack of trust, some families had gone back to the earlier practice (of marriage at a young age and cohabitation few years later).

Jagbiri (RB, 71, Kumhar) believed that *badlā* marriages date back to the late 1960s. She said that as families were not approached with marriage proposals for their sons, they started marrying in *badlā*—a response to the difficulties confronted. Others like Virender (52, Kumhar, M) suggested that *badlā* had a much longer history and was the predominant form of marriage in the "past," with there being a decline in the practice among the present generation of men. He argued that about "50 percent" of men (like him) remained *randwās* because they did not have sisters to have a *badlā* marriage. Some of these men brought cross-regional brides, while others preferred to remain never-married.

Not having a sister for a *badlā* marriage was the reason offered by six of the 11 men in cross-regional marriage. For some, like Ramesh (50, Kumhar, M), having a much older sister and "deterioration in the family's economic situation" made a *badlā* marriage impossible. All of these men were casual laborers, so a marriage was not possible for them without *badlā*. The first cross-regional bride among the Kumhars is believed to have come to Barampur from the Cachar district of Assam in the late 1970s. Six of the 11 men were above the age of 35 years and one over 40 years when they went to other states to get married. After trying and failing to find a local wife, "*jānā parā*" (I was forced to go), Ompal (55, Kumhar, M) told me. The brothers of three of the men in cross-regional marriage had also brought cross-regional brides. Jagbiri (RB, 71, Kumhar) said that cross-regional marriages were not always tolerated. Previously, a cross-regional marriage resulted in outcasting ("*huqqā pānī bandh*"), with caste members refusing to share the *huqqā* (smoking pipe) or accept water from them. She explained that *majbūrī* made men seek wives from outside, and gradually such marriages became acceptable as more brides arrived.

LOHAR AND TELI: ONLY A SECOND MARRIAGE IS DIFFICULT

Lohars were numerically the largest of the five Muslim castes in Barampur. Traditionally they were ironsmiths and some did carpentary and were called

Barhi Lohars. In the past, several Lohar families had been involved in the production of agricultural implements, but they abandoned that work and moved to live and work in the nearby town. The better-off families within the caste owned tractors and worked for Jat farmers, and some were involved in manufacturing machinery, such as flour-milling machines. Poorer Lohars owned small shops of their own in the village or worked as shop employees and as transporters. Several men did welding work in the village or were daily commuters to nearby towns, and some migrated to other cities for this work. Some Lohar men also migrated out to work as factory employees. Most Teli families were poor and men were engaged in casual work. Several Teli men worked in brick kilns as *nikāsīwāle*—they removed fired bricks from the kiln and stacked them. Others worked as rickshaw pullers, masons, and tailors, and some sold jaggery.

Yusuf (77, Lohar, M) explained that when he got married in the mid-1950s, *khāndān* (extended family) was the only consideration in marriage. When his daughter got married in the early 1980s, the prospective groom's employment had emerged as significant in addition to *khāndān*. In the contemporary context, he said that education had become crucial, with at least a class 10 education being essential for a man. Muneera (RB, 32, Lohar) got married in 2003. She talked about how her father was searching for a groom with higher education and salaried employment for her, as her father himself had a private sector job and Muneera was a graduate. Zubeida (27, Lohar, F), however, was of the opinion that education was irrelevant, as she was illiterate. She added that the only consideration for her family was that her husband should be capable of working and feeding his family, or, in Sakeena's (RB, 43, Teli) words, he should be *"hāthon pairon kā mazbūt"* (should have strength in his arms and legs). Thus, physical strength that allowed men to perform hard labor and thereby provide for their families, was a defining component of successful masculinity among the poor.

Teli informants pointed out that few Teli men had attained higher education and a *naukrī*. Other studies on western UP also show that Muslims have been unable to invest in formal education and obtain white-collar salaried employment (Jeffrey et al. 2008). In his study of five villages in Baghpat, Gaurang R. Sahay (2015) noted that the educational attainment of Muslims was mainly primary level. My survey data on educational levels of 60 adult men (Lohar and Teli) show that half (30) were illiterate or had dropped out after completing class five, 11 had a class eight education, and 19 had a class 10 or above education.

Some studies in other parts of north India suggest that Muslim men were also bringing cross-regional brides owing to compulsions similar to those faced by Hindu men—landlessness or marginal landholding and informal sector employment (Chaudhry & Mohan 2011; Ibrahim 2018; Kukreja & Kumar 2013; Singh 2009). In Barampur, however, cross-regional brides among Muslims were exceptional. Muslim men with low levels of education and engaged in casual work (e.g., in the brick kilns) were not facing such difficulty in finding wives as Hindu men (e.g., Kumhar and Chamar also employed in brick-kiln work) were. "*Shādī toh ho jātī hai*" (they get married), several informants told me. There were only two cross-regional brides—one each among the Lohars and Telis. A second cross-regional bride was believed to have come among the Lohars in the early 1960s but had died a few years before my fieldwork. The three Muslim men in cross-regional marriages had been married previously. Of them, one was 60 when he went to Bihar to bring a wife. Informants suggested that additional factors such as children from the previous marriage and "spoiled" reputation made a second marriage difficult for these men. As among the Hindu castes, cross-regional marriages were considered *nīchā* (lower) because of the woman's unknown caste status. Informants also suggested that for Muslim men, getting married in the first instance did not present difficulties, but trying to enter a secondary union was more complex.

Earlier, I indicated that although sex ratios for Muslims are comparatively better than for Hindus, they are still not favorable, so the question that arises: How are Muslim men who may be disadvantaged in ways similar to some Hindu men (who fail to marry) successful in making a regional marriage within a context of adverse sex ratios. Yusuf (77, Lohar, M) explained, "Jats cannot find wives because of *gotrā*. We do not have *gotrā*." What Yusuf points to is that Muslims have a larger marriage circle to choose from. While some informants told me that they were not married to relatives due to preference, or that a "suitable match" (e.g., in age) could not be found within the circle of relatives, some others believed that cousin marriage had increased over the years. Khalida (RB, 45, Teli) held that close-kin marriages were arranged "*jab hotī nahī*" (when a marriage cannot be arranged elsewhere). Yusuf (77, Lohar, M) told me about his *tāu*'s son. "His reputation is well known; no one was willing to give their daughter in marriage to his son, so he got his son married to his wife's brother's daughter." Muslim marriage practices, such as cousin marriage permitted for Muslims but forbidden for Hindus, could be one explanation for why getting married may be less of a problem for Muslim men as compared to Hindu men, but other factors that could explain this need further exploration.

BACHELOR MEN, MARGINALIZED MASCULINITIES

I have shown that bachelorhood (especially among the Jats) was not uncommon in the past, yet during my fieldwork informants insisted that non-marriage for men had different implications in the contemporary context than it did in the past. Some recent studies on India and China have focused on the (negative) consequences of a "male surplus" and involuntary bachelorhood (see Kaur 2016, pp. 14–19, and Srinivasan & Li 2018, pp. 8–9, for a summary of these discussions). Writing on India, Prem Chowdhry (2005), for instance, discusses a "crisis of masculinity" among the unmarried and unemployed in Haryana. She argues that having failed to achieve social adulthood through marriage, such men claim and display masculine identities in the public domain by extending support to "illegal and unconstitutional decisions" of traditional *panchāyats* headed by older dominant caste men, thereby strengthening casteism (p. 5193). Also writing on India, South et al. (2014) focus on a potential rise in crime, specifically violence against women. They postulate that an abundance of males would increase the likelihood of theft, assault, and harassment of women in public spaces. There are also studies, such as Paro Mishra's on Haryana, that critique such studies for their "homogenized portrayal of bachelors as prone to violence" and seek to present a far more complex and multi-dimensional lived reality (2018, p. 27). In Barampur, the dominant discourse centered not on "over-age" bachelors but on the "deviant" behavior of young unmarried (mostly Jat) men who were unlikely to get married in future. The narratives considered such behavior to be a consequence of men's unemployed status and non-marriageability and not necessarily their demographic surplus, however.

People in the village pointed out how young Jat men spent their days "hanging around" for hours at the Jat *chaupāl* harassing women as they passed by, an observation I made as well. By contrast, young Chamar, Kumhar, and Muslim men could not be seen "hanging around" in public spaces. The difference between men of these castes and Jat men was that while the former worked in brick kilns or in other kinds of casual work if they failed to find salaried employment in the government or private sector, Jat young men, in the words of an older Jat male, were "*khālī*" (free). Cecile Jackson notes that for high-status groups, manliness does not involve manual labor, which they consider degrading and a mark of inferiority, but lower social groups widely value physical strength as an attribute of men (1999, p. 101). Chamar and Muslim men, unlike Jat men, thus, had to be employed, as their families were sustained through wages and not through land ownership. The history of caste and economic livelihoods and the inability to study (and "stay out of the sun") meant that for them physical labor, laboring for others, and their sense of subaltern masculinity were intertwined (Chaudhry 2018).

In his work in Meerut, Craig Jeffrey noted that a few unemployed Jat men regarded harassing Dalit women as an especially good means of "timepass" (2010, p. 99). In Barampur too, Jat men harassed women of other castes, a privilege available to them due to their dominant caste status, something that Dalit and Muslim men could not do. Sakeena (RB, 43, Teli Muslim), for instance, discussed how this had led her to withdraw her daughters from school after class five. "Jat girls are getting educated but the daughters of the poor like us cannot. Jat men can take our daughters from school if they want to and our men can do nothing as even the police is owned by the Jats." Young Jat men harassed not only women of other castes but also young Jat women who traveled to schools and colleges to study. Some young Jat unmarried women told me that it was common for groups of young men to board buses from the village to the nearby town and grope women on the bus. Older informants often remarked, "*māhaul kharāb hai*" (the environment is bad) and expressed concerns about their daughters' safety that have had implications for young women's mobility in public spaces.

Informants emphasized that there was something different about the present generation of young men. Rampal (87, Jat, M) told me, "Even earlier men were unmarried, but they never acted this way." What has changed is that young women are pursuing higher education and becoming increasingly visible in public spaces. As masculinities are "defined and redefined in social interaction" (Cornwall & Lindisfarne 1994, p. 3), with the relationship among men in all male spaces being central to the enactment of masculinities (cf. Chopra 2004), such harassment could be read as a response to ideas of "natural claims to such spaces," that is, public space as male space (Srivastava 2012, p. 25). Raewyn Connell (1995) considers that men who harass women are unlikely to think of themselves as "deviant." On the contrary, they usually feel that what they are doing is entirely legitimate—"they are exercising a right" (p. 83) and in the process displaying masculinity.

Kavita (41, Jat, F) remarked that what was also different was that bachelors in the past "had control and *sehanshaktī* (willpower) while the men of today think about sex all the time." She attributed this to pornographic images that they accessed through mobile phones. While on the one hand, people in the village complained about such behavior, on the other, some blamed women for "encouraging men to act this way." My landlady's husband, for instance, commented on how young women had lost their modesty as they dressed in "tight-fitting western clothes," such as jeans, which he considered inappropriate clothing for the village. Likewise, Yusuf (77, Lohar, M) asserted, "Nowadays girls go to colleges and have cell phones. They are having relationships with boys. They leave their houses to study and meet up with boys. No boy has the courage to tease a girl until she allows it." As Sanjay Srivastava (2012) has argued, "the gendered discourse of public spaces represents them as sites where women may both be allowed and afforded security of movement as long as they behave as women should" (p. 26). By this logic, women forfeit the right to (male protection) if they fail to conform to expectations of feminine honor and modesty. Such discourses reveal great patriarchal anxieties regarding "the decline of society" that seem to have become particularly salient in an era of globalization (p. 27).

Rahul Roy (2007) writes that masculinity is "fragile" and the fear of failure to meet desired norms underlies a high level of "masculine anxiety." Martyn Rogers (2008), in his study of Dalit young men on a college campus, explains the performance of hyper-masculinity through sexual harassment of women and engagement in "deviant" forms of leisure as a reaction "to the devaluing of their social status," that is, their subordination within higher education and the "white-collar employment market" (pp. 79, 86, 91). In Barampur, if the unemployed and unmarried were trying to compensate for failing to conform to valued masculine norms by engaging in the aforementioned behavior, as a consequence they were placed even further away from being "eligible" and marriageable and hence from hegemonic masculinity.

Respondents also spoke disapprovingly of young Jat men having sexual relations with in-married women of the household/extended family. It was not clear why this was a matter of concern, as this seemed similar to, though not "sanctioned" in the same way as, the practice in the past when the never-married had sexual access to in-married women of the household. Informants narrated accounts of young men "catching hold of women in the fields" as well as visiting nearby villages and paying for sex. I also heard accounts of older Jat men (married and bachelors) having sexual relations with women who worked as casual laborers on their fields or paying for sex. Some of this current alarm thus seemed unfounded, especially as the sexual exploitation of women by men in positions of dominance is not "new." Sheela's (CRB, early 40s, Chamar) words are telling in this regard: "If a woman goes to the field to work and gets raped, she comes home quietly and says nothing to anyone." Some of my Jat women informants, in contrast, spoke of the relations between Dalit women and Jat men as "consensual" and as something that was widely known to take place. Sarla (RB, 47, Jat), for instance, casually told me, "Usually, Chamars are *kālā* but you will notice that some Chamars have lighter skin than others. These are children of Chamar women and Jat men."

Not only Dalits, but Muslims and Kumhars as well were dependent on employment in Jat fields or households for at least some part of the year and also for fodder for their cattle and wood for cooking. This dependence, combined with the numerical dominance of the Jats, made it difficult for men of these castes to stand up to those who wielded power. Furthermore, as Sakeena above pointed out, "even the police is owned by the Jats"—i.e., heavily drawn from the dominant group and upholding its interests (see also Chowdhry 2007). Importantly, as the writing on caste has noted, the infliction of violence by the dominant castes, on both lower caste men and women, becomes a means of affirming their masculinity by demonstrating control over women from the lower groups and emasculating Dalit men in the process, thereby asserting their own status and power (Kannabiran & Kannabiran 1991).

Apart for the implications for violence against women, informants pointed to the "excessive" consumption of alcohol and drugs among young Jat men. I also heard that some young Chamar and Kumhar men had acquired "bad habits" (smoking, drinking, and gambling) and it was believed that this, in addition to casual work, was likely to hinder their marriage prospects. Yet the dominant narrative focused on young Jat men's "deviant" behavior. I observed young Jat men always well dressed and with consumer goods—mobile phones, motorbikes—despite being unemployed and wondered how they managed to meet their expenses. Amarpal (65, Jat, M) talked about an increase in incidents of theft and the loss of parental authority: "They fight with their parents and even threaten them and take money forcefully from them. There is no respect left. They steal money from family members so that they can buy drugs." It is important to stress that not all unemployed unmarried men were engaging in such behavior. Yet, the accounts focused only on the unmarried. This stemmed from the assumption that marriage has a civilizing influence on men, even though I observed that some married men also "hung around" in public spaces, harassed women, and were rumored to consume drugs.

There were also rumors of young Jat men having sexual relations with other men. Studies show that in rural north India, homosexuality is not considered "odd" or "unnatural," yet it is considered "temporary" (Chowdhry 2011, p. 249), a phase that men are expected to outgrow as they transition to adult heterosexual marriage. Interestingly, it was not only the unmarried who were rumored to be engaging in such behavior, yet in conversations informants always implied that this was not and could not be because of homoerotic desire but was due to heterosexual frustration. This reflected the cultural understanding that sexuality must find expression only within heterosexual marriage, making spaces "outside marriage" unimaginable for same-sex bondings (Tellis 2014, p. 346).

I argue that the "deviant" behavior described above may have to do with the aggressive patriarchal culture of this rural context (of which the sex ratio imbalance is one outcome), caste dominance, youth culture, and/ or a backlash to women's mobility. What the dominant narrative in the village on young unmarried men offers is not sufficient evidence in itself to establish a definitive relationship between sex ratio imbalance, bachelorhood, and male violence.

Bride-Sending Regions

I will now move on to discuss where cross-regional brides come from and what factors drive their migration for marriage. In Barampur, the cross-regional brides I interviewed had originated in 13 districts of five states: Nasik in Maharashtra; Malda, Jalpaiguri, West Mednipur, and South Dinajpur districts of West Bengal; Madhepura and Madhubani districts of Bihar; Hazaribagh, Giridih, Godda, Sahibganj, and Pakur districts of Jharkhand; and Cachar district of Assam (Map 2.1). The sex ratios in bride-sending states and districts are closer to "normal"—950 females per 1000 males (Table 2.7). My informants did not attribute women's migration over long distances for marriage to a surplus of women in the source states, however. Rather, widespread poverty is central in their accounts of becoming cross-regional brides.

In the following pages, as I outline the factors that influence cross-regional brides' marriage migration decisions, I show that given the contexts from where women move to become cross-regional brides, there are instances of the exercise of some *agency within constraint*. I draw on a notion of agency that attends to the "conditions of choice—choice made from the vantage point of alternatives." Such an understanding recognizes the possible

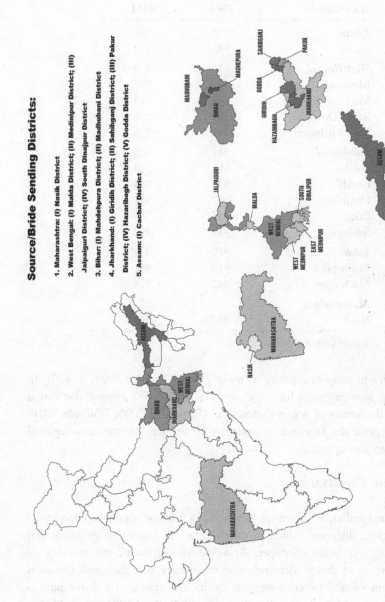

Source/Bride Sending Districts:

1. **Maharashtra:** (I) Nasik District
2. **West Bengal:** (I) Malda District; (II) Medinipur District; (III) Jalpaiguri District; (IV) South Dinajpur District
3. **Bihar:** (I) Mahdehpura District; (II) Madhubani District
4. **Jharkhand:** (I) Giridih District; (II) Sahibganj District; (III) Pakur District; (IV) Hazaribagh District; (V) Godda District
5. **Assam:** (I) Cachar District

Map 2.1. Bride-sending districts.

Table 2.7. Sex Ratios of Bride-Sending States/
Districts, All Ages, 2001 and 2011

State/District	2001	2011
Assam	935	958
Cachar	945	959
West Bengal	934	950
Jalpaiguri	942	953
Malda	948	944
South Dinajpur	951	956
West Mednipur	961	966
Jharkhand	941	948
Giridih	982	944
Godda	926	938
Hazaribagh	987	947
Pakur	957	989
Sahibganj	942	952
Bihar	919	918
Madhepura	915	911
Madhubani	942	926
Maharashtra	922	929
Nasik	927	934

Source: Census of India.

inequalities in people's capacity to make choices (Kabeer 1999, p. 439). In discussing how migrants have the capacity to act with agency, the aim is to "hear the stories of actors themselves" (Constable 2005; Williams 2010, p. 35). I place the factors that explain why women become cross-regional brides into five categories.[7]

ECONOMIC CONSTRAINTS

As discussed earlier, in Barampur, dowry was a primary reason that accounted for "daughter disfavor," which in turn resulted in masculine sex ratios and the consequent bride shortages. At bride-sending areas, the inability of families to meet dowry demands due to poverty was the most common explanation offered by cross-regional brides for marriage in Barampur, as previously noted by other studies (Blanchet 2008; Kaur 2004, 2012; Mishra 2016). Not only did a cross-regional marriage mean a dowryless marriage, but also in such marriages the wedding expenses were met by the groom. Four of the 19 cross-regional brides interviewed said that their families were approached with marriage proposals within their native states, but they settled for a cross-regional marriage because of unrealizable dowry demands. All the cross-regional brides interviewed came from poor families engaged as laborers in casual/informal work in coal mines or quarries, tea planation work, or as rickshaw pullers or brick-kiln workers or in agriculture. Some brides came from families with several daughters, yet they were the only ones of the sisters married in UP.

In their study of cross-regional marriages in Haryana and Rajasthan, Reena Kukreja and Paritosh Kumar found that "birth order" plays a significant role in determining whether a daughter will be married locally or have a cross-regional marriage. They argue that families appear to exhaust themselves of their assets to meet the wedding expenses of the older daughters. Consequently, those lower down the birth order are disadvantaged, as their families do not have the means to marry them locally (2013, p. 19). My data on the marital status of the siblings of cross-regional brides do not reflect such a pattern with respect to birth order. There are other factors (as I discuss below) that shed light on the marriage of some daughters in UP and others in their native states with a dowry. Writing about Bengali families with several daughters, Ravinder Kaur explains a cross-regional marriage for some daughters in terms of a "consumption smoothing strategy"—marrying one daughter with a dowry in West Bengal and sending the others out as cross-regional brides (2010a, p. 18). Renuka (CRB, 33, Chamar) was the only one of my informants who suggested that she was married in Barampur to ease the pressure of providing a dowry for several daughters. She told me that her father did not want to marry her to her husband because he was 40 when he went to Jharkhand to marry and Renuka was only 16. She added that her father was convinced by her *tāu*: "He told my father, where you will get the money from to marry them? There are four daughters, give one away there."

Nine cross-regional brides said that the decision regarding marriage in UP was made by their parents alone. Six others said that they were asked and they "agreed." They were told that they were going to Delhi and did not know where Delhi was—only that it was far away. They spoke with an understanding that marriage was compulsory for them; they could not be left unwed, and extreme poverty meant their fathers could not provide a dowry or pay wedding expenses. Varsha (CRB, 28, Jat) told me, "I thought if there is no choice but to marry, then what difference does it make whether it is near or far?"

"SPATIAL HYPERGAMY"

In the literature, the desire for upward mobility has been considered a motivation for long-distance marriage migration. Writing on cross-border marriages, Nicole Constable points out that majority of international marriage migrants are women and most of them move from poorer countries to wealthier ones, from the less developed global "south" to the more industrialized "north"—from parts of Asia, Latin America, Eastern Europe, and the former Soviet Union to western Europe, North America, Australia, and wealthier regions of East Asia, echoing some of the common patterns of women's labor migration. This she labels "global hypergamy" (2005, pp. 4, 10). Likewise, the writing on long-distance marriage migration within national borders, notes a similar pattern of "spatial hypergamy" (Lavely 1991). Studies on interprovincial marriage in China note that women move from poorer to more prosperous provinces for marriage (Chao 2005; Davin 2008; Schein 2005). Some in fact argue that given women's limited opportunities in the urban labor market due to their low education and skills, for women, hypergamy through marriage may be the only option for "economic betterment" (Fan & Huang 1998; Fan & Li 2002; Gilmartin & Tan 2002). Others suggest that it is women themselves who desire upward mobility and exercise agency in choosing marriage as a strategy to move (Fan & Huang 1998; Fan & Li 2002). Likewise, for India, Ravinder Kaur (2004) argues that women themselves use cross-regional marriage as a strategy to move to more prosperous areas. In a later study, however, she suggests that apart from fulfilling the responsibility of getting a daughter married, parents give daughters in cross-regional marriage believing that they are sending daughters to more prosperous families and states and hope for some remittances at a future point (Kaur 2010a).

However, what distinguishes some women in international marriages from those in cross-regional ones is that in the former, brides are not necessarily poor. Some Chinese, Filipina, and Vietnamese women in cross-border marriages, for instance, are professional and well educated and would be considered middle-class in their countries of origin. Constable writes, "Japan, South Korea, Western Europe and North America, for example are generally considered higher on the ladder of economic development than the Philippines and China, but many Japanese, South Korean, European and North American men who seek foreign brides are poor by local standard" (2005, pp. 10–11).

When talking about the native states of cross-regional brides, people in Barampur often remarked: "*garīb ilākā hai*" (it is a poor region). Satender

(55, Chamar, M) commented: "They call us *dillī ke rājā*" (the kings of Delhi). Similarly, Ramesh (50, Kumhar, M) said: "In Bengal, they know of Delhi and they think that the situation is good in Delhi; their daughter will stay happy." Pramod (21, Kumar, M), the son of a Bengali cross-regional bride, explained that the regions where women like his mother originated from were associated with poverty and backwardness: "They think wrong things about Bengal. They say that people there are starving, naked, and illiterate." Western UP and the northern states more generally undoubtedly are more developed and prosperous than states such as West Bengal, yet women who came from poverty most often ended up in marriages with men who were some of the poorest in the region, an observation also made in the Chinese context (Davin 2008, p. 70; Fan & Huang 1998, p. 246). Delia Davin writes, "Long-distance marriage has developed within a system of balancing of disadvantages and advantages. . . . Regional economic disparities are so great that a poor man in a prosperous area will probably seem a good match to a woman from a poor area of the country" (2008, p. 70–71).

Only three cross-regional brides said that the belief that daughters will have a more comfortable life in UP motivated parents' decisions to give daughters in marriage in Barampur. Some parents were convinced by the go-between that life in Barampur would be free of hardships. These decisions, as Lucy Williams notes for cross-border marriages, are made from a place of "relative ignorance" (2010, p. 56). They did not know where they were going or what life was like there. Vasha said, "*Dur hai* [it is far] . . . and for this reason you believe all kinds of things about *pardesh* [foreign land]." Yet it is important to stress that even though cross-regional brides often ended up in marriages with men who were poor and "disadvantaged" and they did not secure the comfortable life they had imagined, some did find themselves in a situation with less extreme poverty, as Kalawati's (CRB, 40, Kumhar) case demonstrates. She told me about her natal village: "*Wāhā zyadā garībī hai* [there is a lot of poverty there] so they think that the people here are extremely wealthy. Now that I am here, I feel that it is not what I had imagined. I had to do *mazdūrī* [casual labor] there to feed myself and I have to do the same here . . . but I must say that at least here, I am not starving."

FAMILY CIRCUMSTANCES

For some cross-regional brides, their own decisions were influenced by the attractions of distance from difficult situations back home. Varsha (CRB, 28, Jat) explained that apart from poverty, she was married in Barampur as her father, an alcoholic, had absolved himself of the obligation to marry his daughters.

> My *chāchī* [father's younger brother's wife] would tell us sisters
> to run away from home and get married; that my mother would
> not be able to get us married. . . . My father was an alcoholic.
> There was no one to earn. My brothers also did not work.
> Now my natal family has only less than an acre of land. My
> father sold the rest when we were children. He even sold my
> grandmother's jewelry and spent it all on his drinking. Whenever
> anyone visited us at home, they would ask my mother how she
> would get four daughters married. My mother would say that if
> nothing else, she will get us married in *pardesh* [foreign land] but
> that she would not keep us unmarried. She would say this and
> cry . . . now I am married in *pardesh* and so is my older sister.

Deepa (CRB, early 30s, Kumhar) talked about her father refusing three proposals from UP men, yet she ended up in a marriage in Barampur because her father, the only earning member of the family, had an accident. At the time, they were approached with the offer of a dowryless marriage, so her father agreed. Her elder sister was married in her native state prior to their father's accident. Four brides said that their fathers had already passed away when their husbands came to marry them. Radha (CRB, early 40s, Chamar), for instance, told me that her widowed mother agreed to a marriage with her husband, a much older man, only because of *majbūrī*. About her marriage in Barampur she said, "It was how God decided." The older sisters of these brides were married in their native states with a dowry when their fathers were still alive. Two cross-regional brides said that their younger sisters would be married in their native states, because their younger brothers had now started earning and were in a position to provide a dowry.

Two brides from West Bengal, married in the late 1970s and early 1980s, talked about the economic situation of their families deteriorating following floods in their natal villages that made a local marriage difficult for them. At that point in time they were approached by a go-between with the offer of a marriage in Barampur. Hemlata (CRB, late 50s, Kumhar) was orphaned as a child. She lived with her maternal grandmother. She told me,

> When I saw him [husband], he was so old . . . my grandmother
> was worried that he would die and I would be left a widow

but then I thought, I have no other family—mother, brother, or sister. Where will I go after my grandmother dies? I told her to let me go to Delhi.

Likewise, Kalawati (CRB, 40, Kumhar) lived with her older married brothers. She told me,

> I was the youngest of my siblings. My sisters got married then my mother passed away. I thought, for how long will my brothers and their wives keep me? I worked at the house of the manager of the tea planation. I used to cook and look after his children. At home, my brother's wives made me work the entire day. It made me very angry. Then Hemlata [also a CRB from Assam] sent a letter to my brother asking him to send me. She said that I will never go hungry. . . . I told my brother I will go where Hemlata is.

While for these brides their family situations gave them little choice but to enter a cross-regional marriage, it offered them the possibility of escape from insecure dependence on extended family or, in Varsha's case, an alcoholic father.

"INDIVIDUAL ATTRIBUTES"

For some of the cross-regional brides who were the only ones of their sisters to be in a cross-regional marriage, "individual characteristics" such as a physical disability, darker skin, or a previous marriage made a marriage in their native states more difficult. Jameela (CRB, 21, Teli) talked to me about arranging a marriage for her sister's daughter (also a native of Jharkhand) in Barampur.

> Her skin is much darker than mine. People [in Jharkhand] come and see her once and never return. Some have agreed in the past but they ask for ₹60,000–70,000. My sister cannot give so much. Now we have no option but to get her married here because she is of marriageable age.

A larger dowry was demanded as compensation for lacking what was regarded as a desirable attribute (lighter skin) for marriage. Praveena Kodoth makes a similar observation in her study of women in Kerala, where dowry came to be rationalized in cases where women had become "over-age" on account of what was considered a "deficit of normative femininity," i.e., a lack of "healthy good looks" (2008, p. 264). This sheds light on marriage migration of women from Kerala to Haryana (Kaur 2012). Pushpa (CRB, late 30s, Jat) said that she had been left disabled following a childhood accident. Her mother asked her sister (also a CRB) to take her to *pardesh* and get her married there. The literature on cross-border marriages similarly notes that at times, women migrate for marriage as their home communities may not see them as "marriageable" due to being over-aged or divorced (Constable 2005, p. 12; Del Rosario 2008, p. 87).

Cross-regional brides, like Jameela (CRB, 21, Teli), asserted that the decision to marry in Barampur was her own. She explained,

> I was married for three years in Godda [Jharkhand] and even had a child from that marriage. My first husband was an alcoholic and he used to beat me. My father brought me back. I had to leave my daughter. My parents wanted to get me remarried there but I did not agree. My in-laws' home was in the same village as my natal home. I did not want to stay there; *sharm lagtī thī* [I felt shame]. I would have had to fetch water from the same water tap and people would have gossiped about me. I decided that I will go away from there. At least no one here knows that I was married before.

Like Jameela, Maya (CRB, mid-40s, Chamar) was separated from her first husband and did not want a second marriage in Bengal. These women, thus, opted to become cross-regional brides to escape experiences that they were unwilling to accept (see also Constable 2005, p. 7–15; Lu 2008, p. 129). For them, while a previous marriage made cross-regional marriage the alternative, they weighed their options and exercised some agency in choosing that over their other limited options.

DECEPTION

Some cross-regional brides denied any agency in marriage migration to UP. They told me that they had been deceived and brought to Barampur, either by a relative or someone unknown to them. Devanti (CRB, early 40s, Chamar) told me that she was brought to Barampur by her *māsī* (mother's sister), a CRB, under the pretext of looking after her children. Her mother did not know until Devanti visited her natal home with her first child that she had been married off. Similarly, Sita (CRB, mid-40s, Chamar) talked about how she was brought by her *māsī*'s daughter to stay in Barampur for a few days but was then married off. She told me, "When I realized that I was being married off, I thought to myself, what can I do now? I don't know the way to go back. She brought me here and trapped me."

Talking with Sita about her life in her native state revealed that she was widowed and had a son from that marriage. After her husband's death, her in-laws asked her to leave and kept her son back. Her parents had died, so she went to live at her *māsī*'s house. Her *māsī*'s daughter was married in Barampur and she arranged Sita's marriage. The first time I met Sita, she cried and talked about how difficult her life was—her husband was an alcoholic and did not work and feed the family. Kanchan (CRB, 21, Chamar), another bride, left home with her "cousin sister" who was intending to elope with a man (Roshan) from another Baghpat village, a truck driver who traveled to her native state. Kanchan was married to a relative of Roshan called Ratan, who is a resident of Barampur. She told me,

> One day my sister asked me to go with her to the market to buy medicine for her brother. It got late and she took me to the station. I did not have money to go back home so I had to go with her. We traveled to Purnea [in Bihar] . . . then Delhi. When we reached Delhi she got married. Then I thought where will I go? I agreed to marry Ratan.

While Kanchan, like Sita, suggested that she had no option but to get married, her husband told me that Kanchan was aware that she was leaving to get married when she left home. In the course of fieldwork, Kanchan told me that her father had remarried and she had a troubled relationship with her stepmother. She talked about how much she regretted running away, as contact with her natal family was severed. She was troubled by her *sās* and *jethānī* and felt that she did not have the support of her husband. Carol Smart writes, "a reliance on memory can produce an understanding of the past that is filtered through the present" (2007, p. 42). In cases such as these, it is difficult to ascertain whether women made decisions to leave to escape difficult situations back home and concealed that they had been lured with the promise of a better life and hence denied agency, as they now found themselves in unfavorable situations, or they had in fact been deceived.

For some women, conflicting accounts emerged. Pushpa (CRB, late 30s, Jat) told me how she ended up as a bride in Barampur:

> I have been married for 18–19 years. My husband is much older than me. I am from Madhubani district [Bihar]. My father was from Nepal but he settled in Bihar. He was a Rajput. I have three brothers and we are four sisters. Three sisters are older than me. My sister got married before me, here in Shamli [neighboring district]. She brought me here. I came to live with her at a young age. At the time, I neither had breasts nor had I started menstruating. . . . My *jījā* [sister's husband] arranged my marriage in Barampur through his sister, who is also married here.

On a later occasion, when talking about other cross-regional brides from her native state of Maharashtra, Sheela (CRB, early 40s, Chamar) told me about Pushpa: "Did you meet her. . . . Pushpa . . . she lives behind the village temple. Her husband has a defect in one eye. He is Jat. She is also from my village." I asked, "Is she from Maharashtra?" To which she replied, "Did she tell you about a *jījā*? She won't say . . . she lied to you because she is afraid . . . but she was tricked by Asha's (CRB, 55, Chamar) mother and brought here *dhoke se* [through deception], just as I was. . . . When she says *jījā*, she is referring to Asha's husband, who arranged her marriage here."

In some other cases, it was clearer that the women had been trafficked. Samita (CRB, early 30s, Chamar), for instance, was brought to Barampur in the early 1990s. She told me her story:

> I was studying in class five. One day I met a man outside my school. We were three girls. He told us, come with me I will make you meet my daughter. He drugged us. . . . I do not remember. Then his wife and he put us on a train to Delhi. They threatened us that if we talk to anyone they will throw us on the railway track. We reached Delhi. He sold the other two girls before me. We were in Delhi for 10–12 days. We were moving all around the city. They would beat me if I talked to anyone. I tried to run away, but I could not. They sold me to him [husband] for ₹5,000. They had taken ₹15,000 for the other two girls.

Samita was kidnapped by someone unknown to her (professional suppliers of brides) and "sold" without the knowledge of her kin. She told me that she had no memory of where home was and no contact with her kin (chapter 7). As Rajni Palriwala and Patricia Uberoi note, in such long-distance marriages, it is not so much the purchase aspect *per se* but rather "the virtual entrapment of the women" that aligns these brokered arrangements with forms of human trafficking (2008, p. 37).

Conclusion

Cross-regional marriages are a consequence of two separate sets of factors—one operating at source (bride-sending areas) and the other at destination (bride-receiving area). At destination, in this case Barampur, the contemporary inability of some men to marry cannot be explained in terms of demographic factors alone, but needs to be linked to wider changes in the political economy. Men are not all in the same position with respect to either their need to marry or the obstacles they face in trying to get married. The challenges that men face are differentiated by caste, class, and individual characteristics—"various physical deformities" or "blemishes of individual character" (e.g., a "flawed" reputation). On account of such characteristics, men bear a "stigma"—"an attribute that is deeply discrediting" (Goffman 1963, pp. 3–4)—and hence fail to be marriageable. Changes in landholding patterns, caste differences in livelihoods, education, and white-collar employment have a significant bearing on men's ability to marry. Men are positioned differently by virtue of the "social," "cultural," and "economic capital" they possess (cf. Bourdieu 1986). Men who succeed in using the forms of economic and social capital to secure employment are deemed marriageable, as opposed to those who cannot and hence either fail to marry or resort to lesser ways of marrying.

It is important to point out here that "disadvantage" is transmitted to the next generation, with the sons of men in cross-regional marriages often facing issues with regard to marriage. I discuss in detail elsewhere that while the difficulties confronted by sons of cross-regional unions are spoken of as tied to the mother's cross-regional origins, it seems to be closely intertwined with issues around employment, education, and poverty that disadvantaged their fathers and led them to have a cross-regional marriage in the first place. The non-marriageability of sons of cross-regional unions must (at least partially) be explained by the intergenerational perpetuation of inequality (Chaudhry 2019b). While I have outlined multiple explanations for why men failed to marry within the regional context, what I was not able to explore was the affective side (e.g., the desire for companionship) that motivated cross-regional marriages. Due to my age, gender, and marital status, these were conversations I did not have access to.

Men adopted different strategies in response to the difficulties confronting them. These included a relaxation in certain norms of marriage, payment to the parents of the bride instead of dowry, forms of exchange marriage, and cross-regional marriage. While cross-regional marriages were rationalized on grounds of *majbūrī*, nonetheless, these were considered to be the lowest form of marriage because of being inter-caste. Jats, thus, preferred bachelorhood over cross-regional marriage, and hence there were (proportionally) more Jat bachelors in the village than the other castes. Among the Chamars and Kumhars, men were differentiated not only in terms of their need or ability to marry but also by their readiness to have a lesser marriage. Muslim men faced difficulties only in negotiating a secondary but not a primary marriage, and cases of cross-regional marriage were exceptional among them.

While some, across castes, found ways to marry despite the difficulties confronted, others remained bachelors, thereby failing to achieve "successful" masculinity. In a context where marriage represents social adulthood and access to rights, status, and care, such men were marginalized vis-à-vis the married (see also Mishra 2018). A marriage for sex, reproduction, and labor, a marriage so that "womanly" tasks will not have to be performed by men, was a defining component of successful masculinity. Yet what is also crucial in constructing masculinities is not only marriage but a *good* marriage that placed men in relationships of hegemony and subordination to one another. Moreover, despite the moral panic in Barampur around the growing numbers of men who are unable to and would fail to marry in future and the emphasis on its implications, particularly violence against women, there is insufficient evidence to conclude that men's "deviant" behavior is a consequence of the gender imbalance.

At bride-sending states, poverty and the possibility of escaping dowry were the primary factors that explain why parents sent daughters in marriage to Barampur. Other explanations include difficult family situations or insecure dependence on family members and the possibility of a better life and an escape from extreme poverty. Individual characteristics such as a previous marriage, physical disability, or changing economic circumstances of the natal family (fathers passing away or natural calamities, for instance) were reasons offered by some cross-regional brides. This also provides insights on why some women end up in cross-regional marriages while their sisters are married in their native states. As far as agency in decisions regarding marriage in Barampur is concerned, for some cross-regional brides, it was entirely a parental decision, others were asked and "agreed" with the understanding that their families were too poor and remaining unmarried was not an option, others suggested that it was their own decision and they convinced family members to let them go, while some denied any agency by saying that they had been deceived and coerced and married off in UP.

Chapter 3

Making a Cross-Regional Marriage

G iven the difficulties confronted with regard to marriage, some men in Barampur resort to lesser ways of marrying, cross-regional marriage being one. In the previous chapter, I discussed *why* women end up in cross-regional marriages. In this chapter, I address *how* women become cross-regional brides. Through my ethnography, I aim to address whether the lived reality of women who become cross-regional brides, conforms to depictions of them in some media, NGO, and academic accounts as "purchased" and "trafficked" women. I will detail the role of the "go-betweens" who negotiate these marriages, their mode of operation, and the payments involved to address whether cross-regional marriage can be placed in the category of bride-price, bride-buying, or trafficking. In the last part of the chapter, I outline what is regarded as a "legitimate" marriage within this regional context and how these influence local perceptions of whether cross-regional marriages are marriages at all.

Who Arranges? The "Go-Between" or *Bīchwālā*

In Barampur, informants distinguished between a *bīcholīā* who mediated a regional marriage and a *bīchwālā* for intermediaries in cross-regional marriage. In her work on long-distance marriage migration in China, Delia Davin writes, "Like other forms of migration, marriage migration generates 'migration chains.' Marriage migration from one area to another can snowball as successive cohorts of brides arrange matches for their husbands' kin or other villagers with women from their natal homes" (2008, p. 69). Similarly, Ravinder Kaur in her work in Haryana found that many cross-regional brides acted as "go-betweens" by accompanying aspiring grooms to

95

their natal homes and getting marriages performed with sisters, cousins, or neighbors' daughters, thereby creating fairly dense networks (2004, p. 2597). In Barampur, 12 of the 19 cross-regional brides interviewed said that the *bichwālā* was also a cross-regional bride married in Barampur or another nearby village, or the husband of a cross-regional bride.

Some studies note the role of other kinds of "go-betweens" such as migrant laborers (Ahlawat 2009; Kaur 2012), truck drivers, and retired army men (Kukreja & Kumar 2013). Others argue that the go-betweens are professional suppliers of women (Blanchet et al. 2003; Kant & Pandey 2003; Singh 2009), with women being "duped and betrayed as the middlemen lure them out of the sanctuary of their homes with false promises" (Mukherjee 2013, p. 44). In Barampur, one cross-regional bride said that her marriage had been arranged by an army man posted in Assam (her native state). For another bride, a shopkeeper in her natal village had acted as a "go-between" for the marriage with her husband, a truck driver. For two brides who had migrated into Baghpat villages to work with their families, the *bichwālās* were brick-kiln owners. Others said that their marriages had been negotiated by a *rishtedār* (relative) or *jānkār* (acquaintance)—a "*behanoī*" (sister's husband), "*māmī*" (mother's brother's wife), or "*phuphā*" (mother's sister's or father's sister's husband). In these cases, the go-between was not a "real" relative related through blood or marriage. Radha (CRB, early 40s, Chamar), for instance, told me that the *bichwālā* was her *māmī*. I asked her if she meant her mother's brother's wife and she responded, "*gaon ki*" (from the village). When I asked her if they belong to the same village, she said no but that she was a relative of a relative of her *māmī*.

There were other cases where it was difficult to establish who the *bichwālā* was. For instance, for two cross-regional brides married to Chamar men, informants said that they had no information about who brought them and how they came to Barampur and that all they knew was that both brought a child with them when they first arrived. When I talked to one of them, Chanda (early 40s, Chamar, F), she told me that her name was Rukhsana (she was a Muslim) before she came to Barampur. She said she was from "beyond *Chotā Patnā*" (it was unclear where this was) and that she had left home to look for her sister who had "run away to Delhi." In Delhi, she met "a man" who brought her to Barampur. When I probed further, she said she could not remember who this man was and how he brought her to Barampur (see also "deception" in chapter 2).

Eleven of the 19 cross-regional brides said that their husbands went to their natal villages accompanied by the *bichwālā* to get married. Of them, seven said that the "go-between" had either lied or withheld information about their husbands. Deception is common in regional marriages as well (chapter 1), yet as Thérèse Blanchet points out, "The distance involved in the long-distance marriages makes it easier to elaborate a fiction that cannot be checked beforehand" (2008, p. 170). Katharine Charsley makes a similar observation in her work among Pakistani marriage migrants in Britain: that such transnational marriages introduce an additional distance and therefore an additional "risk." She argues that distance may increase the possibility of concealing premarital relationships or other undesirable behavior or traits potentially damaging to reputation and marriage prospects in local contexts (2008, p. 266). Delia Davin, in her study of interprovincial marriages in China, found that "disadvantaged" men sought brides from outside because their disadvantages were widely known, making it difficult for them to find local brides. Another motive was control. Men and their families feared that the bride would run away. However, a woman who had traveled a very long way would find it difficult to do this however disappointed she was in her husband (2008, p. 71).

Renuka (CRB, 33, Chamar) explained that her "sister" (the "go-between") lied to her family about her husband's caste. Her father was told that her husband's caste was *nāī* (barber) like them and not Chamar (Dalit). Likewise, Varsha (CRB, 28, Jat) said that the *bichwālā* told her father that her husband owned four acres of land when in fact he was landless. When I first went to meet Malti (CRB, 16, Chamar), she was a new bride and had arrived in Barampur two weeks earlier from Jharkhand. She told me that her husband was 26 years old. Satender (55, Chamar, M), my facilitator, told me that Malti's husband was in his early 40s and was previously married to a cross-regional bride who "ran away." As I waited for Malti, I started a conversation with her mother-in-law. I asked her if they would go to work in the brick-kiln that year. She responded asking me to lower my voice and said: "She [Malti] does not know we are brick-kiln workers, do not tell her." An account I heard numerous times was Rekha's (CRB, 45, Jat). Rekha was the widow of Satvir. She came from "the hills" when she was about 14, I was told. Satvir, as the story goes, was 70 at the time. He did not go to "the hills" to marry her but sent a "27-year-old, *sundar ādmī*" (beautiful man) to pose as the groom instead. It was on her wedding night that Rekha learned of the deception, yet there was little she could do. I tried speaking with Rekha but she did not want to be interviewed.

There were some exceptional cases, such as that of Deepa (CRB, early 30s, Kumhar), for whom a male relative traveled from Jharkhand to

Barampur before the marriage was fixed to confirm that her husband was not, like the *bichwālā* for this marriage, a Muslim. For most cross-regional brides, whose marriage ceremonies had taken place in their native states, a male relative came with them to Barampur to drop them following the wedding and stayed for a few days to ensure, in Lakshmi's (CRB, late 40s, Kumhar) words, "that he [husband] had a house and family, he did not lie about anything and he would not sell me off to someone else." Virender (52, Kumhar, M) said that his nephew was married to a cross-regional bride and her parents had visited Barampur before the wedding was formalized to ensure that everything was "*thek thak*" (right). This did not seem to be a common practice, however.

With the exception of one cross-regional bride, all said that they had been approached at least once by men or families of their own or other castes to arrange a marriage from their native states. Eight said that they had refused. Radha (CRB, early 40s, Chamar) explained, "If I bring her and she is unhappy, she will curse me." Renuka (CRB, 33, Chamar) remarked, "The men here drink and gamble. There is no *sahī* [literally correct] *ādmī* [man] here." Two others said that they did not want to deceive anyone. Jaya (CRB, 45, Jat) told me, "She will become like us." She explained that she had not returned to visit her natal home for over 20 years (chapter 7). I watched my chaperone Rani (RB, 35, Jat) approaching several of my informants to fix a marriage for her younger brother and failing. She remarked angrily on one occasion, "We will just go to the hills and have our pick."

Nine other cross-regional brides had arranged one or more marriages in Barampur or other nearby villages. Some said that they did so because their husbands or in-laws asked them to. In her work on long-distance marriages in China, Delia Davin (2008) argues that by negotiating marriages, women seek to recruit their own kinswomen and neighbors, seeking to recreate the kinship they have lost. This was the reason offered by Meera (CRB, late 30s, Chamar), who had arranged four marriages. "I thought, why be the only one here? So I brought others." Chhaya (CRB, 55, Kumhar) said, "I thought, *unkā bhī ghar bas jāyegā*" (their house would also become well-peopled and flourish). There were some who believed they were helping out women whose (natal) family circumstances were similar to their own. Kalawati (CRB, 40, Kumhar) told me about the cross-regional bride she brought: "Her parents had died, her family was poor." Kalawati had been in Barampur since the late 1980s. She had visited her natal home only once, when she returned to arrange that marriage. That arranging marriages serves as an incentive for cross-regional brides to visit their natal homes without incurring any travel expenses has been noted by earlier work (Kaur 2004, 2012; Mishra 2016). While this may have been the motivation for some of my informants, they did not offer this as an explanation for arranging marriages.

In her study of cross-border marriages in Taiwan, Melody Chia-wen Lu found that migrant brides who act as intermediaries may be distinguished from institutionalized brokers and individual matchmakers, as they do not do this work on a regular basis and do not earn a living from the profits of mediating marriages. Making profit may not be their sole motivation for matchmaking (2008, p. 133). Ravinder Kaur makes a similar argument for India. She contends that cross-regional brides who bring in other brides are not considered brokers because their motives are different: augmenting their own community and visiting their homes (2012, p. 87). While this applies to most cross-regional brides, there were some, like Asha (55, Chamar, F), who functioned as a supplier of brides and benefited monetarily in the process. About her, informants remarked, "*Dhandā kartī hai*" (she runs a business) or "*dalālī kartī hai*" (she works as a broker). In Barampur, the term *dalāl/ī*—a male/female broker; transporter of human beings often involved in cross-border trafficking, as noted by Thérèse Blanchet in her work in eastern UP, had a "negative connotation" that implied the use of "devious means, telling lies and cheating" (2008, p. 178). Sheela (CRB, early 40s, Chamar) told me,

> Asha works with her mother in Maharashtra. She brings women from there *dhoke se* [through deception] like she brought me and then sells them to men in other villages. Three years ago she brought a young girl here. She must have been 14–15. I brought the girl to my house to drink tea. She came here and started crying. She started talking to me in Marathi. She told me *mausī* [referring to Asha's mother] brought me here. Three days later she disappeared. Only God knows what Asha did with this young girl whether she sold her, she ran away, nobody knows what happened to her. . . . If you talk to Asha, she will not tell you she does this work, even though everyone in the neighborhood knows. She no longer sells them in Barampur but further away.

Satender (55, Chamar, M) told me about Ratanpal (early 70s, Chamar, M), his *tāū's* son, who was married to a cross-regional bride: "Asha brought him a bride in the mid-1980s for ₹2,600. She stayed with him for a year. Then he took the money back from Asha and she sold this woman in another village. This was many years ago but she still does *dalālī*, taking ₹20,000 from some, ₹30,000 from others." Kumhar informants told me about Deepa (early 30s, Kumhar, F), who had arranged several marriages from her natal home in Jharkhand. Before I met Deepa, Pramod (21, Kumhar, M) told me that she would not talk to me, as her motivations were different from mine. "You want *sudhār* [improvement] but she is only concerned about making money," he said. Virender (52, Kumhar, M) also told me that in his opinion Deepa might be afraid to talk to me, as I might report her to the police for "selling women." I did manage to speak with Deepa, unlike Asha (who refused), though only briefly, as she seemed reluctant. Deepa told me that she had arranged only four marriages and suggested that she only did so as there was no other alternative for the women other than a marriage in Barampur. She talked about one marriage she had arranged among the Jats:

This woman eloped with a Chuhra [Dalit] boy in her village. Her parents managed to bring her back but it would have been difficult for her to get married there. Her family was known to my natal family. They asked me for help, so I got her married here.

She added that she was now reluctant to arrange more marriages: "When I go to my natal village, parents of daughters ask me, 'where did you give our daughter?' It's because they [husbands] do not take them back to meet their parents." This was also her response to Rani (my chaperone) when Rani asked Deepa to arrange a marriage for her brother. Deepa told me she visited her natal home in Jharkhand three to five times a year. The next time I returned to meet her after our first meeting, her daughter told me she had gone to her village to bring a bride. Deepa, like Asha, had made a business of arranging marriages, although she functioned in a different way from Asha in that she asked her natal kin to locate a woman in Jharkhand when she was asked to arrange a marriage. She or her husband then accompanied the groom to her native village to have the wedding performed. Informants said that she charged a fee for arranging marriages, yet I never heard the word *dalālī* used for Deepa as it was for Asha. Deepa was functioning akin to a marriage bureau or professional matchmaker that some informants approached when arranging a regional marriage (chapter 1). Yet she was not viewed as such. She was also distinguished from the *bicholiā* who had started making demands for arranging marriages because what was given to the latter was in local understanding still gift and not payment.

A Marriage without Dowry:
Bride-Price, Bride-Buying, or Trafficking?

Writing on the so-called "mail-order brides," Lucy Williams (2010) contends that the discourses that link such marriages to trafficking stem from assumptions about how they came about (through brokering agencies, internet advertising services, etc.). Rajni Palriwala and Patricia Uberoi explain that in much of the academic and activist interrogation of transnational marriages, it is the introduction of material calculations or commercial operations into the process of spouse-selection that self-evidently impugns the authenticity of the marital relationship, transforming marriage from a domestic arrangement in the domain of kinship to a form of human "trafficking" (2008, p. 35).

In the Indian context, Ravinder Kaur (2004) asserts that cross-regional marriages cannot be described as cases of trafficking. She makes a further distinction between bride-buying and bride-price marriages and argues that cross-regional marriages do not fall into any of these categories. Trafficking is purely for profit: in it, women are like any other commodity being bought and sold. These marriages do not fall in the category of trafficking, as the wife is not passed on to others and is not one of several wives thus acquired. More often than not she makes a stable home with a particular man fulfilling the roles of wife, mother, and farm laborer. In marriages by sale and purchase, men who are unable to find wives and need them for their domestic, sexual, and reproductive services buy women from poor families. In such marriages, the man pays the girl's parents to acquire a wife. Bride-price marriages are those where the bride's family is compensated for the loss of her labor. Bride-price marriages are not the same as marriages in which the women are "bought." Bride-price marriage is the accepted practice in an entire community and is not seen as "buying" the bride (Kaur 2004, p. 2598). In her work on Bangladeshi wives in eastern UP, Thérèse Blanchet (2008) noted that while the "sale" of women was acknowledged, the term "trafficking" was used in neither sending nor receiving communities.

In Barampur, it was widely believed that cross-regional brides involved the "sale" of wives. This was primarily predicated on assumptions about the payments involved, irrespective of whether the parents or the "go-between" profited from the negotiation. In eastern UP, Blanchet found that the term "kharīdān awrat" (purchased wife) was used for Bangladeshi wives (2008, p. 167). Similarly, Patricia Jeffery and Roger Jeffery, in their study in Bijnor district, noted that "bahū mol lenā" was used to mean "taking a bride for a price" (1996, p. 231). In Barampur, cross-regional brides were referred to as "*mol kī*" (bought wife).

All the cross-regional brides interviewed said that there was no dowry in their marriages. Chhaya (CRB, 55, Kumhar) remarked, "If my father could give a dowry, then why would I be here?" In these marriages, the grooms met the expenses for the wedding, including the *dāwat* (feast), clothes that the bride wore, and the travel-fare for the go-between as well as a male relative of the bride who accompanied her to Barampur after the wedding. Five cross-regional brides talked about being taunted by their *sās* (mother-in-law) for coming "empty handed" from their natal homes. In Barampur, when a *mūh dikhāī* (face showing ceremony) took place following the wedding, the dowry that the bride had been given was displayed (chapter 1). Most cross-regional brides said that there was no *mūh dikhāī* ceremony for them. Sarla (RB, 47, Jat) believed that this was because families wanted to avoid a situation where remarks would be made about the marriage being not only cross-regional but also dowryless, given the role of dowry in cementing affinal relations and enhancing the prestige of the family.

Kalawati (CRB, 40, Kumhar) explained why in her opinion cross-regional brides were believed to be bought wives: "Men go from here to marry and they spend on traveling there . . . it is expensive because it is far and they come here and tell others that they spent ₹10,000 or ₹20,000 and then people start saying: *woh mol ā rahī haī*" (she is a bought wife). Cross-regional brides, like Kalawati, were aware that women like her were referred to as *mol kī* by others in the village. She also explained that it was because men incurred an expense in getting married that it was believed to constitute purchase. There were some like Santosh (60, Jat, F) who spoke of a "market for women in the east." She added, "Women are made to stand in a line and men go from here and take their pick and pay money to their parents." Neither the brides nor the grooms ever mentioned the marriage having come about in this way. Ramesh (50, Kumhar, M), the husband of a cross-regional bride, explained, "Here they think we give money to the bride's parents but they did not take anything from us." In other words, while those in the village alleged that cross-regional brides entailed purchase, men in cross-regional marriages denied that this was the case. As I discuss below, however, some men did use the language of "buying" when they spoke about their cross-regional wives.

The pertinent question here is: to whom are the payments made and what do they constitute? Husbands or in-laws of some cross-regional brides clarified that they had made payments to the "go-between" but what they had paid was only *kharchā* (expenses). They talked about handing over a certain amount of money to the *bīchwālā* and said that they had not been asked for a fee for arranging the marriage. Cross-regional brides who acted as go-betweens said that they had only been paid the travel fare. Varsha (CRB, 28, Jat), who had arranged one cross-regional marriage, pointed out that it was assumed by others that the *bīchwālā* took money for arranging the marriage, even though it was used only to meet expenses.

> Her [CRB's] husband told people here that when we [Varsha and her husband] took him to Bengal to get married, we took a lot of money from him. You tell me, we stayed there at my parent's home for one month. . . . They gave him a place to stay and cooked whatever he asked for but how long could they feed three people for free? They are poor. He would drink every day. How could they pay for his alcohol? So my husband asked him for money to meet his food and drinking expenses. We did not take any money from him for ourselves but we only asked him to pay our train fare.

Yet in other cases, women said the *bīchwālā* had taken money from the groom for arranging the marriage. Jameela (CRB, 21, Teli) said that it was only after her *sās* taunted her 15 days after the wedding, saying "*tujhe baich kar gaye*" (they sold you and left), that she learned that her husband had paid ₹18,000 to the *bīchwālā*—a "*rishtedār*" (relative). She insisted that her father had no knowledge of this. Similarly, Hemlata (CRB, late 50s, Kumhar) talked about being told by her husband that her natal kin "sold her" for ₹15,000. She said, "I would tell him my family took nothing, it was that *Sonar*" (Sonar is a caste name, but she meant the *bīchwālā*). While brides like Hemlata and Jameela stressed that their parents were unaware that the *bīchwālā* had taken a payment for them, several people in the village asserted that the *bīchwālā* kept part of the payment and gave some part to the parents.

Ramesh (50, Kumhar, M), husband of a cross-regional bride, said he had paid ₹800 to Chhaya (the "go-between") to give to his wife's parents to meet the wedding expenses. He said that his wife told him later that Chhaya gave only ₹30 to her parents and probably kept the rest for herself. When I talked to Chhaya, she told me that she had been given only travel fare, as did some other cross-regional brides. In such cases, it is difficult to say for certain whether the brides' natal kin had received any payment or were even aware that a payment had been made to the "go-between." As discussed in the section above, there were exceptional cases of brides such as Asha (CRB, 55, Chamar) who were known to be carrying out a *dhandā* (business) in brides and profiting from the sale, at times selling and reselling them.

Some said that payments had been made not to the *bīchwālā* but to the bride's parents. Abdul (30, Lohar, M) told me about his relative who married Faiza (CRB, late 40s, Lohar): "He gave ₹5,000 to her parents, he told me himself." When I questioned him further, he added, "They used it on the *dāwat*." Similarly, talking about the cross-regional bride she brought to Barampur, Varsha (CRB, 28, Jat) said,

> They say here that her parents sold her for ₹5,000. Her mother told her husband that she could not afford to get anything made for her daughter so she took money from him. She used the money to get a nose ring and earrings made and the remaining on the wedding feast. She even gave her some utensils and two sets of clothes. She brought everything with her to Barampur. Tell me then, what did her parents take from them?

Kishore (70, Jat, M) told me about his neighbor Satvir (75, Jat, M). "He told me that he had paid the bride's parents not to meet their expenses but in exchange for the bride." He recalled,

> When his wife went to visit her natal home for the first time after the wedding, she did not return for a long time. People in the village started saying to him, "your wife ran away. You are left a *randwā* again." So he would tell them, "I will think that the buffalo that cost me ₹15,000 died."

Cross-regional brides were similar to regional brides, who came without *dān dahej* (without a dowry, negating the ideology of *kanyādān*) and for whom a payment had been made and this was seen as "sale" of a woman. Yet unlike in regional marriages, this was not "hidden" and had implications for women's incorporation in the receiving communities, as I will explore in the following chapters.

What Makes a Marriage a Marriage?
Ritual and the "Legitimate" Marriage

Deepa (early 30s, Kumhar, F) told me that the common assumption about cross-regional marriage was that a wedding did not take place, "*aise hi le aye, yā mol le aye*" (just like that they brought her or they paid for her, i.e., without getting married). Some cross-regional brides talked about being asked "how they got married" when they moved to live in Barampur. Some, like Satender (55, Chamar, M), believed that when men first started bringing cross-regional brides, they were all brought through deception. He added, "*par ab shādī kar ke lāte hai*" (but now they marry and bring them). Unlike Satender, for many, these could not be considered marriages because they were not "proper" marriages in local understanding. Koyal (RB, 16, Chamar), the daughter-in-law of a cross-regional bride (Sheela), for instance, told me about her *sās*:

> *Shādī nahī huyī* [there was no wedding]. They only exchanged garlands. A wedding is one where a groom goes with a *barāt* [wedding party]. Only after you take *pherās* [circling the sacred fire] can you be regarded married. I can put a garland around anyone's neck but that does not mean that I am married to him.

Likewise, Kajri (RB, 35, Jat) stressed that the *pherā* was necessary and the most significant ritual for a Hindu marriage to be socially recognized and validated. She added, "A wedding is one where relatives and neighbors are invited." In Saroj's view (35, Jat, F), a cross-regional marriage was one that was "*ritī rivāj ke binā*" (without rituals and customs).

My cross-regional informants, however, asserted that a wedding had taken place, for most in their native states. Hemlata (CRB, late 50s, Kumhar) remarked, "Who gives away a daughter like that?" Eleven of the 19 interviewed said that a wedding that entailed the exchange of garlands, filling *sindūr* (vermilion in the parting of the hair), and/or *pherās* had taken place in their native states. Faiza (CRB, late 40s, Lohar) said that a *nikāh* had taken place at her natal village. Cross-regional brides said that the wedding ceremony was followed by a *dawāt* in their natal village attended by neighbors and relatives. The groom was accompanied by the *bichwālā* and in some cases a male relative. Four said that they had a "court marriage" (a registered/legal marriage)—one in her native village, and the three others in

Delhi or Baghpat town before they moved to live in Barampur. Of them, the husband of one told me that they had neither a ritual wedding nor a legal/registered one and that his marriage was negotiated by the *bichwālā* and they started living together. Two others said that they exchanged garlands only after moving to Barampur. Of them, one bride said that following the garland exchange, she was taken to a photo studio in the nearest town where a photograph of the couple was taken. Other cross-regional brides said that they did not have a wedding photograph, but five showed me a photograph taken a few months after the wedding. Samita (CRB, early 30s, Chamar), who was deceived and "sold" into marriage, insisted that a wedding ceremony and feast had taken place at her husband's sister's home in Delhi.

Despite what the cross-regional brides claimed, several people remained skeptical of these marriages. This was not only because they believed that the necessary rituals and customs for a marriage to be accepted as legitimate within this regional context had not been performed, but also because some were known to be "court marriages," associated with elopement—a marriage without ritual or parental sanction (Mody 2008). Additionally, they were unlike regional marriages that gained social sanction as they were witnessed by family and community. For cross-regional marriages, there was no way to ascertain who attended and witnessed the ceremony, as it had taken place in a distant place, with the grooms often going to marry unaccompanied by their kin.

There were some who seemed less concerned with ritual but rather suggested that the legitimacy of such marriages was questionable because they involved payment and the woman was "*bāhar se/ki.*" What was implied was that these marriages were less legitimate because they were not "normative," particularly as they crossed caste boundaries.[1] In Barampur, 10 of the 19 cross-regional brides interviewed admitted to being in inter-caste marriages, and two brides married to Hindu men said that their fathers were Muslim. As noted by other studies on cross-regional marriages, the caste and religion of the brides was overlooked when the alliance was made (Blanchet 2008, p. 166; Kaur 2012, p. 84). There is a discussion in the literature on the "acceptance" of cross-regional marriages in caste-bound rural communities, despite their being inter-caste or inter-religious. Writing on cross-regional marriages in Haryana, Ravinder Kaur (2004, p. 2602) explains,

> What possibly explains the differential acceptability is that inter-caste marriage within a village or between neighboring villages impacts the local standing of families much more than when one

spouse is non-local. The 'behaviour' of local women has consequences for both their natal and marital families. The 'foreign' women, whose origins are somewhat suspect, are measured with a different rod; they are tolerated as long as they try to conform sufficiently to local norms.

Paro Mishra, also writing on Haryana, explains that as the bride's family belong to a distant region and only the groom and a few others visit her native village, her caste identity can be easily concealed. When questioned, men say their wife belongs to the same caste, although the caste name is different in her native state (2016, p. 231). Similarly, Janaki Abraham maintains that the caste identity of cross-regional brides can remain "unknown and vague" because they are imported from outside the local region (2014, p. 63). Evidence from Barampur supports these arguments and provides some additional insights. Some informants remarked that the caste of cross-regional brides was insignificant because "a woman has no caste of her own": after marriage she becomes a member of her husband's caste group. Mahipal (68, Jat, M) told me, "The Jat community is like the river Ganges: whoever falls into it also becomes Jat."

Attempts were made to either conceal their caste status or pass them off as belonging to their husband's or a higher caste. People in the village were aware of the caste difference, however. Ashok (39, Jat, M) explained, "These women are *dūr kī* [from far away] so it is easier to keep quiet because we know that their caste is different but we cannot say anything for certain." Likewise, Kavita (41, Jat, F) commented, "You can tell that the caste of these women is different because everyone here knows: where are there Jats in Bengal? Nobody asks these women what their caste is, because when they are asked they say they are Sonar or Brahmin or Rajput [upper castes]." Kavita suggested not only that cross-regional brides could not possibly be upper caste but also alludes to a widespread assumption in Barampur that all cross-regional brides belonged to *nīchī jātīs* (lower castes), although this was not necessarily the case. Satender (55, Chamar, M) told me, "A bride from outside is less valued because a local woman will know our language, *rahan-sahan* [way of life] . . . there the *riti riwaj* [customs] are different." Satender is referring to cultural and linguistic differences between north India and the brides' native states, but his comment could also be about caste difference, because caste is often spoken about in terms of "cultural difference" and "way of life" (Mayer 1996, pp. 59–60; Fuller 1996, p. 12). What the aforementioned suggests is that the caste status of brides, though disregarded when the marriage was arranged, did not completely cease to be an issue for the people in the village, as I will discuss further in the following chapters. Nonetheless, cross-regional brides were accorded the status of wives, mothers, and daughters-in-law, and their children were recognized as legitimate and granted the caste status of their fathers.

Conclusion

Melody Chia-wen Lu (2008) highlights the necessity of distinguishing various types and modalities of commercial matchmaking in order to address questions around "wife-trafficking." For Barampur, a distinction could be made between three kinds of "go-betweens" or *bichwālās* involved in the negotiation of cross-regional marriages: first, cross-regional brides who drew on their natal family and village networks to bring other women as cross-regional brides, similar to regional marriages where women played a key role; second, other kinds of intermediaries (army men, shopkeepers, brick-kiln owners); third, cross-regional brides who either acted as brokers charging a fee for their services or functioned more like professional suppliers of wives involving deception and profiting from the sale of women. As noted by earlier studies, most cross-regional marriages were negotiated by other cross-regional brides who did not arrange marriages on a regular basis and were not driven by benefiting monetarily from the arrangement, though in some cases, they may have.

Can cross-regional marriages then be categorized as trafficking, bride-buying, or bride-price? Apart from a few exceptions, my findings suggest that most marriages do not fit the parameters of trafficking. As for bride-buying, in local perception, cross-regional brides were regarded as *mol ki*, irrespective of who the payments were made to and what they entailed. From the groom's perspective, he had incurred expenses instead of receiving a dowry and having the wedding expenses met by the bride's family, as in a regional marriage. This also influenced evaluations of whether cross-regional marriages were "legitimate" marriages. Even in cases where a payment was known to be made to the bride's parents, people did not speak of it as "bride-price" because within the regional context it was no longer the customary practice even among groups that are known to have previously practiced it. As with regional marriages, all material transactions that were not dowry ("gifts") and moved in the opposite direction (groom to bride) were construed as "sale." My findings highlight the complexities of marriage payments and the difficulties of neatly placing them in one or the other category. The payments involved varied from only travel fare or expenses paid to the go-between, a fee (brokerage) for negotiating the marriage, or a payment as expenses or in exchange for a bride to the parents or a combination of these. It is important to emphasize here that most cross-regional brides did not think of themselves as "bought wives" and asserted that they had been "given away" in marriage and that their parents had not received a payment for them.

In the first three chapters, I discussed how cross-regional marriages differ from regional marriages, as they do not conform to the "rules" of marriage (inter-caste/inter-religious, dowryless), they involve different modes of arrangements and payments (the "go-between" and "sale"), and they result from a specific set of factors at source (mostly poverty) and destination (masculine sex ratios and the difficulties some men have in achieving "eligibility" for marriage). Given this, in part 2, I move on to explore how regional and cross-regional brides' lives are lived in everyday contexts within a context of poverty, caste, and gender inequalities.

PART 2

POST-MARITAL
LIVED EXPERIENCES

Chapter 4

Life in the *Sasurāl*

When I left, in that moment I felt as though that was no longer my
home. . . . I cried till I arrived at my *sasurāl*. I felt sad . . . . I left
everything behind . . . my parents, brothers and sisters. . . . Once
a woman gets married, one's home automatically becomes *parāyā*
[someone else's].

—Ritu (RB, 25, Jat)

Once married, a woman no longer has *adhikār* [rights] in her natal
home and her natal kin no longer have any *adhikār* over her. From
then on, she can go to her *pīhar* only to visit and that too only if her
in-laws allow her to.

—Abha (RB, 25, Chamar)

Following her wedding, as a bride departs from her natal home for her
sasurāl, songs convey the pain and sorrow experienced by her as she
leaves behind those who are "one's own" (Raheja 1995; Jeffery & Jeffery
1996; Narayan 2016). The departure marks a critical life transition for a
woman, who from then on becomes *parāyā dhan* (someone else's property)
as she is transferred in marriage from father to husband in accordance with
the ideology of *kanyādān*. This "gift of a daughter" signifies the "transfer
of rights and expectations of support of married women from their natal
to their conjugal home" (Palriwala 1991, p. 2771). Sarah Lamb writes
that there are significant differences between men and women with regard
to the ways in which they are constituted through relational ties over the
course of their lives. Patri-virilocal marriage means that men's ties are "made
once" and "endure" throughout and beyond their lifetimes, while those of
women are repeatedly altered—"their ties are disjointed and then remade"

(1997, p. 289–290). In this chapter, I begin to explore this process of the "making" and "unmaking" of ties. In the first section, I discuss what the movement from *pīhar* to *sasurāl* entails for women and highlight that this transition is more difficult for cross-regional brides because of not only geographical distance but also cultural difference. I then focus on women's work as a crucial aspect of their day-to-day lives and show that decisions around work are shaped by a range of factors other than regional origins. In the last section, I explore whether a sense of belonging to the affinal home and family is altered over the life-course.

From *Pīhar* to *Sasurāl*: The Transition

Talking about their experiences at the *sasurāl* when they first moved to live there, regional brides said, "*Jī nahī lagtā*" (I did not like it), it felt "*ajīb*" (strange) and "I felt like running away." For, unlike their husbands, who continued to live in their own homes among their kin, women were temporary members of their natal home. They had to leave their homes and childhood relationships and find themselves in a "new" environment among "strangers." Jagbiri (RB, 71, Kumhar) shared, "When I first came here, I did not feel like eating. I ate less than five *rotīs* [Indian bread] in five days. I did not like the taste of the water. It tasted bitter. I could not sleep because you have trouble sleeping in someone else's home." Many talked about "*adjust karnā*" (to adjust) in the *sasurāl*, which seemed to have become common vernacular usage in this part of north India. Promilla Kapur defines marital adjustment as a state of "accommodation in marital relationships." This entails tolerance, compromise, and sacrifice on the part of women with a view to maintaining marital harmony and the interests of the larger family unit (Kapur 1970, pp. 21, 293). The burden fell entirely on the new incoming bride, who was expected to adjust not only to her husband but also to her in-laws. This asymmetrical adjustment is "an affirmation of male dominance in the family" (Tyagi and Uberoi 1994, p. 115). Infact, as Leela Dube notes, in patri-virilocal systems, girls are socialized with an emphasis on the need to "bow before the wishes of the husband and his family," to be submissive and obedient future wives (1988, p. WS-12). A woman is thus conditioned to accept that she will find herself in an unfamiliar setting where her own status will be low. The idea that a woman's behavior in her affinal home will have a bearing on the reputation of her natal family is instilled from a young age (Dube 1997, p. 90).

As new brides, women find themselves at the bottom of domestic hierarchies. Within the patrilineal extended family, the authority structure is characterized by hierarchy on the basis of gender and age—that is, the subordination of female to male and junior to senior. Within the overarching authority of senior men there may be separate lines of control, wherein senior women exercise authority over daughters-in-law and daughters, and elder men over sons (Palriwala 2000, p. 672).[1] Adjustment in the *sasurāl* thus entailed submitting to the authority and control of the husband's kin. For some women, the separation they felt from their natal kin in the early months was exacerbated by the (ill) treatment from affinal women, especially the *sās*. Kumkum Sangari explains this dynamic between mothers-in-law and daughters-in-law in terms of securing "consent" from women by making "certain distributions of power within patriarchal arrangements" (1993, pp. 867, 869). Deniz Kandiyoti describes this power dynamic in terms of "patriarchal bargain," which is the "thorough internalisation" of patriarchy by women themselves. For systems of "classic patriarchy," such as India, she explains that within the patriarchal extended family, the deprivation and hardship that a woman experiences as a young bride is eventually superseded by the control and authority she gradually acquires over her own subservient daughters-in-law as she progresses in her married life. The anticipation of inheriting the authority of senior women leads women to conform to and become complicit with systems that subordinate them (1988, p. 279). Women, thus, "strategize within a set of concrete constraints" (p. 275). These household hierarchies are central to maintaining the unity of the joint family (by preventing the development of strong ties between husband and wife that might result in the son breaking away from the family unit) and preserving the mother–son bond with a view to ensuring old-age support. At times, conflicts arose between *jethānīs* and *devrānīs* (husband's brothers' wives) that mostly had to do with tensions between their husbands over joint household resources. For some new brides, affinal women became a source of support, however (chapter 6).

Regional brides thus contrasted the *pīhar* and *sasurāl* in ways similar to those described by Patricia Jeffery et al. for women in Bijnor: In their parent's village, women "find benefit (*fāida*), affection (*mamtā*), consideration (*khayāl*), succour (*madad*) and peace (*ārām*). But in the *sasurāl*, a *bahū* receives no indulgence (*khātir*) or appreciation (*qadr*)" (1989, p. 32).[2] Kajri (RB, 35, Jat) told me, "Once a woman gets married, she becomes like a buffalo tied to a tethering post." Some others, like her, made a distinction in temporal terms—splitting their experiences between the time "before" marriage and the time "after." The time before was described as a time of "*azādī*" (freedom), while the time after was one dominated by "*chintā*" (tensions/worry), constraint and "burdened with household responsibilities" (see also Bapna 2012).

Shanti (RB, 24, Kumhar) felt that a *sās* treats her daughter and daughter-in-law differently. She explained: "You can see my children are so young, my work never gets finished. No one helps me. If my *nanad* was as troubled with her children and had as much work, I know that my *sās* would have done everything to help her." Women like her believed that they could tell their mothers if they did not want to or could not work, but they could not do the same with their *sās*. In her *sasurāl*, a woman had to work, even when she was ill, under the control and watchful eye of the *sās*. When they first moved to their *sasurāl*, women said they had to seek permission for everything. They had to ask how things had to be done and feared being reprimanded. Khalida (RB, 45, Teli) told me, "I was always worried about doing something wrong or taking too long to finish the work. What if the salt in the food was too little?" She pointed out how a new bride had to adapt to the different food tastes of every member of the household.

In her *pīhar*, a woman did not have to observe *ghūnghat* (veiling) or *pardā* (veiling and seclusion). By contrast, in the *sasurāl* she could not go anywhere or talk to anyone and had to remain veiled and silent in the presence of senior males within and outside the household. About her first months in her *sasurāl*, Aarti (RB, 27, Chamar) said that she felt she was "*qaid mein*" (in detention) and talked about feeling like a "trapped bird." Likewise, Koyal (RB, 16, Chamar) felt that *ghūnghat* was a *sazā* (punishment). They added that over time it became a habit. *Pardā* entailed not only veiling but also restrictions on women's movements and interactions outside the household, respect-avoidance within the home, and certain kinds of feminine modesty behavior such as soft speech, avoiding direct eye contact, and assuming subservient postures (Jacobson 1982; Jeffery 1979; Papanek 1982; Sharma 1978a; Vatuk 1982). *Pardā* varied according to a woman's caste and class status, but also with age and stage in her married life, with young brides being the most constrained. Women conformed due to fear of the ridicule, gossip, and violence that non-conformity invited. They were subjected to surveillance by senior women, who became "complicit" in subordinating them and enforcing conformity to standards of "appropriate" behavior. Young wives were expected to display deference not only to senior men but also to senior female affines through the practice of *pāon parnā* (touching the feet/pressing the lower legs).

Like regional brides, cross-regional brides talked about the sadness they felt when they left their homes and parents to live in Barampur in their husbands' homes. "*Jī nahī lagtā*" and "you have to work in the *sasurāl*," they told me, just as regional brides did. For cross-regional brides, however, marriage entailed not only movement from *pīhar* to *sasurāl* over a very long distance, but additionally adjustment in a linguistically and culturally different region. Renuka (CRB, 33, Chamar) told me, "It was a *dūsrā ghar, dūsrā gāon aur dūsrā desh* [another home, another village and another country]."[3] For Chhaya (CRB, 55, Kumhar), it was "*pardesh*" (a foreign land) and "*alag*" (different). Varsha (CRB, 28, Jat) shared how she felt helpless as she fathomed the distance she had traveled that separated her from her natal kin: "I would sit by myself and cry. I wondered if I will ever be able to see my parents again." Unlike regional brides, whose natal kin came to fetch them a few days after the wedding and who could also avail of frequent visits in the first and early years, several years passed before cross-regional brides were able to return for a first visit to the natal home, and this intensified their isolation making adjustment more difficult (chapter 7).

The literature on cross-border marriages similarly shows that even when marriages are "within community" women often face a challenging process of adjustment in a "new" country. Writing on marriages between ethnically Korean (Chosŏnjok) women in China and men in South Korea, Caren Freeman writes that despite "the myth of ethnic homogeneity—the belief that Chosŏnjok and South Koreans belong to the same people," Chosŏnjok brides discovered immediately upon arrival in South Korea that they did not blend easily with the local population. Readily identified by their style of dress, their patterns of speech and pronunciation, and their unfamiliarity with Korean linguistic and behavioral codes of politeness, Chosŏnjok were for the most part unable to pass as South Koreans (2005, p. 95). Margaret Abraham similarly noted the isolation experienced by recent Indian immigrant brides in the US: "in perception and in reality, a woman feels that she is emotionally and socially alone, economically constrained and culturally disconnected" (2008, p. 314; see also Qureshi and Rogaly 2018, pp. 209–212). In Barampur, Kalawati (CRB, 40, Kumhar) explained how different and alienating life in Barampur felt:

> The first one year was very difficult. I felt alone. I could not understand the language. In Silchar [Assam], we ate rice three times a day but here they eat *rotī* for all meals. When I came here, I could not eat *rotī* because cowdung cakes were used to

make them. In Silchar, we used wood to cook. Here they cook on a *chūlhā* [open stove fueled by dung cakes]. I did not know how to make *rotī* on the *chūlhā*. Here they did not use soap to wash hair or clothes but used *multānī mittī* [soil] instead. There women wore *sārīs*. Here they wear suit-salwar or a long shirt with a *dhotī* [*sārī*]. There they do not observe *ghūnghat*. I did not know how to use a hand-pump for drawing water. It took me more than one year to get used to everything here.

For cross-regional brides then, marriage meant a difficult process of adjustment that entailed learning a new language and adopting the way of life, dress, and food habits of a different cultural context, also noted by earlier studies (Blanchet 2008; Chaudhry & Mohan 2011; Kaur 2004, 2012; Mishra 2016). Like Kalawati, other cross-regional brides talked about having to dress in suit-salwar instead of a *sārī* worn by married women in their native states. Even as new brides, two cross-regional brides were not allowed by their in-laws to wear a blouse but were made to wear a long shirt with a *sārī*, usually worn by older women. Two Bengali brides talked about how they were wearing a set of white conch-shell bangles framing a red one, as worn by married women in Bengal, when they first came to Barampur. They were asked to remove them. Some were given new names more suited to the region they married into. For three others (married to Hindu men), the name change served to both conceal and erase their Muslim identity. Cross-regional brides, then, had to let go of all markers of their pre-marital identity and life.

Cross-regional brides married to Hindu men also talked about fasting on *karvā chauth* (A one-day festival celebrated by Hindu women in north India where women fast from before sunrise to moonrise for the long lives of their husbands). This was not a festival they celebrated in their native states. Sheela (CRB, early 40s, Chamar) talked about Ganesh Chaturthi, which she celebrated in her native state (Maharashtra). She told me, "I cannot celebrate the festivals we do there because no one here does." Two cross-regional brides, both married to Chamar men, were Muslim before they came to Barampur. Both said that their husbands had never asked them either to wear *sindūr* (vermilion in the parting of the hair worn by Hindu women that serves as a signifier of their married status) or to fast on *karvā chauth*. They had, however, to give up their religious practices and undergo a name change. Of them, Samita (CRB, early 30s, Chamar) told me that she continued to perform *namāz* for three years after she got married without the knowledge of her husband, but stopped after the birth of her son, as it became increasingly difficult (see Blanchet 2008, pp. 165–168; and Kaur 2012, pp. 85–86 on Bangladeshi Muslim women married to Hindu men in eastern UP).

Ghūnghat was an adjustment that cross-regional and regional brides alike had to make. The difference between their experiences, however, was that the former had to be told what it entailed and before whom it had to be observed, because *ghūnghat* was not a practice in their native states. I watched Kanchan (CRB, 21, Chamar) in the first few months after her wedding and saw how the *ghūnghat* always slipped off her head. On one occasion when I went to speak with her, she came to the courtyard with her husband Ratan, veiling from me. I asked her why she was doing so and to that Ratan responded, "She will keep *ghūnghat* from you but not when she should" (pointing at the elderly men sitting outside across the street, suggesting that she did not understand the rules of *ghūnghat*). Sheela (CRB, early 40s, Chamar) talked about when she first came to Barampur, and how she wondered why women covered their faces but left their chests uncovered. In her native state (Maharashtra), she added, it was necessary for a woman to cover her chest.

For five cross-regional brides, having to learn the language was the most difficult adjustment. Varsha (CRB, 28, Jat) told me,

> Before I came here, I was worried about how I will talk to my husband. And my sister, who is married in Etah [a district in UP], was also worried about the same thing, but somehow both of us could speak Hindi. In Bengal, we learned Hindi by watching Hindi films. Sometimes I think it was destiny that both of us married in UP could understand Hindi and my younger two sisters cannot. . . . When I first came here, I could not understand the language because I was used to the Hindi of Bollywood films. The language here is different.

Varsha talks about the language in Barampur being different from Hindi because not only is the Hindi spoken in rural areas different from that of Bollywood films but also because of the regional dialect that is spoken in Barampur. While all cross-regional brides had to learn the language, the process was longer and more difficult for some than for others because they could not even speak Hindi when they first came to Barampur. It was easier for brides from Jharkhand and Bihar compared with those from West Bengal and Assam. For Jaya (CRB, 45, Jat), the interpreter between her husband and her had been her sister, who was married in Barampur three years before Jaya was. Lakshmi (CRB, late 40s, Kumhar) said that her husband communicated to her what those in her *sasurāl* were saying. She explained: "When they asked me for *pānī*, I thought to myself, what is *pānī*? My husband lifted a glass, filled water in it and showed me. I then understood that they meant water." Of the 19 cross-regional brides interviewed, 13 told me that they had learnt "*yahā kī bhāshā*" (the language of "here"—Barampur) and that they could no longer speak their native language. This had to do with the nature of their contact with their natal kin (chapter 7).

Another adjustment that cross-regional brides had to make was with regard to food. They pointed out the difference between Barampur and their native states (mostly the rice-eating eastern states): "Here they eat *rotī*, there we ate rice." Almost half of the cross-regional brides interviewed, however, said that they continued to cook and eat rice in Barampur, some more frequently than others. They also talked about the different vegetables or pulses they ate in their natal states. With regard to food, what seemed to be a more difficult adjustment for cross-regional brides married to Jat and Kumhar men (who were vegetarian) was that they had to adopt a vegetarian diet instead of one that included meat and fish in particular that formed a part of their everyday diet in their native states. Muslims and Chamars were non-vegetarian.[4] Thus, adjusting to different food tastes was easier for brides married among these two castes. Brides like Varsha (CRB, 28, Jat) also shared how they had to alter certain habits such as eating rice with the hands the way people did in her native state of Bengal. She added that her *devar* and *sās* taunted her by calling her *Bihārī* whenever she did so. Western UP has a history of Jat farmers employing in-migrant *Bihārī* laborers. During my fieldwork, I heard various accounts that stereotyped migrants from Bihar. They were spoken of as "poor," "backward," "savage," all associations made with cross-regional brides' native states as well (chapter 2). By using a pejorative term, Varsha's in-laws judged her cultural practice as inferior, thereby asserting their own as superior and needing adoption.

Women's Work

Adjustment in the *sasurāl* also entailed bearing the burden of work for all young brides and for cross-regional brides learning new skills related to work. In this section, I will discuss the work that women do alone and with men, but I will focus primarily on the work that women share with other women, an aspect that has not been discussed in the Western literature on domestic labor. This literature focuses mainly on the household division of work, including childcare, between men and women (e.g., Bianchi et al. 2012) or acknowledges the joint domestic labor of other members of the household (older children and youths) but discusses it within the context of a nuclear household (e.g., Gershuny & Sullivan 2014). In this context, with residential units being mainly non-nuclear, there existed a gendered division of labor between men and women but also a division of labor between women that was not fixed but shifted over the course of a woman's life, with seniority being crucial.

In Barampur, cross-regional and regional brides alike distinguished between *ghar kā kām* (housework) and *bāhar kā kām* (outside work). Household work broadly included cooking, cleaning, and washing clothes and utensils. Cattle work (milking the cattle, chopping fodder, and making cow dung cakes for fuel or manure) was also included in housework. Going to the fields to fetch fodder for the cattle, getting wood for cooking, and drawing and bringing water from the public tap were included in outside work. Some men did help with or take responsibility for cutting fodder or milking the cattle (see also Lyon 1988). Women, though primarily responsible for childcare, did not talk about it as work. "The work never finishes" or "I work all day" were oft-repeated to me. Sarla (RB, 48, Jat), for instance, described what household work usually involved:

> I wake up at 5 a.m., then I go to give fodder to the buffalo. . . . I
> return after about 45 minutes and make tea. Then I make food
> for the laborer who works in our field. Then I milk the buffalo.
> It takes 20 to 25 minutes. Then I sweep the floors downstairs
> and upstairs. Then I knead the dough. Then I do dusting in
> the house. Then I make tea and my husband comes to eat. I
> make *rotī* for him. Then I make tea again for my son and myself
> and *rotī* for both of us. By then it is around 8 a.m. I then start
> cleaning the kitchen. After that I wash clothes. By then it is 11
> a.m. Then I start cooking a vegetable and *rotī* for the laborer
> in the field. I simultaneously cook the food for the afternoon.
> Then I dry the washed clothes. I eat lunch at 3 p.m. I go to
> the cattle shed to give water and fodder to the buffalo. Then I
> wash utensils. I bathe at around 4 p.m. Then I make tea again.
> By 6 p.m. I start cooking the dinner. After dinner, I wash the

utensils and by 9 p.m. I go to bed. I spend 15 to 20 minutes every day making cow dung cakes.

She added, "And my husband tells me, 'what do you do the entire day'!" Women's work was highly significant in sustaining their households, yet it was devalued and unrecognized. Sarla was the only woman in her household and she told me on several occasions how she was looking forward to her son's marriage, as then (household) responsibilities would ease as they would be shared with a daughter-in-law.

Some studies on cross-regional marriage have argued that more labor demands are made on cross-regional brides than on regional brides. In her work on Bangladeshi wives in eastern UP, Thérèse Blanchet (2008) notes that in Bangladesh, unlike in UP, women did not work on their husband's land or hire themselves out as laborers. She describes the case of a bride married to a man much older than her who supported three children and an elderly husband who was unfit to work. Her husband owned less than half an acre of land when he married her but, owing to her hard work, he owned thrice the amount 16 years later (2008, p. 161). Similarly, in their work on cross-regional marriages in Haryana and Rajasthan, Reena Kukreja and Paritosh Kumar claim that excessive demands were made on the labor of cross-regional brides. They argue that the absence of kin support made it difficult for cross-regional brides to resist the "abuse" of their labor (2013, p. 49). Further, they write that in their day-to-day lives cross-regional brides were even excluded from decisions about what to cook or eat. They lived in a state of "self-imposed isolation" because they were considered "inferior" to "local women" and preferred to collect firewood or water separately, instead of with other women (p. 54).

Cross-regional brides talked about how they could cook before they came to Barampur but had to learn how to cook different kinds of food. For instance, all mentioned the difficulties they faced in learning how make roti on the chūlhā. They were taught by a jethānī or sās or learned by watching other women. Sheela (CRB, early 40s, Chamar) had been in Barampur for almost 30 years. She told me that she could still not make roti on the chūlhā, a task she previously left to her jethānī, then to her daughter, and now to her bahū. Cross-regional brides also had to be taught how to do cattle work and make cow dung cakes. Learning this work was an adjustment that they had to make, but none of my informants linked their workloads to their cross-regional status. Also, they did not feel that they had ever been excluded from collective activities (such as fetching firewood or water) by other regional brides, as noted by Kukreja and Kumar (2013) in their work. Decisions around work, as I go on to discuss, were shaped primarily by factors such as household composition, stage in the life-course, widowhood, and caste and class status for regional and cross-regional brides alike.

The structure and composition of the household had a significant bearing on the amount and kinds of work that women did. Most women started their married lives living in a *sanyukt* (joint) household with their *sās* and later on became *alag* (separate/nuclear), usually when their husbands' brothers got married and had children. The separation was marked by the *bahū* establishing a separate *chūlhā*, i.e., cooking independently. In some cases, women remained joint with their *sās*, as their husbands had no brothers (see also Jeffery et al. 1989, pp. 49–54). In joint households, work was shared with other women—*jethānī, sās, devrānī,* and unmarried *nanad(s)*, even though *bahūs* remained responsible for most of the work. Koyal (RB, 16, Chamar), a new bride, lived in a joint household with her *sās* and unmarried *nanad*. She complained that her *sās* did nothing, while her *nanad* only helped her with making *rotīs*, leaving her to take care of all other work by herself.

Some women (RB and CRB alike) believed that even though work was shared (with other women) in joint households, they had more work when they lived jointly than after they set up nuclear households. "You have to cook for more people" was one example they gave. These informants had previously lived in large joint families before they became *alag*, in contrast to those like Munesh (RB, 38, Kumhar), who lived jointly only with her widowed *sās* till she died. She pointed to the benefits of joint living, saying that when she was ill, for instance, she could rely on her *sās* but now she had no other choice but to work as she was without help. Older informants, particularly in Jat households, said that they had continued to help their *bahūs* with cattlework—milking the cattle and making dung cakes—even though they no longer helped with other household tasks.

Some said that they could leave children in the care of their *sās* while they took care of the work, while there were others like Shanti (RB, 24, Kumhar), who was left to care for her five young children and take care of the housework with no assistance from her *sās*: "No one helps me," she lamented. I also observed that women were often helped by young girls in the neighborhood, especially with infants. Husbands helped occasionally, but childcare, like all other housework, was primarily women's responsibility. Sarla (RB, 47, Jat) believed that when a *sās* left her *bahū* without help it was a way for her to assert her power over her daughters-in-law, and a *bahū* who had no power within the household had no option but to comply.

In nuclear households, as brides with young children, women were solely responsible for housework, but once a daughter reached the age of 12–13, she started helping with and gradually took over the housework. In households with many daughters, once the older daughter got married, the second one became old enough to do the work. Informants with adolescent daughters told me that they were "free" of housework. Some women continued to help their elderly *sās* with their housework even after becoming *alag*. Thus, in most cases, when women grew older their workload reduced as they were helped by daughters or daughters-in-law. For some informants, such as Jagmati (RB, early 60s, Chamar), however, (older) age did not offer respite from work: she was a widow living in a nuclear household with her two unmarried sons. The burden of housework fell entirely on her. Here the composition of the household had a more significant bearing on work than her age.

It was regarded shameful for a woman to visit her natal home once her pregnancy became visible. Sylvia Vatuk explains that this *sharm* relates to a woman's desire to avoid the situation of her parents having to acknowledge her sexuality and to keep her role as daughter and hence as *kanyā* (literally virgin) distinct from her role as a wife and mother (1982, p. 74). This was also the explanation offered for why women gave birth at their *sasurāl* and not the *pīhar*. Thus, she could not return to her *pīhar* to seek rest and respite from work during pregnancy. For most informants, work continued as usual during pregnancy. For some, the burden of work was eased somewhat, but this varied with the needs of the household, its composition, and a woman's relationship with her *sās*. After childbirth, women said that they were not expected to work for a 40-day period, although they did not usually get relief from work for this length of time. As women delivered at their *sasurāl*, I was also told that during this period, the *nanad* was called from her *sasurāl* to help with the work. Some informants were indeed helped by a married or unmarried *nanad*. Others, however, pointed out that sometimes either the married *nanad* was unable to come or could stay only a few days because she had household responsibilities of her own, was ill, or had very young children. In the absence of a *nanad*, women were helped by their *sās* or a *jethānī/devrānī*. Renuka (CRB, 33, Chamar) said that her *sās* helped only after the birth of her son but not her daughters and so it was her husband who stepped in. In some situations, an unmarried girl or an older female relative from the *pīhar* was called. Some women were helped by their older children when younger children were born and also had some assistance from their husbands (See also Jeffery et al. 1989, pp. 153–158). It was only in exceptional circumstances (conflict in the *sasurāl* and absence of any support from other women) that a woman could return to her *pīhar* for the delivery, as had two of my regional bride informants (chapter 7).

As far as *bāhar kā kām* (outside work) was concerned, new brides (whether CRB or RB) were not sent out to fetch fodder, firewood or water or to buy household provisions. In joint households, usually the *sās* went out, and if the *sās* was not alive, the *sūsar* (husband's father), husband, or *jeth* (husband's older brother). In some cases, young brides were sent out, but always accompanied by older women. In nuclear households, the *bāhar kā kām* was done by husbands in the early years of marriage. After children grew older, women started going out, especially if they lived in nuclear households.

Apart from age and years of marriage, factors such as widowhood affected a woman's work. Abha (RB, 25, Chamar), for instance, was a young window. She did all the *bahār kā kām* with her unmarried *nanad* because her household comprised only her four children, her elderly widowed *sās*, and her unmarried *nanad*. Ordinarily, young brides like Abha would not be sent out to fetch firewood or fodder, but her widowed status and the composition of her household (only adult women and very young children) offered no alternative. Most Jat households owned cattle, but not all among the four other castes (Chamar, Kumhar, Teli, and Lohar) did, so not all households required fodder. Also, in most Jat households, the men brought fodder from their own fields for the cattle. In several households, particularly among the Jats and Lohars, food was cooked using gas cylinders. Thus, some households did not use firewood or dung cakes.

Bāhar kā kām also included paid work outside the household and, in the case of Jat women, (unwaged) agricultural work on the family fields. Jat informants told me that the number of Jat women involved in agricultural work had decreased over the years, apart from a few weeks during wheat harvesting. They attributed this largely to mechanization. It also became evident that with an increasing number of Jat girls pursuing higher education, they were less inclined to be involved in agricultural work. Caste, class, and age were significant in determining women's involvement in paid work. Some Teli, Kumhar, and Chamar women worked as (waged) seasonal agricultural laborers on Jat fields. Some Chamar and Kumhar women also worked in Jat households as sweepers or helped with cattle work for a wage. With the exception of Chamar women who worked in the brick kilns from the first year of marriage, women usually became engaged in paid work only at a later stage in their married life, as their mobility increased. Sometimes compulsion of poverty forced women to go out to work from the early years of marriage, however.

Kalawati (CRB, 40, Kumhar), explained that she worked in the fields of Jat farmers and as payment received fodder for her cattle. She told me that she worked the entire day and even though she did it "*apnī marzī se*" (of her own will), her family could not be sustained if she stopped working. Her husband worked as a potter for part of the year and in the brick kiln for the other part. She said that it was not possible for them to feed their six children with her husband's earnings alone. As their family grew, it became essential for her to go out to work. She told me, "Some women are *dūkhī* [unhappy] and some *sūkhī* [happy]. I am neither *sūkhī* nor *dūkhī*. I am medium. I am not *sūkhī* because I cannot feed my children without working and I am not *dūkhī* because at least my family is not starving."

Due to status concerns, Jat and Lohar women were not usually employed outside the home for a wage, although there were exceptions such as Kajri (RB, 35, Jat), a landless widow with eight children. Like Kalawati, she was compelled by poverty and (additionally for her) widowhood to go out to work. She worked as a sweeper, washed utensils, and made cow dung cakes in three Jat households. She told me, "If my husband was alive, I would not go out to work. We are Jat. Nobody in the village talks about me. They know that I have to work because of *majbūrī*. If I do not work, how will I feed my children?" In her case, poverty and widowhood and not caste status were determining in decisions regarding work.

Due to compulsions of poverty and caste, those regional and cross-regional brides who were married to Chamar brick-kiln workers also worked in the brick kilns with their husbands from the first year of marriage. As discussed earlier (chapter 2), Chamars work as *patherās* in the brick kilns, with their tasks including loosening the soil through wetting and digging up the hard ground with a spade. This is considered heavy work and is done by men. Then there's the packing of the mud into the molds, which is often done by both men and women, and then the stacking of the bricks so molded to dry, which is mostly done by women. Regional brides whose natal kin were brick-kiln workers had worked in the brick kiln before marriage and already knew how to do this work. Others, like Kusum (RB, 47, Chamar), however, shared how she had to learn how to do the work, since her natal family had never worked in the brick kiln. She talked about the first time she went to the brick kiln, when she stayed for only two months. She was constantly taunted by her in-laws as she struggled to do the work and was sent back to her *pīhar*. She said that she had been troubled throughout her married life because of this work and felt helpless, as there seemed no way out of it. "My children were born at the brick kiln and now they all work there," she told me. As it was for Kusum, learning to do brick-kiln work was a very difficult adjustment that cross-regional brides had to make. Radha (CRB, early 40s, Chamar) remarked, "I had not even seen a brick kiln in my dreams until I came here."

Chamar wives (regional and cross-regional alike) shared with me the hardships they experienced in brick-kiln work shaped both by their caste and gender identities. "It is hard labor," Kusum said. They had to work very long hours and, unlike men, they had childcare and other household responsibilities. Renuka (CRB, 33, Chamar) talked about the health problems she developed because of brick-kiln work, as it was *bhārī kām* (heavy work). She said, "This work is for *tākatdār ādmī* [physically strong people], *hum toh kamzor hai, toh lāchārī hai*" (we are weak, so we are helpless). Samita (CRB, early 30s, Chamar), had a miscarriage during the sixth month of pregnancy while working at the brick kiln. Other informants also talked about the difficulties of working in the brick kiln during pregnancy. Women who gave birth to children at the brick kiln talked about having to resume work as soon as ten days after childbirth because brick-kiln work depends on family labor, and the advance received for the work had to be paid back.[5] Wage labor (on Jat fields, in brick kilns, etc.) also made women vulnerable to violence, from which their men could offer little protection, as they were powerless in the face of men in positions of dominance (see also chapter 2).

As far as control over the income that women earned from outside employment was concerned, most said that whatever they earned went into meeting household expenses. They did not have an independent income. Only three said that they kept what they earned and had never been questioned by their husbands on how they spent it. Kalawati (CRB, 40, Kumhar), for instance, used her earnings to buy gifts for her married daughter when she visited, since Kalawati's husband refused to give her the money to do so. Chamar women said that payment for brick-kiln work took the form of a lump-sum advance payment that was made to their husbands, and it was their husbands who determined how it was to be spent.

Incorporation, Home and the Ambiguity of Belonging

I have discussed how women, unlike men, grow up with a sense of temporary membership in their natal homes. Do they then ever come to completely belong to their affinal homes and families? In their work in rural Rajasthan and Uttar Pradesh, Gloria Goodwin Raheja and Ann Grodzins Gold noted that women's songs reflected the fact that "there may be no place that a woman may truly call 'one's own home'" (1994, p. 73). Writing on rural Rajasthan, Rajni Palriwala observed that for a considerable time in their life-course, women were not accepted completely by either their natal or their conjugal families. Nevertheless, with life-cycle changes—as their mothers-in-law aged, their husband's siblings were married, and their husband's sisters spent more time in their own *sasurāl* and the bride became the mother of sons—women became "fixed" in and were increasingly "incorporated" into their marital homes (1991, pp. 2770–2771).

In Barampur, when I questioned regional brides about what they considered their home, *pīhar* or *sasurāl*, the responses varied: after marriage a woman's home is her *sasurāl*; the *sasurāl* feels like home once children were born;[6] a woman has to live and die in the *sasurāl* once married, yet only her *pīhar* is home; or a woman never completely belongs to either her *pīhar* or her *sasurāl* and neither is home. Ritu (RB, 25, Jat) explained,

> Once you get married everyone will tell you, now your *sasurāl* is your home. If I have a dispute with my husband and in-laws and they ask me to leave, I can go and stay at my *pīhar* but after two months my natal kin will start saying that is your home, you must return. They will say *"ab terā kam wahī se chalegā"* [now your needs will be met there]. They will send me from the *pīhar* but here they will tell me, *"tu apne ghar jā"* [you go to your own home].

Ritu points to the accepted view that a married daughter's future lies not in her parental home but in her husband's home, where "she has rights of residence and maintenance" (Palriwala 1991, p. 2764). Leela Dube (1997) and Rajni Palriwala (1991) both argue that women become the source of suspicion for both their natal and conjugal families for a significant time in their life-cycle. Palriwala explains that on the one hand, her affinal kin might suspect that the new bride might attempt to transfer wealth to her natal kin, and on the other, her natal kin might resent their obligation to provide gifts to her irrespective of whether they could afford to or not (1991, p. 2770).

In Barampur, what became evident was that women continued to experience ambiguity about belonging until a much later stage in their married lives, until the "cyclical nature of women's power in the household"

(Kandiyoti 1988, p. 279) enabled them to inherit authority and become matriarchs of their households. As Palriwala notes, the birth of sons was crucial for a woman to establish her rights in her husband's home. Yet while women became increasingly incorporated into their marital homes as they aged, they never completely became kin to their affines.

Some cross-regional brides, like regional brides, said that they felt that their *sasurāl* in Barampur was home: "where your parents give you in marriage, that is home," they explained. Some others, like Kalawati (CRB, 40, Kumhar), however, felt differently. She had been in Barampur since the late 1980s. Kalawati talked of Silchar (Assam) as home even though it had been over two decades since her last visit (chapter 7). She told me, "I remember everything about my village . . . the cinema, the fairs, the circus, the tea gardens. . . . My mother passed away when I was a child. We had no contact with my father. . . . My brothers and sisters were there . . . my brothers worked in the tea factory." Home, as Carol Smart points out, "is tied to memory, to relationships and to events" (2007, p. 163). When I asked her if Barampur felt like home, she told me,

> This is my home and yet it is not. One's home is where one is born even though I have to live and die here now. My parents got me married and I came to *pardesh* . . . now I will have to accept this as my home. This is *pardesh* even now, not *apnā desh* [one's own country]. If someone asks me, "Where are you from?" I will say I am from Silchar, Assam. I came here after marriage, but my home is there. Even for my married daughter, her home is here in Barampur.

Kalawati suggests that a woman's home will always be the place of birth— her natal home. This was an opinion that some regional brides, like Kusum (RB, 47, Chamar), shared: "I am married here, but if you ask me where am I from, I will say *wāhā kī*" (from there—she named her natal village). Unlike Kusum, however, Kalawati also makes a distinction between one's own and a foreign land—Barampur was *pardesh*. Cross-regional brides had adapted to the way of life in *pardesh*, divesting themselves of all markers of a pre-marital identity, yet questions of home and belonging for them cannot be adequately understood in terms of the sense of ambiguity experienced by regional brides.

In her work in Haryana, Prem Chowdhry (2005, pp. 5195–5196) describes cross-regional marriages as "dubious marriages." She writes,

In the present context these women are not necessarily 'wives' in the strict sense of the term. They occupy an unrecognised and indefinable status in contemporary Haryana. . . . Most of these purchased women do not even know the language or participate in any of the cultural activities of this region. With severely limited or even non-existing communication, these women are isolated and experience an extreme sense of alienation from the families they are supposed to belong. Many of them even physically live on the periphery, or in the '*khet*' [fields] of their 'owner.' The other women of the family who have come through a proper ritual wedding and a dowry, refuse to give them any recognition. Not incorporated fully into the rural household, the 'married' status of these women remains highly ambiguous. . . . Some women who find it difficult to adjust or manage the extreme hardwork involving the household, animals and the fields are even resold . . . yet others change hands several times. . . . In the years to come, the children born of such liaisons are going to be a major source of tension and conflict when the question of their inheritance rights comes up.

Similarly, Reena Kukreja and Paritosh Kumar, writing on Haryana and Rajasthan, detail a process of "othering" that defines the experiences of cross-regional brides in their marital villages and present a picture of "widespread intolerance" exhibited by conjugal communities. They argue that the unknown caste status of the women "proves to be the biggest hindrance in their acceptability" (2013, pp. 2, 32). Elsewhere, Kukreja maintains that arguments of "integration" and "assimilation" ignore the "forcible imposition of dominant cultural norms and the violent assimilative process" that women undergo in the shedding of language, dress, food habits, and other cultural markers (2018b, p. 384). Further, she argues that the "internal othering" that women experience is extended to their children.

Other studies, however, argue that cross-regional brides are gradually incorporated. Ravinder Kaur, for instance, states, "The receiving family properly incorporates the bride into the family. Her status is not that of a concubine nor is she discarded after a while or passed into prostitution. The women go on to become mothers and even mothers-in-law. . . . The women adopt the language and culture of the host society and consider themselves a part of that society" (2004, p. 2598). Focusing on the caste of cross-regional brides, Paro Mishra, in her work on Haryana, did not find caste status to be "contentious in itself," although important because marriage into another caste meant accommodating to new caste practices. She noted that caste-based discrimination against the incoming cross-regional bride was rare and that Haryanavi society had accepted the import of brides as a "normal" phenomenon (2016, p. 232–234).

In Barampur as well, cross-regional brides were accorded the status of wives and mothers in monogamous marriages and the terms *bahū, awrat* (literally "woman," but used in this context to mean "wife"), or *gharwālī* (wife) were used for them as for regional brides. They participated in religious ceremonies as wives and attended weddings in their husbands' families and caste communities. Their names were on ration and election cards that served as proof of their marital status. The children born of these marriages were regarded as legitimate, they acquired their father's caste status, and male children inherited their father's property, as did the sons of regional brides.[7] As discussed earlier, decisions around work were not linked to women's cross-regional status. The relationships that cross-regional brides were able to establish with other women were also determined by a range of other factors crucial for regional brides as well (chapter 6). They were not isolated from their affinal kin or others in the village because of their cross-regional status, and marital violence was not an experience peculiar to them (chapter 5). Cross-regional brides were, thus, "incorporated" in these ways, yet, as I go on to show, as far as their sense of belonging was concerned, their experiences were more complex than those of either gradual incorporation or "widespread intolerance."

Jaya (CRB, 45, Jat) came from West Bengal as a bride in the mid-1980s. Here response to my questions about whether she thought of herself as a UP woman and if Barampur felt like home is telling:

> Here people can look at me once and tell that I am *bāhar kī* [from outside]. Everyone knows that I am not a UP woman. Even a cloth-seller who comes to the house will ask me, "Where are you from? You are not *yāhā kī*" [from here]. I still think of myself as a Bengali woman. How can I think of myself as a UP *wālī* [belonging to UP] when no one here accepts this?

Acceptance was crucial to Jaya's sense of belonging, with self-identity being relational. She believed that she could not claim to be a UP woman because those in the village perceived her as *alag* (different). In the village, talk about the appearance of cross-regional brides focused not so much on their different facial features but on the familiar idiom of skin color that was used to accentuate difference. There is wide variation in skin tone across India and most of my cross-regional bride informants were visibly darker than local UP women. Five said they their husbands' relatives and other women had made remarks about their dark skin. When I first went to meet Savita (CRB, late 20s, Jat), her father-in-law was sitting outside in the courtyard. I asked him if I could meet her. He replied, "She is inside." I asked if she was by herself. He replied, "*kālī hai.*" He thought I did not understand, so he repeated in English, "she is black." While for regional brides, skin tone was significant in assessing beauty and attractiveness, for cross-regional brides, it became a visible/physical marker of their (regional) origins and also served as a proxy for (low) caste status as it did for Dalits (chapter 1; see also Chaudhry 2019b).

Other than the fact that they looked different, cross-regional brides said that they could be identified as *bāhar kī* because of language, as their accent was different. They talked about how they had learned the local language and many could no longer speak their native language, but as soon as they started speaking they were questioned about where they came from and told that they did not speak "*yāhā kī bhāshā*" (the language of "here," i.e., Barampur). Lakshmi (CRB, late 40s, Kumhar) had been in Barampur since the early 1980s. She told me that at times she spoke a few Bengali words while speaking Hindi and was taunted for "not letting go of her language."

People in the village said that cross-regional brides were easily identifiable and they could list out to me the brides married within their caste without any difficulty. They did not distinguish between whether they were from Maharashtra, West Bengal, Jharkhand, Bihar, or Assam. For them, they were all *bāhar kī, dūr kī* (from far away), *Bihārī* (from Bihar), or *pūrab se* (easterner). Nine of the 19 cross-regional brides interviewed said that none of this had ever been said to them to their face but they were aware that they were referred to in this way when people in the village talked among themselves.

Sheela (CRB, early 40s, Chamar) expressed her annoyance to me: "The villagers call us *pūrabnī* [woman from the east] irrespective of where we are from. I feel really angry and tell them that I am not even from *pūrab* [the east]. I am from Maharashtra [in the west]. Irrespective of how old I get, I will always be a *pūrabnī.*" Jeeti (73, Chamar, F) had come to Barampur as the wife of a Chamar in the early 1960s. "They call me *pūrabnī* when they speak about me," she told me. Even 50 years of living in Barampur had not sufficed for others to stop identifying her as being from elsewhere.

My facilitator, Satender (55, Chamar, M), would say, "*Bihār side kī*" when talking about cross-regional brides. He explained: "If she is from that side, then we will have to say that she is from there. Most people do not know Jharkhand but Bihar is known to everyone." While Satender suggested that speaking of cross-regional brides in this way did not involve any prejudice, Varsha said that such name-calling made her feel like "*gālī de rahe hai*" (they are verbally abusing us) not only because terms like *Bihārī* were pejorative but also because it made her feel like an "outsider."

When I went to talk to Lakshmi (CRB, late 40s, Kumhar), the first question that her son Pramod (21, Kumhar, M) asked me was if I was aware that his mother was from "Bangla-desh." In the course of the conversation, he told me that he felt that women like his mother were not given the same *sammān* (respect) as regional brides were. He added, "No one in the family ever treated my mother differently, but outsiders do." He believed that this was because women like his mother originated from poor areas. For others, it was because coming from *pūrab* carried associations of belonging to a different (lower) caste, which was raised by people in the village as an issue despite cross-regional brides being granted their husbands' caste status. People in the village, for instance, said that they refused to accept food from cross-regional brides or marry their children. Some of the children of cross-regional couples also mentioned being called the children of *Bihārī* mothers or "bought wives" during a fight. I have argued elsewhere that while references to the differential caste status of brides had more to do with claims to (superior) status and less with actual concerns around caste purity, nevertheless, they do point to a prevailing discourse of caste-related discrimination (see Chaudhry 2019b).

Conclusion

For all women, marriage marks a rupture from their natal kin as they move to a new village to live among strangers. The move from *pīhar* to *sasurāl* entails a painful and difficult process of adjustment for all brides as they seek to make a place for themselves and establish new ties in their affinal homes. For cross-regional brides, this process was much harder, as marriage entailed not only migration over a very large (geographic) distance that isolated them from their natal kin, but also adapting to a culturally and linguistically different context. Marriage in *pardesh*, thus, meant undergoing a resocialization process and acquiring a new "habitus" (Bourdieu 1977).

They had to internalize forms of behavior and bodily practices (adapting to new food tastes and clothing, learning a new language and work-related skills) and transition from feeling that these were newly acquired or foreign to feeling that they had become "habitual" or second nature. Learning the language was more difficult for some depending on the state where they originated (Hindi-speaking or non-Hindi-speaking). The process of adapting to new food habits varied according to the castes of their husbands. For cross-regional brides who were Muslim before they were married in Barampur to Hindu men, adjustment also entailed a name change and letting go of all markers of their pre-marital religious identity.

While there were differences between cross-regional and regional brides with respect to adjustment in the *sasurāl*, exploration of other aspects of women's everyday lives, such as the work that women do, shows other factors were more crucial than regional origins. As far as work was concerned, women were largely responsible for *ghar kā kām* (housework). The composition of the households had a significant bearing on women's work as it was shared between women of the household even though how it was shared related to both the passage of time and seniority. Women usually had less work as they grew older, as they were helped by daughters or daughters-in-law. Due to *pardā* restrictions, young or new brides did not take care of *bāhar kā kām* (outside work). It was usually senior women (the *sās*) or men (the husband, father-in-law, or husband's male relatives) who were responsible for these tasks. Women's outside paid employment was determined by factors such as caste and also age, as women's mobility increased as they grew older. Compulsions of poverty and widowhood largely influenced decisions regarding women's waged work.

Regional brides expressed ambivalence when speaking about what they considered home, but this sense of ambiguity reduced over the life-course as they became more embedded within their affinal homes. Despite undergoing a resocialization process, for cross-regional brides, feelings about home and belonging were more complex and were tied to the understanding that time would neither erase nor alter the perception that they came from elsewhere. This is an issue I continue to explore in the following chapters.

Chapter 5

Husbands

Meri marzī unse kabhī alag nahī hotī [My wishes are never different
from his]. He doesn't treat me like his wife but like his friend and
we talk to each other—*sūkh dūkh kī bātein* [talk of joy and sorrow].

—Aarti (RB, 27, Chamar)

If a woman's husband supports her, then she will never be unhappy.

—Sakeena (RB, 43, Teli)

I came here and my husband kept me well and always supported me,
now I have to support him.

—Mansi (CRB, 33, Chamar)

In this chapter, I turn to women's relationships with their husbands. I
foreground "the (conjugal) couple" not only to discuss how inequalities
shape conjugality but also to explore the "dimensions of intimacy" (Jamieson
1998) that equally come to shape the lived realities of marriage. I begin
by discussing some recent work in the Indian context that has addressed
the question of equality in couple relationships. Much of this literature has
explored whether ideas of marital companionship that have come to frame
marriage have led to more egalitarian relationships between couples.

Jonathan Parry (2001), focusing on the industrial working class in
Chhattisgarh, central India, argues that there had been a shift in the meaning
of marriage. To support his argument, he presents the case of an illiterate
Dalit father and his educated daughter, a school teacher. He contends that
for the father, marriage had little to do with "intimate companionship,
emotional empathy or shared tastes." It was above all "an institutional

arrangement for the bearing and raising of children, and for the management of the household economy" (p. 815). By contrast, for the daughter, "the conjugal relationship carries a much heavier emotional freight," with the relationship being "a bond between two intimate selves." He adds that it is likely that the desire for intimacy in marriage was always to some extent present, especially among women. What seems to be "new" is that "what had formerly existed in a semi-submerged form, as an alternative discourse, has . . . now moved more centre stage" and been appropriated by men (p. 816). He asserts that there is now "a new ideological stress on the couple" that leads to democratization in relationships, as argued by Anthony Giddens (1992).

In suburban Hyderabad, Amanda Gilbertson made an observation similar to Parry's: a desire for intimacy in marriage had moved "centre-stage," but she noted that this was in "constant dialogue with other ideas about the function of marriage" (2014, p. 232). Her informants "described a shift in the nature of middle-class marriage from a hierarchical relationship of respect to a more equal relationship of friendship" (p. 226). They valued gender equality in marriage, seeing it as "progressive" and "open-minded," while at the same time occupying a "moral middle ground," believing that "overly equitable relationships" threatened the durability of marriage (p. 237). Women were expected to adjust and compromise with a view to preserving the "good Indian family" and expressing respectable middle-class femininity vis-à-vis both the elite and those of lower caste/class status. Likewise, Parul Bhandari (2017), in her work among the middle class in Delhi, noted that even in pre-marital relationships the onus of adjustment was on women. For relationships described as "serious," i.e., progressing toward marriage, she noted an unequal dynamic where men exercised control and surveillance over their female partners and also attempted to "tame" them to gain family approval.

Shalini Grover, also writing on Delhi, focused on a low-caste, low-income neighborhood. She compared women in arranged marriages, love marriages, and secondary unions to assess which form of alliance was most democratic for women. She concluded that "women face physical violence, alcohol-related abuse, sexual jealousy and conflicts over money and other matters, which are regular features of unequal marital relations" (2011, p. 203). Neither the choice to enter or terminate relationships nor secure employment reduced women's dependence on men or made relationships more egalitarian. Women were best positioned in arranged marriages, as they could access emotional and material support from their natal kin in situations of marital conflict. In contrast, in love marriages, women "invest more emotion, energy and effort into making their marriages work" due to the absence of exit options (withdrawal of parental support) following the assertion of choice in marriage (p. 207). Further, while the courtship period was more egalitarian, once they are married an "asymmetrical relationship begins to develop" between love-marriage couples (pp. 207–208), an observation also made for other contexts (e.g. Smith 2006 on Nigeria).

Like Grover, Katharine Twamley in her work among Gujarati Indians in urban India and the UK found that "love promotes more adjustment and acceptance on the part of women" (2012, p. 9). Her participants valued love, respect, and equality equally in both contexts and sought to make marital relationships different from their parents'. In part, this reflected global ideas of love associated with modernity and development. Yet she asserts that love is not "new," but rather its place and meaning within marriage had shifted. Women held ideals of egalitarian relationships but were unable to realize them in day-to-day decision-making and household division of labor. The increased emphasis on intimacy possibly contributed to women's inability to negotiate more egalitarian relationships, she argued, because women tended to ignore or rationalize gender roles and inequalities so that the loving foundations of their relationships were not questioned.

In her work among Kerala Muslims, Caroline Osella, like Twamley and unlike Parry, saw love as continuous with older forms of marriage yet part of a "contemporary re-shaping of conjugal expectations" (2012, p. 244) that she locates within the context of economic liberalization, gulf migration, and Islamic reformism. A growing emphasis on conjugal intimacy has led to the cultivation of a new style of conjugality and "gendering" that had undermined the matrilineal extended family and promoted the nuclear family as the ideal family form, with the switch to a neo-patriarchal household requiring the "performances of impeccable heterosexuality and masculinity" (p. 247). Gayatri Reddy, also writing on South India, noted that among the Hijras (so-called "eunuch transvestites") of Hyderabad, a marriage based on companionship and emotional intimacy with (non-Hijra) men described as "husbands" was the "most longed for relationship" (2006, p. 179). Hijras' "bonds of love" with their husbands were "constructed in the image of normative heterosexual marital bonds" (p. 187). Even though built on egalitarian ideals, these relationships were marked by a "very unequal gendered pattern of violence" (p. 188).

The aforementioned studies focus on urban contexts where companionate ideals have come to be prioritized in the making of marriage or have become increasingly emphasized after marriage. In keeping with the findings of studies, from other Western and non-Western contexts (Jamieson 1998, 1999; Hirsch & Wardlow 2006), these studies from India show that women's desires for equality remain unrealized and an asymmetric dynamic defines the marital relationship. Unlike in urban India, in the rural context described here, marriages are not made or premised on companionate ideals, and women and men have little choice over whom and when to marry.[1] Women enter marriage with an understanding that they are and must remain subordinate to their husbands. Furthermore, love and intimacy between spouses has to be kept "hidden" and is not culturally extolled.

In this chapter, I will develop on two of Lynn Jamieson's arguments. First, just because a particular form of intimacy is celebrated in European and North American cultures, featuring self-disclosure and expression of emotion, we must not resist calling forms of love and relationships that are emotionally constrained and taciturn intimate, for they may involve a "repertoire of other practices of intimacy" (2011, p. 8). Second, intimacy can exist despite and alongside inequalities. I will highlight the cultural specificity of this context to show that while in the West, there is the understanding that there will be intimacy in the couple relationship, this intimacy fades with little doing and is undermined by violence (Jamieson 1998). By contrast, in the context studied here, women enter marriage with little expectation of intimacy but with the possibility that there will be violence that is both widespread and normalized. Yet, I argue that *intimacy can develop even within violence.*

In the first three sections of this chapter, I highlight the inequality in marital relations through a discussion of marital violence that includes coerced sex, wife-beating, and verbal abuse and, drawing on Rebecca Emerson Dobash and Russell P. Dobash's understanding, various forms of controlling behaviors (1998, p. 155) such as control over reproductive decisions. The last section explores the meanings of marriage and support to unpack women's desires and yearnings with a view to providing insights on the meanings that women themselves attach to their relationships. I conclude this chapter by arguing that women are not entirely without agency or support, despite the inequality and violence within which they live their lives.

Sex

For women in Barampur, marriage at a young age, lack of knowledge about sexual matters, and the fact that their husbands had been strangers meant that sexual relations were experienced as difficult and were marked by the absence of choice when they first moved to live in the *sasurāl*. Sarla (RB, 47, Jat) laughed about her ignorance:

> When I came here at *gaunā*, I was 16. I didn't know that you get a husband in marriage [laughed]. . . . I didn't know that you have to sleep with your husband. I thought that as I did work in my *pīhar*, I would do work in my *sasurāl*. . . . There was no exposure to television. Mothers wouldn't talk about such things. My elder sister was married, but she felt *sharm* [shame] in talking about such things.

Likewise, Kripa (RB, 75, Jat) commented, "The first time my husband came to me, I thought, why is he teasing me? I threatened to tell my father." Women like Kripa and Sarla learnt about "*ādmī ke sāth sambandh*" (sexual relations with a husband) from a *jethānī* or husband. Both women were married over three decades before my fieldwork. Younger brides, by contrast, said that they had been told about "what would happen" by a friend from their *pīhar* or a female relative: *buā* (father's sister), *bhābī* (brother's wife), or *chāchī* (father's younger brother's wife). All informants agreed that a mother never talked to a daughter about such matters because of *sharm*. Yet, while young brides were aware of "what would happen," being unmarried women, they could not openly share concerns or ask questions about sex. Ritu (RB, 25, Jat), for instance, told me, "I was told that it would hurt but I did not know how much it would hurt . . . you hesitate asking other women."

When talking about their early sexual experiences, many talked about the sense of fear they felt, as their husband was a stranger to them. Jagbiri (RB, 71, Kumhar) commented, "He is a stranger and then he takes you and sleeps with you at night. I had not even seen his face until after the wedding." Even younger brides, like Ritu, who had had some say in her marriage and had communicated with her husband before marriage via a mobile phone, said that she was "*ghabrāyī huyī aur darī hūyī*" (anxious and scared) because marriage meant sex with a stranger. There was also an understanding that the marriage would be consummated on the *suhāg rāt* (wedding night), a matter over which women had no say and to which they had to submit. For instance, Abha (RB, 25, Chamar) told me, "I think that when women get married they are most afraid because other women tell them that this will happen." Hemlata (CRB, late 50s, Kumhar) said she was married at the age of 15 and recounted her experience of submitting to coerced sex:

The man does not think, she is still young . . . *ādmī toh chortā nahī* [your husband does not leave you alone]. He [husband] was *thādā* [used to describe a tall and well-built man] and I was like a child. . . . He must have thought, what can she do?

Likewise, Koyal (RB, 16, Chamar) talked about pleading with her husband to let her be, as she was menstruating on the wedding night and did not feel well, but "He said, he cannot wait. The next morning, I was not even in a condition to get up from the *khāt* [bed]." Other women, like Hemlata, were often married at young ages when their bodies were not prepared for sex. Kalawati (CRB, 40, Kumhar) had not attained puberty when she had sexual relations with her husband:

> I must have been 12–13 when I first came here. When I had come here and I was living in his house I had to stay here and stay with him [husband]. What could I do? Even my *sās* did not think about this. *Bahut dar lagā thā* [I felt extremely afraid]. No one told me this will happen. *Jab aise aise kām hone lage* [when these things started happening], I went to Hemlata [the go-between for her marriage] and told her. Hemlata said, "this will happen now that you are married." A few days later I started menstruating. *Bahut zyadā taklīf huyī thī* [it was very difficult].

Even until the early 1990s, when women were married at much younger ages, they were kept at the *pīhar* and not sent to live at the *sasurāl* until after they had attained puberty. A regional bride would not share Kalawati's experience of having to consummate the marriage prior to puberty. It was a *sās*'s responsibility to ensure that sexual relations did not take place until the bride returned for cohabitation. Though married post-puberty, most of my regional bride informants were married below the age of 18 (the legal age at marriage) and some consummated their marriages at ages under 16 (the legal age of consent). For them, too, sexual relations in the initial months caused *taklīf* (trouble) or *pareshānī* (difficulty). Abha (RB, 25, Chamar) started cohabiting with her husband at age 14 and had to seek medical help because of the physical pain she experienced during sex for the first three months of marriage. Similarly, Shanti (RB, 24, Kumhar) was about 16 when she moved to her husband's home. About her early sexual experiences, she said, "*sharīr par bahut zor partā hai*" (the husband's physical force on the body is very great). Women could not complain if they were hurt during sex or it caused them pain or discomfort. Of the informants who talked to me about sex in the early years, none said that their husbands had acted considerately in this regard.

I attempted to understand whether women came to think of and experience sexual relations differently over the course of their married lives. Women's accounts of their sexual lives ranged from force or coercion, through lack of interest, compulsion, duty and submission, to desire and pleasure. Not all of my 38 regional bride and cross-regional bride informants talked to me about their sexual lives, however. In neighboring Bijnor district, women mentioned being caused "trouble" by their husbands demanding sex and sang songs that contained explicit sexual references, yet "discussing sex much further proved immensely difficult" (Jeffery & Jeffery 1996, p. 127; see also Ahearn 2001, pp. 72–73). I had anticipated that my unmarried status would present additional difficulties and I approached the issue by asking women about "choice" with regard to the number and timing of children. I was surprised at the ease with which some women talked to me about their sexual lives. Yet, with others, I found it difficult even to raise the subject. On one occasion, a Jat woman reprimanded me: "Do you not have any shame, talking to women about such things." Some women were uninterested or less open in talking after my first or second visit. Studies on rural north India note that women's songs were filled with references to marital pleasure and frequently spoke of the intimate loving relationship between a man and his wife (Gold 2006, p. 312; Wadley 1994, p. 49). In Barampur too, women's songs contained explicit sexual references, yet few women mentioned desire and pleasure when talking about sex. I wondered whether this was a way to appear respectable, given the cultural expectation that modest women must not express desire. It may have also been a way to instruct me on what was appropriate, as premarital sex was taboo and as an unmarried woman I was to feign ignorance. At the same time, reflecting on my conversations, I realized that some women talked about their experiences of sex following on conversations about other topics (such as beating) and not always in response to questions I asked about sex.

Ritu (RB, 25, Jat) opined, "*Shādī kā matlab yahī hai*" (the meaning of marriage is this, i.e., a sexual relationship). She elaborated:

> Sometimes the husband desires sex and sometimes the wife. It is not as though women have no desire. Women probably lose interest once their children grow up but women like me, of my age, have no problem. . . . Having children is a separate matter

and sexual relations another. Sometimes the husband wants to
have sex and the wife does not. The wife then has to explain to
herself. I have never given my husband a reason to complain.
I have never refused sex and I think that a woman should not.

Like her, Muneera (RB, 32, Lohar) believed that there would be problems
in a marriage if there was no sexual relationship: "The sexual relationship
helps both the man and woman to put all their tensions and tiredness
aside. I feel that I want to have a sexual relationship with my husband,
not that I have to have it" (see also Grover 2011, pp. 55–56). For Ritu,
the assertion of desire was intertwined with a sense of (wifely) duty, while
Muneera's account was one of both desire and pleasure. Ritu distinguished
between sex for procreation and the desire for sex, as did Kanchan (CRB,
21, Chamar), who was the only informant who described sex as "*pyār karnā*"
(making love). Urmila (RB, 32, Jat) believed that sex could fortify the
marital relationship. Her husband had been in a relationship with another
woman for a large part of their married life. She said, "I wanted to have
sambandh [sexual relations] with him so that he would come back to me."[2]

Veena Das describes such bonds created by sexual relations, "the base
relation of sexuality" between husband and wife, as threatening a man's
ties to his natal kin (1976, p. 10). Attempts are thus made, especially by
a woman's female affines, to control the development of intimacy between
husband and wife. Studies on rural north India point out that a woman's
female affinal kin at times controlled sexual access to the wife (Jeffery et al.
1989, p. 29; Minturn 1993, pp. 82, 209; Narayan 2016, p. 55). In Punjab
and Tamil Nadu alike, a husband and wife were expected to conceal familiarity and observe avoidance in the presence of others (Hershman 1977;
Trawick 1990; see also Madan 2011, pp. 119–120). Shazia (RB, early 70s,
Lohar) told me that such avoidance in public included veiling from the
husband, while Kripa (RB, 75, Jat) talked about avoiding mentioning the
husband's name (see Minturn 1993, p. 45). This, however, had ceased to
be the practice among women like Sakeena (RB, 43, Teli), who had been
married for almost three decades when I first met her. On one occasion,
she happily posed for me with her arm around her husband's shoulder.
When my landlady saw the photograph, she called Sakeena "shameless" for
her open display of affection. As for sex, Sakeena had discussed with me
how sexual relations had to be carried out discretely: "Even our children
who sleep in the same room don't know if their father and mother were

on the same *khāt* [bed]. We don't do *besharmī* [to display shamelessness/
immodesty] in front of our children."

While some women saw sexual relations as central to the conjugal
relationship, most said that they neither desired it nor did sex bring them
pleasure. I often heard women refer to sex as *ādmī kā kām* (man's work),
suggesting that sex was thought of as a task of which they were passive
recipients and not something that was experienced as mutually pleasurable.
Kripa (RB, 75, Jat) told me, "*nafrat thī*" (I felt revulsion). Similarly, Sakeena
(RB, 43, Teli) told me,

> *Ab zyādā nafrat hotī hai iss kām se* [now I feel more repulsed
> by this work than before]. . . . He used to beat me because I
> did not go to him. He was very short tempered. I used to be
> afraid of him. Women have relations with their husband because
> they have to. You cannot say no to your husband, no matter
> what. . . . if you refuse, they say, "What did you come to do
> here, then? What will I do with you? Run away from here
> and go back to your *pīhar.*" You cannot tell your natal family
> this. . . . You have to agree.

Sakeena points out both that a woman cannot talk to her parents about (the
difficulties of) sex because of *sharm* and that this would not be accepted
as a legitimate reason for leaving her husband and expecting their support.
Like Sakeena, some others also talked about being beaten for refusing sex.
"After being beaten, I have to have sex," Pushpa (CRB, late 30s, Jat) stated.
Some women talked about being made to engage in sexual acts they did not
want to partake in. One morning Koyal (RB, 16, Chamar) told me that her
husband had made her watch animal pornography on his mobile phone the
previous night. She was disturbed and asked me if that was "*māmulī bāt*"
(common) and something that husbands did. Similarly, Anita (mid-40s, Jat,
F) told me that her husband only had sex with her "*galat tarāh se*" (the
wrong way), referring to anal sex, and said she experienced physical pain and
taklīf. She added that this was the reason why she never conceived a second
child, as "that was the only way he did it." "*Mānnā partā hai*" (you have
to agree), "*karnā partā hai*" (you have to do it), "*majbūrī*" (compulsion),
and "*kise ko achchā nahī lagtā*" (no one likes it) were common responses to
questions about sex. Some informants referred to their husband as "*mālik*"
(owner/master) in conversations.

This discussion resonates with Carol Pateman's (1988) arguments about the power relations in heterosexual marriage. Her arguments have been widely debated and critiqued, but I find them relevant for the context described here. Pateman argued that marriage enables men to enact patriarchal privileges by giving them not only rights to women's labor but also sexual access to their bodies: the marriage contract alone "can turn use of sexual property . . . into the use of a person. It is not the wife, but the husband who has use of a person" (1988, p. 172). The consent of the wife to sexual relations is thus seen as irrelevant because marriage becomes the "proxy for consent" making marital rape a "categorical impossibility" (Basu 2015, pp. 170–171).

In Barampur, some women asserted that they had never been "forced" but spoke of consenting to sex in terms of their duty as wives. Khalida (RB, 45, Teli) told me, "My husband is a decent man; he is earning and feeding us. I have to stay with him. We had a *nikāh*." Others believed that sex was *thīk* (fine/correct) when it served the purpose of procreation or in the early years of marriage. Some like Mansi (CRB, 33, Chamar) commented, "*Ab toh kyā sambandh*" (Now what relations?). As children had grown older, several others complained that their husbands' demands for sex had not ceased as they aged. The marriage of children did not mean that sexual relations would end, yet it was a matter of great shame for a woman to become pregnant once her children were married (see also Minturn 1993, p. 211).

Additionally, women felt uninterested in sex for several reasons such as the fear of pregnancy, violence, work, health problems, and the absence of emotional intimacy (see also Schensul et al. 2018). Koyal (RB, 16, Chamar) felt that sex aggravated her ill health: "This work is for people who are physically strong. I do not get enough to eat. It is not for people like me. Nothing happens to the man, but the woman suffers." Sakeena (RB, 43, Teli) felt exhausted after a day's work and felt no desire for sex: "I start my day at 5 a.m. . . . work never ends. At the end of the day, is this the only thing left to do?" Shanti (RB, 24, Kumhar) had had five children and she was afraid "*bachchā nā reh jāye*" (that the child might stay—i.e., that she might get pregnant), as her husband neither accepted responsibility for limiting the family size nor brought her contraception, an issue I discuss in the following pages.

For women in western contexts, studies noted that sex was more than simply a physical encounter but was tied to the emotional dimensions of the relationship (Gabb and Fink 2015, p. 63; Jamieson 1998, p. 168). For women in Barampur, like Sarla (RB, 47, Jat) too, her lack of desire was explained by her husband's absence in their marriage. Sarla had spent more than half her married life at her *pīhar* because her husband was in a relationship with his *chāchī*. In our conversations, she always referred to sex as *būrā kām* (bad work), but on one occasion she told me,

> I feel very bad that my husband doesn't stay with me but what could I say to you? Now at times he wants to stay here at night and asks me to have sex but I am no longer interested. I spent my youth alone. . . . I feel that without a sexual relationship there is no marriage unless marriage means taking care of the housework and cooking. If my husband *ne sāth diyā hotā* [had supported me] even, I would have been interested in having a sexual relationship with him. I feel that I had a married life only for one month. It was the only time when my husband showed some consideration toward me.

Unlike Sarla, Munesh (RB, 38, Kumhar) had come to experience sexual relations differently over the course of her married life as she developed intimacy with her husband based on respect, understanding, and support.

> Initially, *būrā lagtā thā* [it felt bad]. I felt I came to someone else's home and I did this [sex]. I felt shame. I no longer feel this way. I started staying here and with him [husband]. Earlier when he would come to me, I would think, why has he come? *Pehle marzī nahī thī, āb toh hai* [At first I did not want to, but now I do consent]. Now it has been 19 years. . . . My husband kept me well. *Sāth nibhāyā* [supported me]. He never raised a hand to me. If I'm not feeling well he doesn't expect me to have sex. I tell him that I'm not well or I don't feel like it. He never forced me.

To summarize: lack of choice, fear, anxiety and difficulty were used by women to describe their experience of sexual relations in the initial months of marriage. While some came to experience sexual relations as desirable or pleasurable over the course of their married lives, most used the language of duty, revulsion, lack of interest, compulsion, submission, or coercion when they spoke about sex with their husbands. Crucially, for all women, their experiences of sex were primarily shaped by factors such as emotional intimacy or the absence of it, the fear of repeated pregnancies, work, and violence.

Wife-beating and Verbal Abuse

I knew that men beat their wives because I'd seen my father beat my mother.

—Kajri (RB, 35, Jat)

In our *mohallā* [neighborhood], getting beaten is like a *paramparā* [tradition]. This isn't the case only in our household.

—Shanti (RB, 24, Kumhar)

A man can beat his wife but a woman cannot raise her hand to her husband. If she does, even her natal family won't support her.

—Kusum (RB, 47, Chamar)

In Barampur, violence within the domestic sphere was normalized and accepted. Other studies also note the widespread acceptance of violence against wives. In neighboring Bijnor, women remarked, "No one here escapes a beating," with "wife-beating regarded by men as a necessary and legitimate means of controlling their wives" (Jeffery & Jeffery 1996, p. 127). In rural Haryana, men justified inflicting violence on wives as a way "to keep the women in line" (Chowdhry 2012, p. 45), while Shireen Jejeebhoy found that wife-beating in Uttar Pradesh and Tamil Nadu was justified as a "woman's due and her husband's right" (1998, p. 855). In this section, I develop my discussion on marital violence through a focus on *pītnā* (beating) and *gālī denā* (verbal abuse).

Women offered a range of explanations for why they believed they were beaten by their husbands. For cross-regional and regional brides alike, their experiences of violence were shaped by similar disputes related to alcoholism, bad temper, suspicions of infidelity, expectations related to women's work, men's sense of entitlement to punish their wives for wrongdoing, and tensions around livelihood concerns and poverty. Sakeena (RB, 43, Teli) told me, "Whenever there's a problem . . . like tension . . . a woman always bears the brunt of the man's anger." As she elaborated, it became clear that violence became an outlet for the frustrations that poor men like her husband faced with regard to the struggles survival and fulfilling their "provider" roles. Women talked about being beaten and verbally abused if they did not meet their husbands' demands on time: for instance, not serving food on time, not heating water for bathing, or if dirty clothes were lying around, and, as discussed earlier, women were also beaten for refusing sex. Answering back to the husband or speaking up to the *sās* or *nanad* was considered an affront to their authority and beating became a means to suppress insubordination (see also Srivastava 2002, pp. 258–262). Some explained beating in terms of the intergenerational transmission of violence (cf. Kalmuss 1984)—their husbands had grown up watching their fathers beat their mothers.

Ten (CRBs and RBs) of my 38 key informants said that they had never been beaten by their husbands. Three others (two RBs and a CRB) said that they had never been beaten, but their husbands had slapped them a few times. This they considered irrelevant when I asked questions about wife-beating. Abha (RB, 25, Chamar), for instance, commented, "My husband never beat me . . . you know, like other women here get beaten . . . *dande se* [with a stick]. He only used a couple of slaps here and there whenever he was angry." Some others, in contrast, described their experiences of being beaten *būrī tarah se* (excessively/brutally). Sheela (CRB, early-40s, Chamar) told me,

> There is not a bone in my body that has not been hurt. He has done very bad things to me. He broke my arm five times. [I asked her, you mean the bone?] . . . He did all of this [she showed me injury marks]. Last month, one night he was drinking and he hit me on the head with a wooden stick. I collapsed and had to get eight stiches.

Anita (RB, mid-40s, Jat) told me, "Once he threw a wooden ladder at me. Another time he beat me with an iron rod and broke the bone in my arm and on the same day he made me bathe the buffalo with the broken arm." Varsha (CRB, 28, Jat) talked about being beaten by her husband when she was pregnant with her second child. "He kept kicking me hard on my stomach." Sarla (RB, 47, Jat) described a similar experience of being kicked while pregnant. Hemlata (CRB, late-50s, Kumhar), a widow, said,

> My husband would beat me with whatever he could find. My body would turn blue with the bruises. I passed my days with a lot of difficulty. When you become old you suffer because you have been beaten in the past. My husband stopped beating me when he fell ill and could not do anything on his own. In

all those years, he did not do anything for me but at least the beating stopped.

Similarly, Kajri (RB, 35, Jat), also a widow, talked about being beaten every day while her husband was alive. "Even now my arms and legs hurt when I wake up in the morning because I was beaten so much by him. I have not been happy since I got married." I recalled a conversation I had with Sarla (RB, 47, Jat) about what she told her *devrānī* when her husband died. "I told her, why are you crying? Now at least the beating will stop." Nicola Harwin and Jackie Barron point out that violence within the domestic domain is not a "one-off event or incident but part of an ongoing pattern of controlling behaviour" (2000, p. 206). Several talked about being beaten from the first year of marriage. For some, the beating did stop as their children, particularly sons, grew older. There were women, like Sheela (CRB, early 40s, Chamar), however, who had been married for over 25 years, for whom the beating continued with alcohol and suspicions of infidelity being the main reasons for marital conflict:

He drinks and *būrī būrī gālī detā hai* [bad-bad swearing] and beats me even now but I'm no longer afraid. I'm not afraid because I think, for how long can he beat me? Now I speak up to him. He accuses me of staying with other men, even more now than before. If I wear a bangle or *bindī* [worn on the forehead by Hindu women], he asks me why I'm wearing it. He asks me why I change my clothes every day.

Shalini Grover noted in her study in Delhi that suspicion was mainly a "male preoccupation." It can be real but was often imagined, "baseless and a mode of exercising male control" (2011, p. 51), as Devanti's (CRB, early 40s, Chamar) case illustrates. When I first met Devanti in September 2012, she was a widow with two married daughters and she lived in a household with her three minor sons. She talked to me about her difficult marriage to her deceased husband, a "much older" man who was an alcoholic and violent toward her. A month later she confided in me about her relationship with another (unattached/separated) Chamar (Suresh) from the village whom she met in 2009 while working at the brick kiln. Subsequently, she had managed to maintain contact through her mobile phone. She talked about wanting to marry him but feared that this would be contentious. Her husband's relatives were aware of her relationship with Suresh and had threatened her with consequences if she tried to elope. She talked about the life she had imagined with Suresh and how much *pyār* (love) there was between them. A few weeks later, I heard that Devanti had eloped and had a "court marriage" with Suresh. They stayed away from Barampur for a few months and then returned. I met her ten months into my fieldwork in her new home that she then shared with Suresh. She told me,

> He is a different man now. He doesn't let me go anywhere or talk to anyone, not even with other women. He keeps an eye on me. He's always fighting with me saying, "Why were you standing there? Why were you looking at him?" He's suspicious. He thinks I'll run away with another man. He beats me excessively.

By eloping with Suresh, Devanti had left her sons behind and severed ties with her married daughters and husband's kin. She told me that her natal kin supported her marriage to Suresh but they were far away and contact was infrequent. The freedom that Devanti had attained as a widow with married daughters and being the head of her household she lost with her marriage to Suresh and she found herself extremely isolated and controlled. This resonates with Grover's findings on what she describes as consensual secondary unions in a low-income neighborhood in Delhi: many remarriages in low-income settings are prompted by unsatisfactory primary marriages, but if the freedom to remarry may appear liberating and synonymous with choice (in entering and terminating relationships), it nevertheless entails "grave risks for women" (2014, pp. 328–329). In other words, secondary marriages reproduce the violence and gender inequality of the primary marriage (p. 209), and intimate partner violence is not restricted to arranged marriages.

In her work on domestic abuse among Pakistani women in Scotland, Nughmana Mirza (2015) argues for recognizing the "specificity of South Asian women's experiences of family abuse" (2015, p. 394). In critiquing mainstream (Western) conceptualizations of domestic abuse, she takes issue with the focus on the nuclear family and confinement of women's experiences of abuse to intimate/partner relationships. Even in the UK, South Asian women tend to live their married lives in or close to patrilineal extended households, and she notes the role of female affinal kin (the mother-in-law in particular) in instigating (and even perpetrating) violence (pp. 397–398). Mirza's observations are valuable for the context described here because beating by a husband often followed provocation by affinal women (*sās*, *jethānī*, or *nanad*) for several of my informants. To understand marital violence, it is thus essential to shift our focus away from the dyad of husband–wife to other affinal kin who may both perpetrate and instigate violence.

Koyal (RB, 16, Chamar) insisted that her husband was *bahut achā* (very nice) even though she was beaten by him: "He does not beat me when I do something wrong, no matter how big the mistake, but only when his mother [Sheela, CRB, early 40s, Chamar] makes him. His mother taunts him and says, 'Are you not a man? Do you not know how to beat your wife?' " Koyal added that on one occasion her *sūsar* chased her with a *dāntī* (sickle) and even her *nanad* raised her hand to her. I heard from her neighbor that one morning Koyal was being beaten by her *sās* and *sūsar* as neighbors gathered around. Despite the public nature of the violence, neighbors did not intervene in this case. Furthermore, for her, being verbally abused by those in her *sasurāl* was an everyday experience: "My *sās* tells my husband, 'why are you running after this *randī* [whore]? They accuse me of having a *yār* [lover]. I have been having trouble conceiving a child so my nanad calls me a *hijrā* [eunuch]." Koyal believed that if she was living *alag* [literally separate, meaning in a nuclear household] her husband would not beat her and there would be no problem between them. There were women, however, who had managed to set up nuclear households following conflicts yet this did not necessarily help them evade violence for, as Leela Dube has noted, even nuclear households embedded in patrilineal kinship are considered part of the larger extended family (1997, p. 93). While it was usually female affines who instigated and perpetrated violence, in some instances, male affinal kin were also involved, as in Koyal's case.

Kān bharnā (constant ear-filling, meaning complaining about the daughter-in-law) was often the form taken by the provocation. One after-noon, when I went to see Kanchan (CRB, 21, Chamar) she was sleeping. Her *jethānī* remarked that she "sleeps all the time." She started yelling at Kanchan telling her to wake up and threatened to send for Ratan (Kanchan's husband). She sent her daughter to get Ratan. Within minutes Ratan was in the room asking what the matter was. Her *jethānī* said that Kanchan had refused to wake up. I saw Ratan grab the wooden stick in the room and I intervened. These were tactics used by affinal women not only to exert their power but also ways to prevent the development of intimacy between husband and wife. For the Pandits of Kashmir, T.N. Madan observed that the more influence that a woman was seen to exert over her husband, the greater the resentment her in-laws harbored toward her (2011, p. 115).

Women were also verbally abused by their husband's kin and mocked for not bringing enough dowry or gifts from their natal kin. Sarla (RB, 47, Jat) shared her experience of being made to work incessantly. She added,

My husband's *chāchī* would say, "She is a *bāndhī* [slave/servant].
If we send her to her *pīhar*, then who will do the work?" The
day my son was born there was no one with me. When I started
having pains, I told her to call the *dāī*. She said to me, "When
a *kuttiyā* [bitch] gives birth, who comes to help her, she gives
birth on her own."

Being subjected to verbal abuse was an experience that cross-regional brides
shared with regional brides; however, the former were abused in ways that
served to remind them of where they came from and/or that a payment
had been made for them. Pushpa (CRB, late 30s, Jat) had been called
bānjh (barren) for being childless (just as had some regional brides) but her
husband's relatives would insult her by saying, "*Bihāran kā bachā bhī nahī
hūā*" (the woman from Bihar could not even have a child). Varsha (CRB,
28, Jat) shared how her *devar* often repeated to her that anyone could "buy
a bride in exchange for a bottle of alcohol" in Bengal (her native state).
She added, "He gets drunk and *būrī būrī gālī detā hai*" (then engages in
bad-bad swearing).

For cross-border marriages, Lucy Williams writes, "It is clear that
many migrant women are more vulnerable to domestic violence and abuse
than their citizen peers and that violence when it happens is likely to be
more severe" (2010, p. 94). Some studies on cross-regional brides also focus
specifically on the violence that such brides suffer in their marital homes
(Ahlawat 2016). In Barampur, some cross-regional brides pointed out that
while some men beat their wives in their native states too, it was "not like
here" (UP). As discussed above, women's experiences of marital violence were
diverse. Not all regional brides suffered violence, just as not all cross-regional
brides did. Some cross-regional brides described experiences of being repeatedly and "badly" beaten, as did regional brides. The crucial difference was
that cross-regional brides were left more vulnerable in situations of abuse
because of the absence of natal kin support (chapter 7).

Women's voices diverged when they spoke about whether they thought
that it was acceptable for men to beat their wives. Nasira (RB, 26, Lohar)
said, "Even if a man beats his wife their marriage is *thīk thak* [OK/alright]
because it happens in anger. Yet they stay together." Sakeena (RB, 43, Teli)
remarked: "So what if a man beats his wife? It is *jāyez* [legitimate]. I think
merā ādmī hai, mār le [he is my husband, let him beat me]. He beats me
but he also loves me a lot. . . . A woman should not leave if her husband
beats her. Fights take place in every household." On another occasion she
told me, "If my husband beats me and I don't speak to him then he will

get angrier." These women had "accommodated" to the violence. There were others, like Koyal (RB, 16, Chamar), who had internalized the idea that it was acceptable to be beaten for *galtī* (wrongdoing), yet she was critical:

> I can't understand . . . if someone does something wrong she's beaten but when I do nothing wrong, why should I get beaten? They [in-laws] say I talk back to them. You tell me if someone does an injustice to you, would you not speak up? Will you remain silent?

Some like Kamlesh (RB, late 20s, Kumhar) were critical of the power relationship that legitimized such violence. "A woman is beaten not because it is her fault, but men beat their wives because they want to and can." Similarly, Abha (RB, 25, Chamar) told me, "It makes me angry that a woman cannot do anything against a man's will, all she can do is fight. But I never fought with my husband, as I was afraid of being beaten." She expressed her defiance through silence. "The first time he hit me, I felt very bad. Even my father had never raised a hand to me. I would not talk to him for the next five days whenever this happened." Sarla (RB, 47, Jat), however, did not suffer silently whenever her husband beat her; she refused to do the housework. "He would then apologize and would say he would not beat me again. He did and then I would do the same. I believe that irrespective of how much a man does for his wife, if he beats her, he is *nālāyak* [good-for-nothing]."

Some cross-regional brides talked about how they felt like going away when they were first beaten. Some others said that their husbands would beat them and tell them to "go away." They felt that they were beaten so much because their husbands were aware that they had nowhere to go. Yet I also heard something similar from regional bride informants like Aarti (RB, 27, Chamar), who told me, "I felt angry when he beat me but what difference does it make whether he beats you or keeps you *pareshān* [troubled]. You have to stay here, where can you go?" Having nowhere else to go, however, had different meanings for regional and cross-regional brides (chapter 7).

Reproductive "Choice"

> When I had my first child [son], I was not even 16. I was a child myself. My husband had been told that because I was very young, I

would have trouble giving birth and that I should be taken to the
hospital for the delivery but he did not pay any attention. My son
died after birth. . . . After that I had three daughters and then I
gave birth to a son but lost him a month later. Then I gave birth to
another son who survived but I lost another son after that and then
gave birth to two more daughters. . . . After my fourth child, I did
not want to have more children and I wanted to get sterilized but my
husband did not agree. He said he wanted another son. . . . Look at
what has happened to my body. If you have a child every year, your
body becomes useless . . . your husband never thinks about you.

—Hemlata (CRB, late 50s, Kumhar)

Getting pregnant at a young age, delivering at home,[3] lacking access to
healthcare, losing children, multiple pregnancies and deliveries taking a toll
on the body, and having no say in decisions around contraception, the issues
that Hemlata's account points to, are issues that emerged in conversations
with several women and will be explored in this section. Maya (CRB, mid-
40s, Chamar) told me, "I did not want to have eight children but children
were just born. . . . When the man does not agree . . . I told my husband
several times that I did not want so many children, but men do not think."
Women, like Maya, explained that they had no control over childbearing
decisions because they had no control over sexual relations and, as Sakeena
(RB, 43, Teli) asserted, "*Aurat kī nahī chaltī iss māmle mey, mardon kī chaltī
hai*" (A woman's wishes in this connection do not prevail, only the man's).
Khalida (RB, 45, Teli) had seven children. She talked about how the *dāī*
had explained that she would not get pregnant if she did not have sexual
relations with her husband during some days of the month but her husband
never agreed to this: "I felt angry but what can you do? A woman is a
woman and a man a man."

When talking about their reasons for wanting fewer children, women
talked about the embodied suffering that came with giving birth, "*bahut
dūkh hotā hai*" (*dūkh* literally translates as sadness but here they used *dūkh*
to express the physical pain experienced during childbirth). Some talked
about being poor and not getting enough to eat after childbirth, and that
adversely affected their health and bodies, particularly as they grew older.
Kajri (RB, 35, Jat) suffered from polio and spoke about the difficulties she
experienced in giving birth to eight children, but she could not say anything
to her husband because she was afraid of him.

Some women talked about getting pregnant at a young age and within the first year of marriage and thinking "*jaldī ho gayā*" (it was early). Many said that they did not have any knowledge about contraception until a much later stage in their marriages. They learned about them when their mobility increased and they started sitting with other women. By then, they had had several children. Some could not use contraceptives because their husbands did not want them to. Aarti (RB, 27, Chamar) had two children—both sons. She told me that she did not want more children, but would not undergo sterilization because her husband was of the opinion that it caused problems. "He does not use anything and I do not take the *golī* (birth control pill) because he says it causes side effects." Aarti told me that both she and her husband had wanted only one child and that the second pregnancy was unplanned. She did not share what she and her husband were doing to prevent future pregnancies. Shanti (RB, 24, Kumhar) wanted to be sterilized, but she alluded to practical considerations: that after the operation a woman needs rest, but she could not because there were five young children (including an infant) to be cared for. For Chhaya (CRB, 55, Kumhar), it was a problem of access. She had asked her husband for the *golī* but he never brought it for her. Radha (CRB, early 40s, Chamar) said that she had no knowledge of contraception in the early years of marriage but learned about the *golī* from the village *dāī*. After she had four children, she took the *golī* and did not get pregnant for two years, but then she did again even though she was taking the *golī*.

Elderly informants, across castes, talked about younger married women being more aware of contraception. "They have fewer children now" was often repeated to me. Women of the three Hindu castes, in their 20s and early 30s, talked about wanting fewer children because of *mehangaī* (increasing expenses) and the desire to educate their children. They also talked about being more aware of contraception because of the radio and having access to oral contraception through the ASHA. "If you have too many children, you can't educate them," was repeated by some Muslim women as well.

Limiting the family size to two to three children, due to poverty, was why Varsha (CRB, 28, Jat) had an abortion. She had two children—a son and daughter. She told me that she would not have more children. She talked about not being able to take the contraceptive pill because of the side effects, but her husband was unwilling to use a condom. She pointed out that her husband had absolved himself of his responsibility, and limiting the family size through either contraception or termination was solely her responsibility. She added that if she became pregnant she could not abort without her husband's consent. She wanted to get sterilized but she said she could not because there was no one to do the housework while she recovered.

Like Varsha, Ritu (RB, 25, Jat) had an abortion. She had one child—a daughter. She talked about how the second time she was pregnant she had an ultrasound and learned the sex of the fetus and her husband forced her to have an abortion because it was a girl. She told me, "*Bahut būrā lagā thā* [I felt very bad], I did not want to do it, but he made me." For Sarla (RB, 47, Jat), her circumstances (marital conflict) had forced her to abort. She had one son. She had an abortion the second time she was pregnant. She told me, "I decided not to keep it because I knew that I would have to return to my *pīhar*. Who would raise my two children in the *pīhar*? I felt very bad at the time. I would have liked to have a second child . . . maybe a daughter. If my husband was with me, I would have kept the child."

Some Muslim informants, like Faiza (CRB, late 40s, Lohar), believed that their religion did not permit them to use contraception. Faiza had eight children. She told me that if she had not reached menopause, she would still be having children. Khalida (RB, 45, Teli), however, distinguished between *jāyez* (legitimate) and *nājāyez* (illegitimate). Contraception, she said, falls in the former and abortion in the latter. She added that even among Muslims, young couples were having fewer children and using contraception to limit family size due to poverty. Sakeena (RB, 43, Teli) had six children—five daughters and one son. She told me, "According to our religion if you abort a child, *toh namāz qabūl nahī hotā* [your prayers are not accepted]. This is written in the Quran." Yet she admitted to having an ultrasound for the purpose of sex determination and having an abortion in 2001, three years before the birth of her youngest child, because it was a girl child. She said that when she was pregnant with her youngest child (also a daughter) she thought of aborting again, but could not because the doctors told her that it would be life threatening for her (although she had previously blamed her *sās*). She added that not getting sterilized was her own decision and that if she wanted to, her husband would not have a problem with it. Patricia Jeffery et al. (2008) noted that in the early 2000s, Muslim women in neighboring Bijnor rarely adopted "modern" contraceptive methods, and sterilization in particular was uncommon. Almost two decades later, Muslim women's use of "modern" contraceptive methods had increased substantially, but sterilization remained uncommon and contraceptive failure was quite common (Patricia Jeffery, personal communication). It is important to note that Muslim villagers' contraceptive practices are certainly colored by what they believe to be "Islamic doctrine," but "Islamic doctrine" on contraception is not monolithic (Jeffery et al. 2008, p. 538).

Women talked about feeling pressured to conceive soon after the wedding. They explained that if a woman did not have a child within the first two years of marriage, those around her (other women and in-laws) would start saying that she would never have children, "*kamī hai*" (there is a lack—suggesting that she was reproductively challenged), and that her husband should leave her and remarry. Childlessness was stigmatized and a childless woman was called *bānjh* (barren). It was always assumed that it was the woman and not the man who was infertile. As Susan Seymour noted in her study in Bhubaneshwar, Orissa, childlessness was a "tragedy" for a woman. To bear a child, especially a male child, was not only personally rewarding but also enabled a woman to secure her position in her husband's home by producing the next generation of patrilineal heirs (1999, p. 70; see also Jeffery et al. 1989, pp. 87–89; Narayan 2016, pp. 63–64, 118; Raheja & Gold 1994, pp. 58–59).

For some, the use of contraception was not permitted by the *sās* until a woman had produced one or two sons (see also Robitaille and Chatterjee 2017). In fact, several women told me that they continued to have children they did not want (especially daughters) "*larke ke leye*" (for a son). Sakeena (RB, 43, Teli) explained,

> I think that a woman should have only three children: two sons and a daughter. But now I have so many [six]. . . . My husband never felt happy at the birth of daughters and my *sās* would taunt me about having so many daughters. . . . My son was born after two daughters. Everyone in the family had started saying that only girls were being born. . . . My husband wanted two sons [paused] . . . even I wanted the same thing. I had two daughters after my son and then I took an oral contraceptive for nine years and then I got pregnant again and I had an abortion . . . then again I was pregnant and I wanted to have an abortion but my *sās* said not to because it might be a son but then another daughter was born.

Almost half of my informants had multiple pregnancies and had lost a child or children because of the pressure to produce one or two sons. Some failed to achieve full-term birth, while others were struggling to conceive and were under constant pressure to produce a son. Kanchan (CRB, 21, Chamar) was married in June 2012 (three months before I started fieldwork). During my initial visits, Kanchan told me that she was having trouble conceiving a child because of *sūjan* (inflammation) in her uterus and her husband told her that he would keep her only if she did. She underwent treatment and in September 2013, she gave birth to a boy. Koyal (RB, 16, Chamar) was also married in June 2012. Her story followed a different trajectory. In early October 2012, she talked about having had a miscarriage. In mid-December 2012, she told me about getting pregnant a second time and then having an incomplete miscarriage requiring an abortion. A few months later she told me,

> I've been married for almost a year now. Women in the neigh-
> borhood tell me that those who got married at the same time
> as me have already had a child. I don't know what the problem
> is. The child never stays. When they [in-laws] are not willing to
> spend money on my treatment, then how will I have children?
> I went to the doctor and she told me that my uterus is weak.
> I don't get enough to eat.

Like Komal, Pushpa (CRB, late 30s, Jat) was taunted for being childless, but she had not given up hope:

> For the last 18 years, I have been hoping to conceive a child.
> I got treated in the first few years of marriage yet I couldn't
> conceive. My husband says that there's no *kami* [shortcoming]
> in him. Those in the *kunbā* [extended family] and neighborhood
> call me *bānjh* [barren]. I feel very bad. I had to discontinue my
> treatment because we are very poor. My husband also tells me
> sometimes, "you cannot have children, run away from here."

For women like Pushpa, childlessness added to her vulnerabilities as a cross-regional bride because the need to carry forward the family had necessitated a cross-regional marriage for her husband (an only son) in the first place. In case of desertion, she could not call on her natal kin to intervene or provide refuge (chapter 7). Some like Nasira (RB, 26, Lohar) were struggling to have another child after they had their first child. Nasira had been married for nine years. She had an eight-year-old daughter. She got pregnant for the second time three years after the birth of her daughter. She lost her second child and four children after that. She told me that she had been consulting a *hakīm* (practitioner of *unānī* medicine associated with Muslims who also often prescribe allopathic medicine) and failed to understand why the infants did not survive. When I first met her in April 2013 she had given birth to a stillborn baby eight days before. She had been advised by doctors not to conceive for the next six months. She told me that neither her husband nor she was using contraception. She added that losing children had been very difficult for her to cope with, yet she had to conceive again because it was necessary for her to have a son because that is what both she and her husband wanted.

Ritu (RB, 25, Jat), like Nasira, had one daughter. As discussed earlier, she had had one abortion. During my fieldwork, she was pregnant for the third time and she said that she was carrying a male child. In the fifth month of her pregnancy, she had a miscarriage. I saw her a week later and she talked to me about how pregnancy was very hard for her and that she felt extremely ill during it. Despite the difficulties she had faced, however, it was essential for her to have a son. Muneera (RB, 32, Lohar) shared her experience:

> Four months after my wedding my *sās* started asking me if I was pregnant. I started getting tensed. After one year, I got tests done and the doctor told me that I will never be able to have a child. Then I got treated from a *hakīm*. Women would come from the neighborhood and comment on how I was unable to conceive. I gave birth to my daughter four years after. My *sās* and *nanad* started taunting me saying that my daughter was born after a *barā* [big] operation [C-Section] and it was a girl. . . . When my daughter turned one, I started being pressured to get treated to conceive again. . . . I have been getting treated for two years now but there is nothing yet. . . . I am worried.

Urmila's (RB, 32, Jat) older two children were daughters. She recalled that her in-laws believed that she had not given birth to a son because of her husband's shortcoming (he was a drug addict) and she was pressured at the time to have sexual relations with her (married) *jeth* to produce a male heir. She added that fortunately she managed to give birth to a son. Urmila's case was different from the women discussed above because it was accepted that the problem lay with her husband; nevertheless, she was expected to produce a male heir,[4] as the necessity of a son was strongly felt across castes. Women felt insecure about not being able to produce a son and the possibility of their husbands leaving them and remarrying. I heard of several instances when this had in fact happened.

In sum, women did not desire several children for reasons that included poverty, the damaging effects of repeated pregnancies on their bodies, rising expenses and the desire to educate their children, and marital problems. However, childbearing was influenced by women's own lack of control over sexual relations, knowledge of and access to contraception and (infertility) treatment, and the husband's capacity to determine on matters of contraception, termination of pregnancy, and sterilization. The pressure to produce a child in the early years of marriage and the necessity to produce a male child were vital in shaping reproductive decisions.

In the discussion so far, I have shown how the conjugal relationship is highly unequal. In what follows, I attempt to shift the focus away from the negativities of marriage onto the possibilities for support and care—as "practices of intimacy"—to develop and exist despite inequalities.

Sāth Denā: The Meanings of Marriage and Support

I asked women "What is a marriage?" to which some responded, "getting a husband," "leaving your parents' home," or "having children," while some others retorted, "the matter of marriage is *bekār*" (useless) or "*shādī barbādī hai*" (marriage is ruination). However, most responses reflected ideas and expectations around marriage as a relationship. Abha (RB, 25, Chamar) described marriage as a "*milan*" (union of souls). For Jagmati (RB, early 60s, Chamar), it meant having a "*jīvan sāthī*" (life-long companionship) and "*rishtā nibhānā*" (maintaining a relationship/commitment). Ideas of support were central to women's understandings of the meaning of marriage. "A marriage is *sāth denā*" (to support/a supportive relationship), several told me. There seemed to be a consensus among women that it was a husband who does and/or should support his wife. Different women articulated in different ways what support entailed, and as they spoke it became clear that they did feel supported in some ways and on some matters, even though their relationships were far from egalitarian.

Informants like Jagbiri (RB, 71, Kumhar) assessed support from a husband in terms of the fulfillment of the provider role for the family. She commented,

> My husband was *kālā*. He would not even walk with me. Others often made comments about my light skin in contrast to his. My husband earned and fed the family. He never raised a hand on me. For me, he was *bariyā* [very good]. What difference does skin color make? He brought me whatever I asked for.

In contrast, Jaya (CRB, 45, Jat) felt unsupported because her husband was a drug addict and had "never worked and fed the family." Studies similarly note how the failure of a husband to meet expectations related to providing for material needs can be a major source of marital conflict and even breakdown (Grover 2011; Qureshi 2016; Vatuk 2015). The importance of material support emerged as particularly crucial in conversations with widowed informants, who felt that the most difficult years were those following the death of husbands. Kajri (RB, 35, Jat), for instance, talked about how her husband was an alcoholic and spent all his earnings on his drinking. She had eight children. Her neighbors made jokes, saying that while her husband was alive, the only thing he did was produce children. She told me, "Happiness was not in my destiny, only beating." Yet she shared how she felt that her life would nevertheless have been easier if her husband were alive: "He would have fulfilled his responsibilities." Being Jat, Kajri had never worked for a wage, yet poverty forced her to go out to feed her children after her husband's death. More than once she told me, "You must get married." I asked her why, given her own experience, and she said, "It is very difficult to go through life alone. . . . *Dikh toh rahe the*" (at least I could see him). It became clear that Kajri cherished not the relationship itself but the idea and security of having a companion. Jagbiri (RB, 71, Kumar), also a widow, missed the companionship: "I am alone now because of my bad fate . . . you want someone of your own to sit beside you."

Hemlata (CRB, late 50s, Kumhar) was a widow too, but she felt differently:

> I think that I am better off now my husband has died because while he was alive there was only fighting and beating. I could never talk to him when I felt sad. Other women's husbands console them and reassure them, but mine didn't do anything.

Talking about feelings, being comforted, and sharing *sükh aur dükh* (joys and sorrows) figured in several women's accounts of support.[5] Many compared their husbands to other women's husbands ("not all men are like this" suggesting that they were aware of men who supported their wives), as though they were providing a rationale for regarding their expectations as reasonable. In western contexts too, the "asymmetry in intimate emotional behaviour" has been noted with women expressing discontent around their husband's emotional absence and their failure to provide emotional reassurance and comfort (Duncombe & Marsden 1993; Jamieson 1998). Understanding each other or each other's troubles was considered by some to be an important dimension of support. Women emphasized that being supported at particular junctures and during trying times (e.g., illness or miscarriage or child deaths) was highly valued. Mansi (CRB, 33, Chamar) felt supported because her husband had shown consideration toward her:

> I have been ill for the last few months. My husband is hand-
> icapped. I used to go out to work as we couldn't manage on
> his earnings alone. He can't do much work but he never says
> to me, "Why don't you do any work?" He understands that I
> can't because of my illness.

Not just sharing and knowing but "trust, faith that confidences will not be betrayed and privileged knowledge will not be used against the self" was a fundamental dimension in building intimacy (Jamieson 1998, p. 9). Jameela (CRB, 21, Teli), for instance, talked about confiding in her husband about a previous marriage in her native state and added, "He's the only one who knows this and he didn't let this be known to anyone. If my *sās* found out, she would tell him to leave me." For Sakeena (RB, 43, Teli), *sāth denā* meant sharing but also *salāha karnā* (consulting each other/joint decision-making). In a context where decision-making and control of household finances lay in the hands of men, Radha (CRB, early 40s, Chamar) felt trusted and respected by her husband because he handed his income to her and never questioned her on how she spent the money.

Shanti (RB, 24, Kumhar) felt supported because her husband had provided practical care when most needed. She said, "When I fall ill, he tells me to lie down and he does the work. He brings me medicine and takes care of the children." In contrast, Kalawati (CRB, 40, Kumhar) talked about the lack of consideration that her husband had shown her throughout their married life:

> I can be extremely unhappy but it makes no difference to him.
> Not all men are like this. If I tell my husband to bring vege-
> tables from the market, he will tell me he can't. If I ever fall
> ill, he never says, "Come, I'll take you to the doctor," or "Lie
> down, I will make you a cup of tea." My husband never said
> to me, "Let me bring you a set of clothes that you can wear."

If he never supports me, *toh kyā mard?* [Then what husband is
he?] . . . I worry that in future if my hands and feet become
useless, I can't say about my children for certain, but I know
that my husband wouldn't even give me food to eat.

In saying, "*kyā mard?*" Kalawati conveyed that her husband had failed, as
he did not meet the expectation of providing support. She spoke of his
failure in delivering practical care and the lack of thoughtful gestures (such
as buying a set of clothes or making a cup of tea).

For most women, it was extremely significant whether or not their
husbands spoke up for them and trusted their word over what others told
them, for instance, when there were fights with their husband's kin. In
Jameela's words (CRB, 21, Teli), "*Dūkh dard mein, larāī mein, merī taraf
bole, yeh hi hai sāth denā*" (In sadness and pain, in conflict/fights, he stands
up for me, that very thing is support). Sarla (RB, 47, Jat) explained,

When a woman comes as a new bride then her *sās, nanad,* and
devar find fault and criticize her, her husband should tell them
not to criticize her. That's *sāth denā.* If a woman wants to go to
her natal home and her mother-in-law doesn't give her permission, her husband should tell his mother that he will send her.
That's *sāth denā.* If there's too much fighting in the household,
then he should support his wife and set up a separate household.
That is *sāth denā.*

Muneera (RB, 32, Lohar) felt that her husband had always been supportive—he had never beaten her and he stood by her in difficult times. She
praised him, saying "Here usually the man has the final say in all matters
but if I feel that I am right, I don't agree with my husband. Unless there
is a compromise between two people the marriage can't work. My husband
doesn't think that only the woman should make the adjustment. He agrees
with me as well." Her only complaint was that when she and her *nanads*
and *sās* had an argument, her husband chose not to get involved.

I feel angry that he doesn't speak in support of me irrespective
of what they say to me. . . . Last month my husband wanted
to buy gold earrings for me. My *sās* and *nanads* heard of it and
started filling his ears. He changed his mind. I feel like sitting
with my husband and sharing a meal. If we lived in a separate

household, I could, but now it's not possible. Sometimes my
husband buys things for me, but he does not let it be known
to his sisters.

Muneera's case demonstrates both the cultural expectation that a man must
prioritize his ties to his own natal kin over his wife and conceal affection for
her and that his affinal female kin may attempt to prevent the development
of intimacy between the couple. Thus, for women like Muneera, a husband
siding with them in conflicts was significant because it was considered a
public declaration of a man's loyalty to his wife vis-à-vis his own affines.

Fidelity was also central in discussions of a "good marriage" and this
had been a concern for many of my informants. Sarla's husband had been
in a relationship with his *chāchī* throughout their marriage: "If a man goes
to another woman, it's only for his own *sūkh* [pleasure]. Such a man has
no respect for anything: neither his wife nor the marital relationship," she
remarked. Likewise, Urmila's (RB, 32, Jat) husband had been in a relationship with another woman for the first 15 of the 18 years of their marriage.
She told me, "It's difficult to find a woman who is happy from the first
year of marriage." She talked about her husband "returning to her" and her
relationship changing: "*pyār barne lagā*" (love started growing). She added,
"He tells me now that if he'd realized how *bariyā* [good] I am, he wouldn't
have troubled me so much. Now he doesn't even eat food without me."

In Barampur, love is not the basis on which marriages are made,
yet "love between husband and wife is expected to grow as the relationship develops" (Mody 2008, pp. 7–8). Also, love is neither verbalized nor
celebrated as in Western contexts. I was interested in the part love plays
in the marital relationships, yet I did not ask questions about *pyār* (love)
because I wanted to see whether this was something women brought up
themselves, and some did. For Nasira (RB, 26, Lohar), a "good marriage"
was one where two people lived together "*pyār mohabbat se*" (with love and
affection). Likewise, Kripa (RB, 75, Jat) believed it was one where "*dono
kā pyār banā rahe*" (love remains intact). Sakeena (RB, 43, Teli) was in a
violent marriage. She told me,

> My husband really loves me. . . . He beats me only when he's
> angry or I say something wrong. Usually, the beating is because
> of one issue—when I refuse sex. I think that even though my
> husband beats me, my marriage is *thīk thak* [OK]. What's the
> point of complaining about your husband? After all, you have

to stay with him. . . . I feel that he always supported me when
there was a fight with my in-laws. He never let them raise a
hand to me. Today I returned from my natal home after five
days. My husband came there to bring me back. He doesn't like
it here without me. He gives me expenses, he makes me laugh,
he sits and eats with me and our children and fetches water for
me to bathe when I fall ill. This is good, isn't it?

Likewise, Koyal (RB, 16, Chamar) said,

My husband says that I'm the first woman that he's been in
love with. He tells me that he becomes very sad when I go
away from him [to my *pīhar*]. He can't stay here without me.
My in-laws trouble me a lot, but I'm here because of him. He
never stops me from talking to anyone. He even gives me his
mobile phone to talk to my friends. He has never suspected
me. . . . He is *acchā* [nice] and loves me. He beats me only
because he believes his mother and sister easily when they fill
his ears. He only beats me because they make him.

When talking about love, women like Sakeena, Urmila, and Koyal also
referrred to the dimensions of support that emerged in other women's
accounts (fidelity, trust, fulfillment of provider roles, support in conflicts
with affines, etc.) but also to eating and laughing together and fetching
water when ill. In their work on long-term couple relationships in the UK,
Jacqui Gabb and Janet Fink (2015) see these everyday ordinary moments,
mundane routine tasks, and small thoughtful acts as part of "relationship
work" crucial to sustaining couple relationships. In the context described
here, such small everyday acts become particularly meaningful, as they
serve as evidence of love and care in the relationship for women who rarely
experience articulations of love or feelings or ongoing emotional support
and do not have the choice to leave a violent relationship. Lynn Jamieson
writes that "elements of practices of intimacy can be transposable, that is,
one practice of intimacy is sometimes able to stand in for others, making
it as-if other practices of intimacy were also in place" (2011, p. 3). In this
context, such acts did not "stand in for others" but served to somewhat
diminish the negative experiences of violence, as in Sakeena and Koyal's
cases. For them, these were sufficient for them to perceive their relationships

and husbands as "good" despite "deficits in the repertoire of practices of intimacy" (pp. 3–4).

Conclusion

In Barampur, marital relations were highly inegalitarian, yet women expressed a yearning for more equal and intimate relationships. Most women both recognized and were critical of the power relationships that placed them in positions of vulnerability and violence. At the same time, they were aware that their lives were lived "within largely unalterable structures" (Jeffery & Jeffery 1996: 16). I have attempted to unpack the meanings of marriage and support within this cultural context to argue that women are not entirely without support, or at least hope, and they may experience some forms of intimacy even within contexts of inequality and violence. Their yearnings may not be achieved in all ways, but there are glimpses of the importance of small everyday "practices of intimacy" when they talk about their marriages. These experiences should not be written off as some kind of false consciousness but understood as complex ways in which women endure hardship and cope with the realities of their lives.

In recognizing the work of *endurance*, my aim is not to underplay the oppressive contexts in which women live but rather to broaden under-standings of gendered agency beyond the dominant conceptualizations that uncritically limit agency to individual notions of choice, autonomy, and independence (see Burkitt 2016). In doing so, I follow scholars who critique Western-based and liberal feminist understandings of agency such as Saba Mahmood, who, in her work with a women's mosque movement in Cairo, emphasizes the need to think of agency as "a capacity for action that specific relations of subordination create and enable" (2001, p. 210). For her, endurance can contribute to the process of self-making. For Soran Reader, women endure, "because it is often not in their power to flee or fight. . . . Endurance is the only option. It is not action, it does not show positive capability, it is not chosen or independent. Nevertheless, it is a way to be a person in adversity. Far from being an easy or self-deluded option, endurance is *difficult and courageous*" (emphasis mine) (2007, p. 597).

Similar ideas have also emerged in the writing on South Asian women. Clarinda Still, in her work among Dalit women in South India, for instance, writes about "*bhada*"—ideas of female suffering as a particular "cultural resource" that married women draw on and perpetuate, as it enables them to tolerate violenc without necessarily internalizing it (2014, pp. 178–180). In urban Delhi, Geetika Bapna found that the "doing of marriage" entailed *nibhānā*.[6] *Nibhānā*, as dutiful observance, she argues, although tied to a "generalised negativity" and "resignation," could not be reduced to it, as it simultaneously served as "a complex site of interpellation of desire, aspiration and affect" (2012, pp. 111–112).

In her work on chronic illness among Pakistani women in Britain, Kaveri Qureshi discusses the ethic of *sabar* (patience). She writes, "Doing *sabar* meant not complaining about one's pain, not talking about it to other people, not letting others realize what you are going through, being strong and carrying on" (2019, p. 193). Embodying *sabar* was spoken of in terms of being a good Muslim and a good woman. Yet Qureshi argues that *sabar* was not simply about bearing suffering in silence but rather was navigated creatively by women in everyday domestic contexts. *Sabar* demanded acknowledgment from others, allowing those who exercised it to claim a moral high ground and thereby secure attention and care from their families (see also Qureshi 2016). Notions such as these—the necessity to keep marriage intact through *nibhānā*, suffering in marriage and through it, exercising *sabar*, marriage bringing *sūkh* but also *dūkh*—came up in several of my conversations. These ideas become an anchor of sorts for women to pull along in marriages or circumstances where escape routes are few and far between. In the chapters that follow, I discuss why, in the context described here, women do not have the option to "flee or fight."

Chapter 6

Children and Other Women

> A woman gets married and has children and then her children become
> the source of her happiness.
>
> —Aarti (RB, 27, Chamar)

> *Yahā merā sāth dene wale bahut haī* [here there are many who support me].
>
> —Maya (CRB, mid-40s, Chamar)

This is the first of the two chapters where I explore other forms of intimacies beyond the couple that are crucial in women's lives. The first part of this chapter focuses on women's relationships with their children and the second on relationships between women. While I will show that both can be conflict ridden, my aim here is to also examine these as relationships of support available to women in their marital villages and in everyday contexts. In attending to women's relationships with their children, I further develop on Lynn Jamieson's (2011) argument that forms of love and intimacy may exist even if they are neither verbalized nor culturally celebrated. When discussing the relationships between women, I begin by focusing on women of the household before moving on to incorporate a focus on relationships forged between unrelated women. I thereby shift the focus away from the household and relationships established through blood and marriage, the lens through which relationships within the South Asian context have mostly been studied. I interrogate ties of support between women beyond the household as friendship relationships rather than as "fictive kinship."

Anthropological writing has attributed the lack of scholarly attention to friendship to a preoccupation with kinship. Sandra Bell and Simon Coleman

167

ask whether the disciplinary expertise in the study of kinship has resulted not only in the neglect of other forms of human association but also in privileging its distinctiveness as a means of organizing social relations (1999, p. 6). Evan Killick and Amit Desai make a case for retaining an analytical distinction between friendship and kinship while acknowledging that the two are not mutually exclusive, and they note the "close intervening" and at times "inseparability" of the two concepts (2010, p. 2). They contend that by subsuming friendship under kinship, "we miss what friendship does differently for the people who practice it" (p. 5). Like Killick and Desai, I argue that friendship should be studied in its own right, but not because friendship does something different from kinship; I will show that relationships with both kin and friends usually contain a mix of "dimensions of intimacy" (Jamieson 1998, p. 173). I use "friendship" rather than "fictive kinship" because while terms such as "fictive kinship" extend the boundaries of kinship beyond biology, they do not necessarily imply closeness or provide insights on the quality of the relationship, while "friendship" assumes some form of intimacy.

Some writing on Western contexts shows that when women fail to feel emotionally fulfilled by marriage, they turn to build emotional lives with their children and friends, apart from their husbands (Duncombe & Marsden 1993; Harrison 1998). Some others that focus on friendship among those who live "outside the conventional family" (heterosexual and nuclear) note a "deliberate de-emphasizing of the importance of the couple relationship" and a "clear prioritizing of friendship over and above sexual partnerships" (Roseneil & Budgeon 2004, pp. 146, 150). The findings of these studies cannot be applied to the very different cultural context described here, yet they raise some interesting questions: is it useful to think of relationships with children and other women as alternative structures of support to the couple relationship? Are these relationships more significant for women than the conjugal relationship? I will return to these questions in the concluding section. I begin by discussing the mother–child relationship through a focus on young children before turning to examine women's relationships with their adult children.

Motherhood and Mothering

When I asked Kamlesh (RB, late 20s, Kumhar) about how she felt about becoming a mother, she said, "What is there to tell . . . to feel happy about . . . everyone has children." Likewise, Kripa (RB, 75, Jat) remarked, "children were just born." Both women spoke with some emotional detachment, suggesting that the birth of children "naturally" followed marriage. Some others, like Kajri (RB, 35, Jat), expressed their desire for a child and talked about the happiness they felt at the birth of the first child—a feeling that diminished with each successive pregnancy: "Every woman wants to become a mother, but after my fourth child [sighed] . . . when a child is born in difficult circumstances, you feel sad but what is in your destiny, you cannot help. . . . We do not even have enough to eat."

Kajri had eight children. Shanti (RB, 24, Kumhar) had five. During one of our conversations, she held her infant daughter out to me and said, "Take her away with you . . . we are laborers . . . how will we get so many daughters married." These women should not be seen as devoid of maternal sentiments; rather, such responses need to be understood within the specificities of this context, as "mother-child and adult-adult attachments are not given—they are socially, historically and culturally produced" (Scheper-Hughes 2014, p. 230). The meanings of motherhood for my informants were shaped not only by cultural expectations but also by the lack of control they had over the timing and number of children (chapter 5) and by the compulsions of poverty and the struggles of survival. Though they received help and assistance from other women, older children, and at times husbands, mothers were the primary carers for their children, especially infants. While I was at Shanti's house, I watched her struggle to do the housework while simultaneously watching her four children and a crying infant. She told me,

> There is never a time during the day when I can sit and rest on the *khāt* [bed]. My children are so young my work never gets done . . . one will go to the toilet, one has to be bathed, for which I have to heat water and then there is housework. . . . I wake up in the morning, make tea and cook, then I get two children ready for school, then I cook again, wash utensils and sweep, then I wash clothes . . . by then it is evening and I again start cooking the night meal.

That women, especially young mothers, were often burdened with household work meant that childcare was one of the many things they did during the day. I observed that young children were left lying on the cot or to crawl on the floor while women continued with work. Patricia Jeffery et al. noted something similar in neighboring Bijnor: childcare was slotted into the interstices of their other work or done in tandem with it. They were told, "We don't rear our children. Children rear themselves" (1989, p. 171). Shanti's case also draws attention to the difficulties entailed in raising several children. Kamlesh said she felt *pareshān* (troubled) by her (four) children: "What can I do? Where can I leave them?" It was no surprise, then, that women, like Shanti and Kamlesh, did not describe mothering young children as a pleasurable or gratifying experience. More children meant not only more mouths to feed and a strain on scarce household resources, but also more work for women. They could not devote themselves entirely to attending to their children's needs; "child-centred rearing" was not a possibility (see Seymour 1999, p. 82). It was unlike the "intensive parenting" described by Henrike Donner for the urban Indian middle class in Kolkata, where motherhood dominates the lives of women. Donner writes that her middle-class informants held a version of relationships between mothers and children which was not only labor intensive but was also built on trust and was described by mothers in terms of friendship (2008, pp. 32, 124, 132; see also Croll 2006 on the wider Asian context).

The Bengali mothers in Donner's study were heavily implicated in their children's educational practices with a view to ensuring their children's future success (p. 129). In the village, too, there was a greater emphasis placed on education, with wealthier families and Jats in particular investing in the education of their children, which was tied to future livelihood strategies and marriageability (chapter 2), but few were educated enough to be involved in the education of their children. In poor families, children were unable to continue or complete their education. Among the Chamars, for instance, children as young as ten migrated with their families, contributing to work in the brick kilns, and had to drop out of school. Older children, especially daughters, across castes, were also involved in assisting with housework and caring for their younger siblings. Concerns around guarding the sexuality of young daughters from dominant-caste men at times resulted in the withdrawal of young girls from education. Thus, there are significant differences in parenting between rural and urban contexts, with caste and class also making for significant variation.

Love for a child or motherly love did not come up in conversations and displays of physical affection between mothers and children were rare. This does not imply that emotional bonds were absent, but rather that visible demonstrations of affection were not an expected part of this cultural context. In her study of a Tamil family, Margaret Trawick (1990) noted that a mother's love for her child had to be kept "contained or hidden" (1990,

p. 42). Susan Seymour made a similar observation in her study in Bhubaneshwar in the eastern state of Orissa. She explains that the love between mother and child had to be "controlled" just like the relationship between husband and wife so that it did not threaten the collective well-being of the family unit (1999, p. 85). While the unity of the larger family was an important concern, my informant Shazia (RB, early 70s, Lohar) offered another explanation. In her opinion, women did not show love for their children in the presence of others because of *sharm* around sexual relations, something that Veena Das also found in her work on Punjab: "children were the fruits of their parents' sexuality and hence parents felt 'shame' in fondling them or playing with them" (1976, p. 11). At the same time, there was considerable bodily contact between mothers and their children in the mother's delivering of care—in holding, feeding, bathing, putting the child to sleep, and so on. Hilary Graham reminds us of the "dual nature of caring"—as labor (the work of caring) and as love/feelings (1983, p. 16). While the boundaries between the two may shift and the emotional dimensions of caring often carry complex and contradictory meanings (Morgan 1996, p. 98), nevertheless, the intimacy enabled by such practical acts of caring must not be understated.

The attachment between mother and child also became evident when women talked about the death of a child or children and singled it out as having caused them *bahut dūkh* (immense sadness). Hemlata (CRB, late 50s, Kumhar) told me, "If you lose your first child, you lose all hope . . . he would have been a young man now." When Khalida (RB, 45, Teli) talked to me about the death of her daughter from an illness, I could tell that the loss was deeply felt. "We could not save her. . . . It was the hardest time in my marriage. I was very ill. Everyone thought that I would die too." Women's emotional connectedness to their children became visible when they talked about not wanting to be separated from their children even if it meant staying in abusive marriages (chapter 7). I got a better sense of the emotional tenor of the mother–child relationship when women talked about their adult children.

Adult Children

As discussed earlier, the birth of children reduced women's sense of ambiguity around belonging, making them feel more embedded in their affinal homes and villages. Motherhood also marked the beginning of the transformation in a woman's (low) status from young bride/daughter-in-law to that of mother, and women gained status and authority through sons (cf. Hershman 1977). Sarah Lamb argues that as women age, they can gain a social identity from being the mother of their sons as much as or even more than they gain from being the wives of their husbands (1999, p. 558). The birth of sons not only enabled a woman to secure her position in her marital home, but also had implications for her long-term security. I was told that daughters would get married and depart to their in-laws' homes, while sons would uphold the ideal of intergenerational reciprocity by providing old-age care and support. Women hoped that sons would maintain them in situations of widowhood (as they inherited property), stand up in support of them in situations of violence, and enable them to have more control over decision-making, especially once they became primary breadwinners of the household. For cross-regional brides, sons were even more important, as claims to the marital home or shelter could be called into question, a concern that Pushpa (CRB, late 30s, Jat) shared:

> I cannot tell you how unhappy I am. I don't have children.
> My natal kin are not with me. Where can I go? I have no
> one. . . . No money, no property in my name. . . . What will
> I do if my husband asks me to leave tomorrow?

Pushpa felt insecure, as she had failed to produce a child, especially a male child, which is often a ground for men leaving their wives and remarrying (chapter 5). She reveals how she was economically vulnerable, as she was completely dependent on her husband and had lost contact with her natal kin and could not call on them in case of desertion in future (chapter 7). Also, being childless, she could not hope to be supported by a son in future, either, and widowhood would add to her vulnerabilities (see Lamb 1999, pp. 548–549, on childless widows). Adult sons were thus a woman's "most critical resource" and ensuring their loyalty became an enduring concern (Kandiyoti 1988, p. 279).

Based on a review of the writing on family change across East, Southeast, and South Asia, Elisabeth Croll noted fears that owing to modernization, urbanization, migration, and Western values, individual over collective family interests would be prioritized by the younger generations, eroding filial obligations. She argues, however, that the intergenerational contract has been renegotiated and remains intact, as parents have adopted several "identifiable strategies" that include "intensification of investment in young children" (2006, pp. 478–479). She points to "a shift from the notion of filial piety to filial care, with nurturance preceding obedience" (p. 483). Appeals to traditional authority have, thus, been replaced with "practices of intimacy" (Jamieson 2011, p. 6) as a calculation to ensure old-age care.

In Barampur, women talked about how sons were failing to provide support or expressed fears that in future filial obligations may not be maintained. Kalawati (CRB, 40, Kumhar) told me that she never felt supported by her husband and had no expectations of support from her eldest son (age 20). She believed that it was because her son felt anger toward her, as he was made to work from a young age and was beaten by her as a child. His childhood was not one of indulgence or investment but was navigated within hardship and deprivation. She had pinned her hopes on her younger son. Kajri (RB, 35, Jat), a widow, was forced to seek paid employment after the death of her husband in order to provide for her eight children. When I met her, she had two adult sons who migrated out for work:

> My eldest son doesn't tell me what he earns. . . . If something happens to me, I don't feel that my older sons will take the responsibility of getting my daughters married or looking after my younger sons. . . . I have been asking my son to give me some hot water since the morning so that I can take my medicine, but he hasn't yet given it to me.

Likewise, Hemlata (CRB, late 50s, Kumhar), also a widow, complained that her son was not contributing his earnings to the household: "How much can a woman do on her own?" Instead of easing the burden of responsibility on them, both women remarked that their sons had turned out to be *nālāik* (good-for-nothing). Hemlata, like some others, also spoke about the weakening of the mother–son relationship once sons got married. The marriage of sons transforms a woman from mother to mother-in-law, investing her with authority and control over junior women, especially daughters-in-law. However, some complained about the lack of care and respect shown by daughters-in-law. Hemlata said, "My daughters are with me now, but they will get married and I will be left alone. I don't think my daughter-in-law will do anything for me. She won't even give me a glass of water." Maya (CRB, mid-40s, Chamar) commented, "My daughter-in-law was not even willing to make a *roti* for me. Before my son got married, I could say anything to him, but now I feel my children are not my own." Similarly, Sheela (CRB, early 40s, Chamar), whose daughter-in law is Koyal (RB, 16,

Chamar), remarked, "He is his wife's now . . . she came two days ago *aur uskī chūt ke pīchay phir rāhā hai*" (and he is chasing after her vagina/for sex). During each of our meetings, Sheela asserted, "*nihārā kar dongī*" (I will make them nuclear—i.e., she was not willing to keep her *bahū* in the same household with her, as is usually done in the early years of marriage).

Daughters-in-law were central to maintaining household harmony because they were the ones who were expected to perform the actual work of care for their in-laws, but also because it was believed that they had the power to turn sons against their parents (see also Vatuk 1990, p. 76).[1] Such intra-household and intergenerational tensions can be explained in terms of the conflict between "the ties created by sexuality and the previously existing biological ties with a mother." Veena Das explains that while the suffering and sacrifice that the mother has undergone in giving birth and bringing up a child endow the mother–child relationship with a greater "moral claim," the strong bonds created by sexuality between husband and wife cannot be denied (1976, p. 10), as is evident in Sheela's suggestion that her son was overpowered by sexual desire.

In contrast, there were also those such as my landlady Sarla (RB, 47, Jat), for whom her relationship with her son was her most important relationship. Sarla had spent most of her married life at her *pīhar*, eventually returning to Barampur with her son. The support from an adult son had enabled her to live in her marital village as a separated woman and offered her protection from violence (chapter 7). She told me, "It's just us—mother and son. . . . I don't talk with anyone about my problems—not my natal family, sisters, or other women here, but I share everything with my son." As I shared a household with them, I was able to observe their daily interactions for almost a year. Here "mutual disclosure" was just one of the "dimensions of intimacy" (Jamieson 1998, pp. 8–10); trust, affection, emotional support, and practical care were other dimensions that fostered and sustained closeness in this relationship. Sarla had anxieties about her son's marriage in future: "I cannot think of separating from him," she said, and hoped that she would be able to continue to rely on his support.

Women like Sarla were in a minority, however. Sheela (CRB, early 40s, Chamar) commented, "daughters are better than sons," a sentiment echoed by several informants. Daughters were not desired at birth, yet they were considered more reliable than sons and especially daughters-in-law in providing care. Women talked about the help they received with housework from their unmarried daughters. Daughters also provided much-needed practical care and emotional support (see also Narayan 2016, p. 119).

Sheela was beaten by her husband throughout her married life, and she asserted that it was only her adult daughter, Babli, and not her sons who supported her. She added that her sons were afraid of their father but Babli was not, even though Sheela's husband verbally abused her. Sons were often unable to stand up to fathers; this had to do with the authority structure within the patrilineal extended household, with senior men being heads of the household and in control of finances and resources—although this did vary with caste, household assets and wealth, the relative earnings of the two generations, and the health of the senior men (Sharma 1989). When I spoke to Babli, the bond between mother and daughter was evident; she told me that she did not want to get married: "What will happen to my mother? Who will give her food to eat or medicine when she's ill or injured?" Marriage complicated the relationship between daughters and parents, as on marriage a daughter is "given away" and becomes *parāyā dhan* (someone else's property). Sylvia Vatuk explains (1990, p. 77):

> reliance upon a daughter married out of the family is considered
> shameful and demeaning. Unlike a son, the out-married daughter
> has no reciprocal obligations to her own parents; her duty is to
> serve her parents-in-law. For her parents to ask her assistance
> from her means, in effect, relying upon the resources and good
> will of the family to which they gave her in marriage.

Women continued to receive emotional support from their married daughters but the practical care they could expect was limited. Ritu (RB, 25, Jat) talked about the difficulties of caring for her elderly ill mother, as visits to the natal home had to be negotiated:

> I have three brothers—one lives in Baghpat town, the other
> migrates out for work and the youngest lives with my mother
> in the village. We are desperately trying to get my youngest
> brother married so that there will be someone to care for my
> mother. There is a lot of love between my mother and me, but
> I can't do much for her. . . . I can't go to visit or stay without
> the consent of my in-laws. My in-laws hardly ever let me go
> because of work but also because my mother-in-law stays ill.

In the event of widowhood, women became economically dependent on their sons. While sons did not always provide for their mothers or contribute toward maintaining the household, daughters could not. Women had no rights to the labor of their married daughters, as on marriage it was transferred to her in-law's family, and in the absence of support from an adult son or male kin, they bore the burden of earning a living. This is different from the situation described for certain urban north Indian contexts where mothers continue to rely on the labor of daughters after marriage (Grover 2011; Vatuk 1972).[2] Daughters were themselves dependent on their husbands and affinal kin and were in no position to maintain their mothers. Furthermore, given the norms of deference, a mother was forbidden from even visiting a daughter in her in-laws' home (other than in exceptional circumstances), and thus moving to live with a married daughter was "the least satisfactory arrangement and a matter of shame" (Mand 2008, p. 290). She consequently had to remain in her affinal village with her son or had the option to return to her natal home, but this was uncommon (chapter 7).[3] Thus, despite the bonds of affection between mothers and daughters, for women, daughters were not a "critical resource" in the same way as sons were. I now move on to discuss women's relations with other women in their marital village.

Women, Friendship, and the Life-Course

In the South Asian context, there is an emerging literature on friendship, with studies focusing on friendship among young men (Nisbett 2007; Osella & Osella 1998) or girls, with adolescence in particular being a time when deep friendships are formed (Dyson 2010; Narayan 1986). More recently, studies have discussed friendship among young female college students (Krishnan 2015; Patel 2017). Studies in the South Asian diasporic context have examined friendship among separated, divorced, and elderly women in some detail (Mand 2006; Qureshi 2016). In rural Indian contexts, however, married women's ties with other women have been described primarily in terms of "fictive kinship" (Lambert 1996; Raheja & Gold 1994; Sharma 1978b), with some exceptions (e.g., Froerer 2010).

In Barampur, when I asked young brides about friendships with other women in their *sasurāl*, I was often told, "I had friends in my *pīhar* . . ."[4] Kirin Narayan describes female friendship in rural Kangra, Himachal Pradesh, as a "liminal category" and as providing emotional support during a "disorienting life cycle transition," i.e., patrilocal exogamous marriage (1986, p. 70). My informants did not dwell much on the nature of the friendships of childhood and adolescence, yet in some conversations, *pīhar kī saheliyān* (friends of the natal home) came up when women talked about being told by their girlfriends about "what the husband would do" (referring to sex) or what a *sās* would be like. As in Narayan's study, such talk in some ways helped prepare women for marriage.

"Girls are like birds . . . they all fly away," one of Narayan's informants told her (1986, p. 54). My informants explained how *pīhar* friendships become difficult to sustain because friends rarely met, as they were married in different (at times distant) villages and visited the *pīhar* at different times, when the demands of their respective *sasurāls* permitted. Koyal (RB, 16, Chamar) was the only one of my informants who said that she talked to her *pīhar* friends regularly using her husband's mobile phone. While the role of technology in facilitating contact must be acknowledged, Koyal was a new bride. I wondered about the fate of her friendships as she advanced in her marital life and became more tied to her affinal household and village.

Earlier village studies showed that even though a woman moved following marriage, leaving her kin and friends behind to live among strangers in her *sasurāl*, she was not completely isolated. In their work in rural UP and Rajasthan, Gloria G. Raheja and Ann Gold noted that married women actively and intentionally constructed relationships for themselves "from the direction of the natal village." These natal ties were described by them as "closer" than the marital relationships of the conjugal village (1994, p. 107). Such relationships provided them with a site for negotiating relations of power with senior affines when their own natal villages were distant or when their own fathers and brothers were unable or unwilling to show support for them (p. 109). Similarly, Helen Lambert found that in rural Rajasthan, "fictive" kin relationships were recognized to exist automatically between women who came from the same natal place. She also observed "female cross-caste relationships"—adoptive kin relationships between unrelated married women of different castes in their conjugal village. All members of the adopting household became consanguineal kin of the in-married woman (1996, pp. 96, 102). Such ties were valued "as sources of social support to women in their conjugal homes" (p. 120). Ursula Sharma, in rural Himachal, also found that every young bride was encouraged to make a bond of "ritual kinship" with some other young wife who came from her own natal village or was already related to her in some way. These relationships provided a young wife with the moral support when she was getting used to her new household and "learning the ropes" of village society (1978b, p. 276). Leigh Minturn, too, writing on rural UP, found that women without relatives in their marital villages adopted a ritual sister. Women mutually chose each other for this relationship because they had become good friends. The sisterhood was formalized through the exchange of gifts. She writes, "The value of a ritual sister as a confidante was the one most often mentioned and was clearly considered to be more important than the help with work or money that a ritual sister provided" (1993, pp. 60, 63).

In Barampur, new brides were not encouraged to and could not establish ties with other women outside their households. Jagbiri (RB, 71, Kumhar) explained, "Your in-laws don't let you talk to anyone, you can't go anywhere and no one can visit." Koyal (RB, 16, Chamar) added, "I only go out to fetch water at the public tap, but I never talk to anyone because if I do, my in-laws fight." Reflecting on the early years, Jagmati (RB, early 60s, Chamar) said, "I would think at the time, for how long will I have to stay within the four walls of the house? I only went to the fields to defecate and my mother-in-law accompanied me." Several informants remarked that their mothers-in-law would ward off other women by saying, "*humārī bahū ko sikhā diyā*" (you taught our daughter-in-law to be rebellious, or taught her tricks). Women said that even if they had opportunities, they feared talking with women outside because if their in-laws or husbands heard of it, it would result in a fight. Kusum (RB, 47, Chamar) explained, "I was afraid of my mother-in-law. You have to be afraid when you are a new bride."

The sociological writing on friendship highlights the significance of wider social contexts and "cultural scripts" in structuring friendships (Adams & Allan 1998; Allan 1989). Friendship is not "solely the result of individual agency but also depends on the structural circumstances under which people live out their lives" (Allan & Adams 2007, p. 13). In this context, *pardā* restrictions meant that the mobility of young brides was restricted and they were mostly confined to their households; thus in the early years they did not have opportunities to establish relationships of support with other women beyond their households. Moreover, being at the bottom of household hierarchies, new brides had to be obedient to senior affines, particularly senior women who, in adopting "surrogate patriarchal roles" (Sangari 1993, p. 871), exerted their authority through the surveillance of younger brides.

Writing on cross-regional brides in Haryana and Rajasthan, Reena Kukreja and Paritosh Kumar argue that although "local brides" were also secluded to varying degrees, the "shadowing of each and every move of the new bride" was restricted to cross-regional brides (2013, p. 52). Similarly, in her work on Bangladeshi wives in eastern UP, Thérèse Blanchet argues that "purchased wives" were "carefully watched" for fear that they might escape (2008, p. 161). Of my 19 cross-regional bride informants, only three said that their husbands or/and in-laws "kept an eye on them" when they first arrived for fear that they might run away,[5] while other cross-regional brides described experiences similar to those of regional brides discussed above.

Some, like Urmila (RB, 32, Jat), had devised strategies to counter her isolation. Urmila told me, "There is a Jat woman in the adjoining household. Whenever my *sās* left the house, I would run up to the terrace and call her out to talk." However, for most brides (regional and cross-regional alike), it was only at a later stage in their marital trajectories (as their mobility increased and they most often had set up nuclear households) that they were able to form friendships. For Sheela (CRB, early 40s, Chamar), it was after she had three children; Jagmati (RB, early 60s, Chamar) said she was "let out of the house" when she had been married for eight to nine years; and Chhaya (CRB, 55, Kumhar) recalled that it was after she had her seven children. Studies on Western contexts note how practices and patterns of friendship are heavily influenced by age and stage in the life-course (Allan 2010; Davies 2011; Pahl & Spencer 2004). Here, not only age and seniority but also household composition became crucial in determining the relationships that women could establish with other women, both within the household and outside. I begin by discussing relations between women of the same household.

Women of the Household

As women moved to live in their *sasurāl*, they found themselves in a position in which they could not readily capitalize on the social capital of childhood relationships. As unmarried women, they did not have much power, yet they had more allies in their *pīhar* than they could rely on than in their *sasurāl* (Chaudhry 2019a). As new brides, their mobility was extremely restricted, so they could not build new social capital by establishing supportive relationships with those outside of the household. Thus, in the early years, relations between women of the household became crucial for a young married woman to counter her isolation. For some, these relationships proved to be vital structures of support, but for others they became a source of conflict. As discussed earlier, women's relationships with their daughters-in-law were strained. Several of my informants also described their relationships with their own mothers-in-law as hostile. Kusum (RB, 47, Chamar) told me,

When we lived in a joint household, my *sās* used to fight with me all the time about work, money and my health. I was very ill for the first five years of my marriage and I would be sent off to my *pīhar* to get treated. They did not want to spend on my treatment. The hardest for me was brick-kiln work. My natal kin did not work in the kiln and I did not know how to do brick-kiln work and for that reason there were constant fights in the house. . . . I had to go to my *pīhar* for my first delivery because my *sās* refused to help. I felt shame.

Every time I met Sheela (CRB, early 40s, Chamar), she complained about her *bahū* (daughter-in-law): "We were doing well and our household was flourishing and then we got *this* [her emphasis] *bahū*. She fights and argues constantly." Sheela also complained about her own *sās*: "She used to trouble me a lot. She would beat me and make my husband beat me." Sheela's *bahū*, Koyal (RB, 16, Chamar), told me the same about her. Women like Sheela, who had suffered mistreatment at the hands of their *sās*, now mistreated their own daughters-in-laws. In this context, Sarla (RB, 47, Chamar) opined,

A *sās* feels if she faced difficulties, for instance, in terms of her workload then her *bahū* should face the same problems. A *sās* will complain saying, "I worked in the fields, collected fodder and took care of the cattle, why should my *bahū* only cook and wash dishes? I had to stay in *parda*, why should my *bahū* move around wearing *salwar kameez*?" A *sās* feels that a *bahū* should have to experience the hardship she experienced as a young wife.

Ursula Sharma (1978b, p. 277) explains,

A woman who has progressed from the lowly status of a nobody as a bride to the position of a respected matriarch is at last compensated . . . she might be expected to sympathise with her own daughters-in-law for their weak position in the household, but she is much more likely to attempt to keep the younger women in their places.

Women thus "bargain" with patriarchy because they have "an actual stake in certain positions of power available to them" (Kandiyoti 1998, p. 143). It was not only the *sās* but relations between *devrānīs* and *jethānīs* were also often marked by competition and disunity. Parvati (45, Kumhar) and Lakshmi (late 40s, Kumhar) were both cross-regional brides from Bengal and were married to brothers and moved to live in Barampur on the same day. Parvati told me that Lakshmi provoked Parvati's husband to beat her. Both women were new brides yet, as Parvati's *jethānī*, Lakshmi was senior (in relation) and adopted a position of power available to her in the absence of a *sās* (who had died) or another senior woman in the household. Thus, whether cross-regional or regional, as they progressed in their marital lives, all women were incorporated into household hierarchies and hoped that eventually they would come out on top.

In some cases, it was self-interest that motivated women to oppress other women. Kanchan (CRB, 21, Chamar), for instance, told me, "Here there is no one who supports me. The women around are all in relation of *jethānī* to me. They talk about getting me beaten." When I probed, she explained that her *jethānī* (a widow) was at her *pīhar* when Kanchan first arrived as a new bride. She added, "Ratan [husband] treated me with a lot of love, he never raised a hand on me. Even my *sās* was fine but since my *jethānī* returned things are different . . . she is constantly provoking Ratan to beat me." Kanchan believed that her *jethānī* felt angry because after she was widowed, she was to be settled in a marriage with Ratan in a levirate marriage, as was the common practice here, but Ratan had chosen to elope with Kanchan instead. She believed that her *jethānī* thought that if she troubled Kanchan enough, Kanchan would eventually leave.

Likewise, Hemlata (CRB, late 50s, Kumhar) believed that her *jethānī* provoked her husband to beat her because her *jethānī* wanted Hemlata to leave. She added that before Hemlata's marriage, her *jethānī* had a relationship with Hemlata's husband and he would hand his earnings to her *jethānī* but this changed after Hemlata's arrival in Barampur. Similarly, Sarla (RB, 47, Jat) said that she was ill-treated by her husband's *chāchī* in the hope that Sarla would permanently return to her natal home because the *chāchī* was in a relationship with Sarla's husband. She hoped that Sarla would remain childless so that her children would inherit Sarla's husband's land: "His *chāchī* and her daughter cried and mourned loudly in the cattleshed the day my son was born." Urmila (RB, 32, Jat) shared her experience:

> After my wedding, I came to stay at my *sasurāl* for three days. Usually a woman does not have relations with her husband until after the *gaunā* but my *sās* sent my husband to me at night. I was only 15 at the time. My parents had agreed to send me at

gaunā as per custom only a year or two later, but I got pregnant. I could have stayed at my *pīhar* for a year if my husband had not come to me. My *sās* did not think about me . . . she knew that if I got pregnant my parents would leave me at my *sasurāl*. This is what she wanted because there was no one here to cook and do the housework.

Thus, there were differences in interests between women, as Ursula Sharma has noted, that made it unlikely that they would unite as women to form a solidarity group (1978b, p. 277). Some, like Sarla (RB, 47, Jat), felt that senior women ensured that junior women did not develop solidarity among themselves. Sarla said that her *devrānī* was ill-treated in the same way that she was, yet, if they attempted to talk to each other, they were both beaten. Ritu (RB, 25, Jat) felt that her two *jethānīs* were united in their dislike for her. The reason Ritu offered was that she was favored by her *sās* over her *jethānīs* because she had brought a "satisfactory" dowry. She added, "They troubled me a lot. Whenever my *sās* went out, they made me do all the work."

Hemlata (CRB, late 50s, Kumhar) and Kalawati (CRB, 40, Kumhar) were related because their mothers were sisters. Hemlata had acted as the go-between for Kalawati's marriage. When they both talked to me individually, they expressed a lot of sympathy for each other's problems, but they saw each other only occasionally. Hemlata told me that she did not go to Kalawati's house because Kalawati's husband disapproved. Kalawati told me that if she talked to Hemlata, her *devrānī* or *jethānī* complained to her husband and created a fight between them. This was like the experiences described by regional brides with married sisters in Barampur, who said that they were prevented from maintaining close ties with their sisters by other affinal women of the household.

However, not all women shared this experience. For some such as Abha (RB, 25, Chamar), a young widow with small children, the experience of marriage and widowhood was largely shaped by the support she had from her *sās* and *nanad*. Abha said that if it had not been for her *sās*, who supported her and not her own sons, in a dispute she would have lost what rightfully belonged to her children and would have had to return to her *pīhar*. Even when her husband was alive, her *sās* never let him raise his hand to her: "There is a lot of love between me, my *nanad* and *sās*. I do not have a mother, but I have always thought of her [*sās*] as my mother." She added that her *nanad* was married but had continued to support her: "She has offered to help with money or if I have any other problem." Musrat (RB, 32, Lohar) talked about how she and her *devrānī* supported each other in conflicts with their *sās* and *nanad*. "I wanted to protect my *devrānī* from suffering the way that I had," she told me. Jameela (CRB, 21, Teli) said that even though her natal family was far away, she never felt alone in Barampur because she had the support of her *jethānīs*, who sided with her in all conflicts with their *sās*, and she reached out to them in times of difficulty (e.g., during an illness). Mansi (CRB, 33, Chamar) shared how she could not visit her *pīhar* as often as she would have liked because it was far away, yet she felt comforted by the support that she had from her *jethānī*, who took Mansi with her to her own *pīhar* for visits. Similarly, Jagbiri (RB, 71, Kumhar) told me how she had taken two of her (cross-regional) *devrānīs* with her to her *pīhar* on several occasions over the years.

Women Outside

Women also talked about supportive relationships they developed with unrelated women in other households. These were not necessarily women with whom they could trace ties through their natal villages, as noted by earlier studies, but were women of their own caste—or of other castes. Urmila (RB, 32, Jat) talked about relying on her Jat neighbor: "If I told her that I was troubled because my husband did not give me money to buy provisions for the house, she would lend me money. I used to sell milk so I would pay her back as and when I had the money. I tell her all my problems and she has never mentioned anything to anyone." Here not only material support but also confiding and trust were important dimensions of the relationship. Talking and sharing problems also emerged in several informants' accounts when they talked about being supported by other women. Varsha (CRB, 28, Jat) referred to Sapna (RB, late 30s, Jat) as her friend (using the English word): "I talk to her about the problem with my *devars* [referring to being pressured to have sexual relations with them]. She is the only one I can trust with such personal matters."

For rural Kangra, Kirin Narayan writes of women of more-or-less equal caste statuses singing together, where singing was described as an outlet for "exchanging confidences" and "doing sorrows and joys" (2016, p. 142). In Barampur, I often saw groups of women sitting together and talking in the *galis* (alleys/lanes) in the afternoon. I first learned about the content of such conversations in my interviews with individual women. In some of the conversations I sat in on, women discussed routine violence and sex and consulted each other on contraception. In the sitting together talking about what was difficult, women sympathized with each other, were able to engage in a process of unburdening, and bonded on the basis of shared experiences. The sitting together at times became a space for gossip, however. Shalini Grover noted something similar in her work in a low-income neighborhood in Delhi. She writes that women were able to cope with battering with the support of neighbors. Women met in all-women groups comprising neighbors, friends, and fictive kin and confided in each other and compared notes. This, she argues, strengthened their resolve to cope with or contest the violence (2011, p. 54).

Sociologists have argued that friendships can be formed through joint activities (Feld & Carter 1998). In Barampur, fetching water at the public tap and wood and fodder from the fields not only provided women opportunities to talk and share grievances but also forged ties among them as they relied on each other's assistance. Women went for casual (agricultural) work in groups and this, they said, made them less vulnerable to harassment and violence. In her work in a tribal village in central India, Peggy Froerer similarly noted that it was in the "doing things together" that friendships between adult married women were commonly formed, as joint activities (laboring in the fields, fishing, hunting etc.) served to foster "familiarity, trust and reciprocity" (2010, pp. 147, 149; see also Dyson 2010 on the production of friendship among young girls in rural Uttarakhand forged through the work of leaf collection). Affective bonds were also created in the giving and receiving of practical care. Jagbiri (RB, 71, Kumhar), an elderly widow, lived alone. She spoke fondly about Kalawati (CRB, 40, Kumhar), her neighbor, who often made her a cup of tea or a meal when she felt unable to cook. She suffered from a heart condition and relied on Kalawati to accompany her to the government hospital in Baghpat town.

The writing on migration and displacement has drawn attention to "friendship loss" that occurs following migration and of the significance of establishing social networks at destination (e.g., Sirriyeh 2013; Westcott 2012). The literature on marriage migration also explores how migrant brides attempt to counter their isolation by forging ties with others who also come from "back home" (Davin 2008; Schein 2005). For cross-regional brides, who were cut off from networks of natal kin support (chapter 7), making relationships of support in their marital village became significant. None of my informants suggested that they intentionally attempted to create ties only with other cross-regional brides or brides originating from their native states, however. In fact, as the cases of Varsha and Kalawati, mentioned above, and those below demonstrate, cross-regional brides at times established the closest ties with regional brides.

Maya (CRB, mid-40s, Chamar) told me, "My natal family is not with me but there are many here who support me. When my husband used to beat me, the elderly woman in the house across the street would intervene . . . she would ask him, 'Why are you beating her?' and she made him stop." Neighbors did not usually intervene in this way, especially young brides who were equally powerless within their households. It was a woman's natal kin who were called on in such situations (chapter 7). For cross-regional brides, like Maya, however, such intervention was crucial in providing some relief from the violence. Pushpa (CRB, late 30s, Jat) said that the only support she had in Barampur was from a Jat (RB) neighbor who had died two years prior to our conversation. She was tearful when she told me, "It was the only time in my life that someone had shown me *kuch hamadardī* [some empathy]." Poonam was in a unique and difficult position, as she was completely without any support and felt extremely isolated. She was childless and had lost contact with her natal kin, her only friend had passed away, and she did not feel supported by her husband.

In her work on marital breakdown among British Pakistanis, Kaveri Qureshi found that, having experienced disappointment, control, or exclusion from their natal families, some of her informants drew on the "idiom of kinship to create new, voluntary forms of kinship" with their female friends transforming these friendships into kin-like relations among "sisters" (2016, pp. 215, 217). Likewise, for some of my cross-regional brides, women friends became like extended kin. Chhaya (CRB, 55, Kumhar) told me about Sapna (RB, late 30s, Jat): "We are like *jethānī-devrānī*. We share everything." Sheela (CRB, early 40s, Chamar) said, "Asha [CRB, 55, Chamar] is not only my friend but she is like a *sagī behen* [real/blood sister] to me. When I fall ill, she forgets her own troubles and supports me. I can never say anything bad about her. She supports me in good times and bad." Being supported in times of hardship and at particular junctures was described by many women as a mark of an *achī* or *puccī dost* (good or strong friend or deep friendship). In contrast to these women, for some others the use of kin terms did not necessarily denote emotional closeness in the relationship. Chhaya (55, Kumhar) and Parvati (45, Kumhar), for instance, were both brides from West Bengal. Parvati's daughter addressed Chhaya as *māsī*. Yet, when I asked Chhaya about her relationship with Parvarti, she said, "We don't support each other but we feel happy when we meet since we are from the same village." Likewise, Kalawati (CRB, 40, Kumhar) remarked,

> If I was the only one here, I would think, look where my native home is and where have I come. Now there are so many here—she is also from my village, as is she. When I am with Mamta [CRB from Silchar like Kalawati and also her *devrānī*] I do not say that she is my *devrānī*. I say that she is my *behen* [sister] because she is from my native village. But if you ask me, "Does Mamta support you?" I will say, "No."

Like Chhaya and Kalawati, some other cross-regional brides did not describe those from their native states as friends but talked of them as women with whom they only shared a sense of belonging to the same place. For them, while shared background or ties to a common place were sufficient to establish kinship, they were clear that their relationships were not intimate. For Varsha (CRB, 28, Jat), however, belonging to the same place was more meaningful. She explained that because Parvati also belonged to Bengal, she was, for instance, able to understand her cravings for non-vegetarian foods. She said that when her *sās* went out, she asked Parvati to bring her eggs from the market that they ate together. Furthermore, she also relied on Parvati's daughter's help with housework when she fell ill. She said that she didn't share her problems with Parvati yet she referred to her as a friend during our conversation. Women like Varsha, to borrow from Ray Pahl and Liz Spencer, had a range of types of friends in their "friendship repertoires" (2004, p. 207). While Parvati assisted her in practical ways, others like Sapna, as mentioned earlier, provided Varsha with emotional support and a space for exchanging personal confidences, something Varsha felt she could not trust others with. In Varsha's understanding there was also distinction between (fictive) kinship and friendship. When I first met her, she addressed me as *dīdī* (elder sister). Months later during a conversation she said, "We are now like friends, we have a relationship of trust." For Kangra, Kirin Narayan argued that unlike men who have friends all their lives, women have friends in the years before marriage. The intimacy that exists between friends is not thought to be accessible to a married woman. For women, "the category of friendship gives way to fictive kinship" (1986, pp. 66, 68). While women in Barampur too mentioned the loss of child-hood friendships, unlike in Narayan's study, they were able to form new and intimate friendships in their marital village that became a vital source of support for them.

There were others, however, who had either failed to establish friendships with other women or for whom friendship had involved "negative relational practices" (Davies 2011, p. 82). Radha (CRB, early 40s, Chamar) remarked, "No one is a friend here. . . . There is no one who supports me." Nasira (RB, 26, Lohar) described sitting together with women talking as "timepass," not friendship. Likewise, Khalida (RB, 45, Teli) said, "If I am troubled about a personal matter, I won't talk to anyone about it." When I asked why, she told me, "There will be a hundred women who will appear to sympathize with you. They will ask you about your troubles and show concern and as soon as you turn your back, they will tell other women about it." Khalida points to a lack of trust that prevented her from sharing or confiding in other women. There were some like Kajri (RB, 35, Jat), who told me that she had been "betrayed" by a friend with whom she had shared personal secrets. Confiding was an essential dimension of an intimate friendship, yet this came with an understanding of "*trust*, faith that confidences will not be betrayed" (Jamieson 1998, p. 9). For some, the "negative relational practices" included being verbally abused by other women during a fight. For cross-regional brides, such abuse served to remind them of their "outsider" status and that they were "bought wives." Sheela (CRB, early 40s, Chamar), for instance, told me, "Sometimes in the middle of a fight, women will say, 'Why are you talking so much, after all *tuh mol ā rahī hai*' [you have come for a price/are a bought bride]." Varsha shared, "The woman in the house across the street passes comments like *'Bangāl walī kitnā boltī hai, rehegī toh Bangāl kī*' [the woman from Bengal talks so much; nevertheless, she will always be the woman from Bengal]."

Conclusion

As far as women's relationships with their children were concerned, women were most often supported by their daughters, even though their long-term well-being depended on being cared for by sons. The marriage of children complicated the relationship between women and their sons and daughters, albeit in different ways. As for relationships with other women, few women felt supported by affinal women within their households. The discussion on friendship has helped to demonstrate the significance of non-kin relations as sources of support. For a woman, even though her female friends could do little with respect to offering exit options or relief from difficult situations, they provided her with much-needed emotional, practical, and/ or material support. Friendships were both intra-caste and cross-caste. An important finding is that for some cross-regional brides, the closest bonds were established with regional brides. Some others had friendships with other cross-regional brides, even though most agreed that they did not intentionally attempt to create ties only with those who came from back home. Some spoke of negative experiences, with cross-regional brides having their "outsider" status reiterated in interactions with women outside their households. Nevertheless, for all women (whether regional or cross-regional), stage in the life-cycle and household composition had a significant bearing on their opportunities to establish supportive ties with other women. At times, mother–child and friendship relationships were marked by conflict and experienced as disappointing. Yet most women were not completely isolated and could rely on their children and/or other women for support. This, of course varied across the life-course.

Returning to the questions raised at the start of this chapter: should relationships with children and other women be understood as alternative structures of support to the couple relationship? Do these relationships become more significant for women vis-à-vis the conjugal relationship? As discussed in chapter 5, for women in Barampur, the conjugal relationship was not the most intimate relationship despite women's desires and expectations that it should be. My informants, unlike those described in the Western studies, were not consciously exercising choice in prioritizing ties apart from the conjugal one. For women, their relationships with their friends or/and children did seem to provide the emotional succor and care that husbands often did not. As their natal families were either absent or unavailable, many asserted the importance of these relationships. It is, however, important to emphasize that women did not speak of these relationships as significant vis-à-vis the conjugal relationship or relationships with natal kin, but valued them in themselves as forms of everyday support. While there was considerable variation in women's experiences, I conclude that in their marital villages women were sustained through their relational lives with their children and other women.

Chapter 7

Natal Kin

While your parents are alive, you can go to your *pihar* as many times as you want.

—Kusum (RB, 47, Chamar)

When he [husband] came to marry me, I thought my parents have to get me married . . . near or far, what difference does it make. At the time, I didn't understand that if I go far away, I will not be able to come back.

—Varsha (CRB, 28, Jat)

In this chapter, I focus on women's relationships with their natal kin. I will show that despite the emphasis in north Indian kinship on the isolation of a married woman from her natal kin and her incorporation into her husband's family, a woman's ties with her natal kin are not permanently "unmade" (Lamb 1997). While a woman's natal kin are not called upon in day-to-day contexts, they play a significant role in sustaining ties with a daughter's affines, in providing gifts on visits, at life-cycle rituals and festivals that help her secure her position in her marital home, and most crucially in moments of crisis and marital distress. While both regional and cross-regional brides migrate following marriage, I will highlight that the geographic distance separating the natal and affinal homes of the latter amounts to more vulnerability for cross-regional brides as compared to regional brides, as it limits the support available to them. However, I will also argue that over the life-course, regional brides might find themselves in a similar situation—without natal kin support. I begin with a discussion of some of the key debates on natal kin in the writing on South Asia and the diaspora.

189

The quality of a married woman's contact with her natal kin was discussed in several early studies that contrasted the north and south Indian kinship systems to examine how different forms of marriage alliances determine women's contact with their natal kin following marriage. They argued that in the north, unlike the south, due to local exogamy and the prohibition on close-kin marriage, women were married over larger distances that resulted in the "complete dissimilation of the bride from her family of birth and her complete assimilation to that of her husband" (Trautmann 1981, p. 291). Tim Dyson and Mick Moore argued that the greater distances over which marriages are arranged in the north compared to the south "tend to constrain or erode the personal links between a married woman and her natal kin," and the absence of support structures diminishes women's autonomy (1983, p. 46).

One problematic aspect of Dyson and Moore's study is that it reflects a Hindu bias. Muslims in the north permit both intra-village marriages and marriages between close kin (e.g., Jeffery 1979). In their work in rural Bijnor, on Hindus (generally married distantly) and Muslims (usually married into nearby villages), Patricia Jeffery et al. (1988, 1989) noted that Muslim women usually did not favor intra-village marriage, as they feared that it might result in interference from their natal kin in their daily lives. Yet they saw being married close to their natal kin as an advantage, as they felt less cut off from their natal families than the Hindu women. Yet Jeffery et al. see distance as only one element in married women's relations with their natal kin. A married woman's access to her natal kin was determined by several considerations, including obtaining permission (from her husband and older affinal kin), finding someone to do the work in her absence, and having a man from her affinal village with enough time to act as her chaperone. Also, her natal kin were expected to pay her travel expenses (1988, p. 324).

The north–south contrast as a basis for understanding access to natal kin support may also be questioned, because studies on south India show that close-kin marriages and proximity to natal kin do not necessarily imply better treatment for women or protection against violence (Kapadia 1991; Rao 2015; Vera-Sanso 1999). Natal families may be less willing to intervene for fear of jeopardizing kin ties. Studies on Muslims also show that close-kin marriages, generally arranged within a small geographical radius, do not necessarily guarantee a woman's well-being after marriage (Jeffery 2001) and may also break down (Vatuk 2015).

Several scholars argued that even though on marriage a woman loses her rights (of maintenance and residence) in her natal home, she neither becomes kinless nor completely ceases to belong to her natal home. Leela Dube writes that while the transfer of a girl from one family to another is supposed to be "total," the brother–sister tie is held to be "life-long" (1997, p. 90). Pauline Kolenda (1967) argued that a woman's close ties with her natal kin enhanced her bargaining power, enabling her to break away sooner from her husband's joint family. Ethnographic studies showed that the bonds between a woman and her natal kin were sustained through visits and gift-giving, starting at the wedding and continuing through the course of a woman's married life (Jeffery et al. 1989; Jeffery & Jeffery 1996; Palriwala 1991; Raheja & Gold 1994; Sharma 1980; Vatuk 1975). Further, in situations of marital distress, a woman could seek temporary refuge at her natal home that enabled her to negotiate better treatment from her husband and in-laws in future (Grover 2011; Jacobson 1977; Jeffery 2001).

Studies also found that women at times made periodic visits to their natal homes to assist with work. In her study in a central Indian village, Doranne Jacobson (1977) found that married women constantly moved back and forth between their natal and marital homes, serving as a shifting labor supply, particularly in poor agricultural households. Similarly, in her study in a Rajasthan village, Rajni Palriwala questioned the notion of "women as fixed residents of their conjugal homes" (1991, p. 2763). She showed how in the phase in the life of young married women described as *"aoni jaoni"* (coming–going), women stayed for alternate periods of varying length in their natal and marital homes, allowing both sets of kin to access their labor.

Writings on urban north Indian contexts note a tendency toward "matrilateral asymmetry." In her work in urban Meerut, Sylvia Vatuk found that close proximity combined with neolocality (following migration for work) allowed for "considerable visiting" and "mutual aid" between daughters and their parents with daughters' greater reliance on their mothers, particularly in times of need (1971, pp. 287–307; 1972). More recently in her study in a low-income neighborhood in Delhi, Shalini Grover noted that kinship was an "everyday and immediate affair" for the urban poor. The marriage of daughters over short distances and within easy reach helped sustain regular contact and supportive ties, especially between mothers and daughters (2011, p. 205).

As with studies from South Asia, in her study of marital breakdown among British Pakistanis, Kaveri Qureshi noted "a shift towards matrilateral asymmetry" as separated and divorced women turned to their natal kin, who stepped in "to pick up the pieces" and provided accommodation, childcare, and financial support (2016, pp. 30, 300). Grover and Qureshi also discuss how natal kin support may vary depending on the type of marriage—love marriage or arranged marriage: in an arranged marriage, natal kin support may be viewed as an "entitlement" yet requires "continual and intense negotiation" (Grover 2011, pp. 60, 63; Qureshi 2016, pp. 123–124). Likewise, in his work in a garment city in Tamil Nadu, Geert De Neve explores the significance of post-marital kin (material) support for men, too, in fulfilling aspirations of "mobility, entrepreneurship and success in a post-liberalisation environment" (2016, p. 1220). He notes that a parentally arranged endogamous marriage rather than a love marriage is considered the best way to ensure parental and material support, though it may not always materialize (on loss of natal family support, see also Ahearn 2001 on Nepal; del Franco 2012 on Bangladesh).

Like the aforementioned studies on urban kinship, studies on matrilineal systems and uxorilocal residence (in or near the wife's home after marriage) show that women benefit from proximity to their natal kin. In Kerala, among a matrilineal Muslim community, Caroline Osella noted the help with domestic work and emotional support of mothers, sisters, aunts, and cousins that was available to (stay-behind) wives of migrant men because of belonging to a matrilineal *tharavadu* (joint household)—where men had little rights and their status remained always "marginal" (2012, p. 248). In Bijnor, a man at times moved to live in his wife's natal village as a *ghar jamāī*,[1] usually if a woman had no siblings, especially brothers. Such a man was likely to find himself in a "weak position," and this was a situation that most men considered should be avoided (1988, p. 328). Men believed that being an in-living son-in-law undermined their ability to control their wives and be masters of the house, and they would lack both the normal backing from their kin and freedom from their in-laws' interference. However, for a woman, such an arrangement meant greater access to her mother and sisters than she could have had from her affinal village (Jeffery & Jeffery 1993, p. 76). Similarly, in her work on marriage migration of Pakistani men to Britain, Katharine Charsley (2008) noted that these men found themselves in an unusual position of being the "lone incomer," while their wives started their married lives with their parents and siblings "close at hand" (2008, p. 274). This undermined a man's authority over his wife, disrupting conventional power relationships, and meant greater support for women in conflict situations.

It is clear, then, that a married woman's relationship with her natal kin is complex. In this chapter, I contribute to these debates by comparing post-marital kin contact for regional and cross-regional brides and consider the implications of geographic distance for women's position within marriage. In doing so, I also highlight commonalities with women in cross-border (international) marriages.

Visiting the *Pīhar*

> Every time she meets her brother when he comes to visit her or to get her at her husband's village, she weeps as she embraces him. When she returns from her husband's village, she weeps ritually on her mother's shoulder, chanting the misery of her separation and recalling their mutual sorrows.
>
> —Kolenda 1984, p. 111

This description aptly captures the emotions that women experience as they depart from and return to their natal homes in the early years of marriage. For regional brides in Barampur, the first visit to the *pīhar* would take place a few days after the wedding, when her natal kin came to her *sasurāl* to collect her. Most of my informants said that they made frequent visits to their *pīhar* in the first year or early years of marriage. Visits by a young bride to her *pīhar* eased her adjustment in a new village and among a household of strangers, as noted by earlier ethnographic accounts (Jacobson 1977; Jeffery et al. 1989; Jeffery & Jeffery 1996; Palriwala 1991). Khalida (RB, 45, Teli) told me that for her, these visits were crucial in dealing with the difficulties she faced with regard to sexual relations: "It felt bad. For this reason, I would stay for eight days with my husband, then thirteen . . . and go to my *pīhar*." The frequency of visits to the *pīhar*, however, decreased over the course of women's married lives. Women said that following the early years, they started visiting their *pīhar* once or twice a year and gradually only once in two years.

A visit to the *pīhar* was described as a time of rest that offered women respite from work and, as Patricia Jeffery and Roger Jeffery noted in Bijnor, "a break from the rule of the mother-in-law and husband" (1996, p. 188). Many said that their brothers' wives did not let them work when they visited. It was only during lengthy stays that they helped out with work. Moreover, they enjoyed the freedom of not having to observe *ghūnghat* in their natal villages. Women could go to their *pīhar* only if their in-laws, particularly the *sās*, gave them permission to go. Young brides had to rely either on their husbands to drop them or on a relative being sent from the *pīhar* to collect them from the *sasurāl*, as previously noted by Patricia Jeffery et al. (1988). As women advanced in their married lives and their mobility increased, they could travel on their own.

The most common reason for not being allowed to visit their natal kin was household responsibilities or if the *sās* or someone in the *sasurāl* was ill. Women usually started their married lives in joint households where work was shared. Visits to the *pīhar* became shorter and less frequent once they set up nuclear households, as they became solely responsible for work (housework, cattle-work, and childcare). As poor Kumhar, Chamar, and Teli women were also engaged in waged work, visits were limited. For Chamar women who worked in the brick kilns, visits to the *pīhar* were possible only at the end of the brick-making season, which lasted for six to eight months.

Across castes, women visited their *pīhar* and could be visited in their *sasurāl* by their fathers and brothers except when women were pregnant and their pregnancy became visible. During pregnancy, contact between a woman and her natal kin was curtailed, and this cut her off from the emotional and practical support she could receive from them (see also Jeffery et al. 1989, pp. 72–74, 255). There were practical constraints as well. Shanti (RB, 24, Kumhar) had five children and she said she felt *sharm* in visiting her *pīhar* with "so many children": "My biggest problem now is that I cannot go anywhere. All my children are so young. I cannot get on a bus with them by myself without thinking, 'What if one gets left behind?'" Visits became fewer once the number of children increased and as daughters became *jawān* (mature) and could not be left at home alone. Women talked about how visits became even more occasional after parents passed away, and once brothers got married, as they felt that their ties with their brothers weakened. Kajri (RB, 35, Jat), a widow, told me that her parents had passed away several years ago:

Now my brother and his family are there in my *pīhar* but I no longer go. I do not want to be a burden on anyone. My brother's wife is from a wealthy family and she does not want to associate with poor people like me. I have not seen my brother for over two years. His wife does not let him come here. I only had my brother's support but even that has been lost.

Likewise, Khalida (RB, 45, Teli) said,

For many years, I felt that my *pīhar* was *apnā ghar* [one's own home] but since the last few years, I don't feel the same. Earlier I never felt like coming back here from my *pīhar*. Your parents are your parents after all. You go as long as they are alive because things change once they die.

Most women spoke of the natal home as the *parental* home and they regarded the death of parents (especially fathers) as a defining change in their relationship with their natal kin. Shazia (RB, early 70s, Lohar) talked about how there was no one in the *pīhar* left to visit, as not only her parents but even her brothers had died. When we met, she could not recall when she had last visited her *pīhar* but only that it was for her nephew's wedding.

Older women believed that husbands had come to have a greater say vis-à-vis the in-laws with regard to sending their wives to her *pīhar*. What was implied was the greater sexual restraint and *sharm* that men of earlier generations had as opposed to young married men, who openly asserted their right to sexual relations with their wives. Kripa (RB, 75, Jat), for instance, remarked, "When I first got married, I would go and live at my *pīhar* for as long as four to six months but the men of today are not willing to leave their wives in the *pīhar* even for two days."

As far as visits by the natal kin were concerned, it was male members from the *pīhar*, usually the father and/or brother, who visited a woman in her *sasurāl*. It was not considered appropriate for a woman's mother to visit her. A mother only visited, for instance, to express condolence when there was a death in the daughter's marital family. It was considered extremely shameful for a woman's kin to accept anything, including hospitality, from their affines. Iravati Karve noted that in north India, a father must not accept even food at his daughter's marital home when he goes to visit her. "The relationship is that of givers and receivers. One who gives the daughter should not receive anything" (1994, pp. 58–59). During my fieldwork, respondents married for over 30 years (before the early 1980s) said that their fathers did not and still do not accept food in their *sasurāl* but their brothers did. Young married women, however, said that this prohibition no longer existed. Accepting hospitality at a daughter's *sasurāl* was also influenced by whether she lived jointly with her *sās*. Ritu (RB, 25, Jat), for instance, explained that her mother did not accept food and water in Ritu's *sasurāl*, but did in Ritu's sister's because her sister's in-laws were no longer alive.

Women met their married sisters on occasions such as weddings in their natal or marital families. Given household responsibilities and the fact that permission had to be sought from the in-laws, it was rare that married sisters visited their *pīhar* at the same time. It was also not common for women to visit their married sisters in their *sasurāl*, especially when the sister's in-laws were alive and lived jointly with her. Three of my informants had sisters who were also married in Barampur, yet they rarely visited them because their in-laws did not allow it. One of my informants, an elderly widow, said that she was free to do so now that there were no in-laws to seek permission from.

As for cross-regional brides, there were variations among them with regard to natal kin contact. Some studies argue that "bought brides" were unlikely to or were not allowed to visit or maintain contact with their natal kin (Jeffery et al. 1989; Chowdhry 2005; Kant & Pandey 2003). Writing on Bangladeshi brides in eastern UP, Thérèse Blanchet (2008) noted that brides were denied the right to visit their natal homes on the ground that their husbands had made a payment for them. Also, for Muslim women married to Hindu men, return to the natal home was difficult. Ravinder Kaur (2012), in her study of Bangladeshi and Bengali brides in eastern UP, points out that the latter were better placed than the former. Husbands of Bangladeshi brides were unable or disinclined to visit Bangladesh, as it is a different country and visiting it posed additional difficulties (p. 87). Some other studies show that cross-regional brides maintained contact and visited their natal homes, even if not frequently (Chaudhry & Mohan 2011; Kaur 2004; Mishra 2016).

In Barampur, cross-regional brides could be placed in three categories as far as visits to the *pīhar* were concerned. The first category is those who had made visits to their natal homes more than once and talked to me about an impending visit. Most brides could be placed in this category. This included brides who had visited two to five times since they had been married, those who went to their natal home once a year (as did most regional brides), and exceptions, such as Deepa (early 30s, Kumhar), who had acted as a go-between for several marriages from her natal home in Jharkhand, which made it possible for her to visit her natal home three to five times a year.

In the second category are brides who had visited once but had not been to their natal homes for several years. When I first met Kalawati (40, Kumhar), a cross-regional bride from Assam, she had not visited her natal home in over 20 years. She had visited only once—three months after her wedding when she returned to arrange a marriage for her *devar*. Her brother had visited her in Barampur once when her second child was six years old (in 1994). She told me,

Earlier my heart would ache thinking about my natal kin. I would tell him [husband] to take me once to meet my family but he never did because he did not want to spend money. He would say we will go on *Diwālī*, on *Holī* [Hindu festivals] . . . he kept putting it off with excuses. Then I gave up hope. I no longer think about my family because my parents are not there. I received a letter a few years ago about my elder brother's death and I do not know if my younger brother is still alive. If I go, where will I go? My brother's children were young when I left . . . they must have grown up now . . . they will not recognize me.

Kalawati's marriage was arranged by Hemlata (also from Assam). She said that before Hemlata was widowed, Hemlata's husband wrote letters to Kalawati's brothers and would read the letters her brothers sent to her. Kalawati was illiterate but her daughter was educated. Yet she could not ask her daughter to write letters, as Hemlata had lost Kalawati's brother's address: "I feel sad that I never go, there is no news from there and letters don't come." For cross-regional brides, like Kalawati, ties with her natal kin were eventually severed. Chhaya (CRB, 55, Kumhar), like Kalawati, had not visited her natal home (in Bengal) for over two decades and was told by her husband that her kin would fail to recognize her. Unlike Kalawati, however, she had managed to reestablish contact with her natal family:

> In the first year of marriage, I visited my *pīhar* twice, both times to arrange marriages. Then my husband did not take me for 26 years. I was *dūkhī* [sad] for all those years. For that reason, I decided to go with Durga [CRB also from Bengal] without telling my husband. I told my youngest son and he went to drop me to the railway station. Shakuntala [a Jat woman in the neighborhood] gave me the train fare. I had no trouble finding my natal home after all those years. My husband used to tell me not to go there because my relatives would not recognize me, but my brothers did. Everyone from the village came to see me. When I arrived there, I learned that my mother had died three years earlier. . . . My natal family did not contact me for all those years because they did not have the address. My *māmā* [mother's brother] who had come to drop me here after my wedding had died.

Like Chhaya, Sheela (early 40s, Chamar) shared her experience of returning to her natal village in Maharashtra ten years after she first left and resuming contact with them: "My relatives cried when they saw me for the first time. My mother, brother, mother's brother, and grandmother were there when I arrived . . . it had been so many years . . . they thought I was dead."

In the third category are cross-regional brides who never returned to their natal homes to visit and had no contact with their kin and found themselves in an extremely vulnerable position. Kanchan (CRB, 21, Chamar) had run away from her home in Bihar with her "cousin," who was intending to elope with a man from UP. Her cousin arranged a marriage for Kanchan in Barampur. Kanchan told me that she regretted running away and had made several attempts to contact her parents but they were unwilling to communicate with her: "They say I dishonored them. I cannot go there and show my face. What difference does it make if I am happy or not? I do not have parents anymore, I have no one . . . you tell me, where can I go?" Her husband told me that her family could cause him harm if he took her to visit them because they would assume that he had eloped with her. Samita (CRB, early 30s, Chamar) likewise had no contact with her family. Her account of how she ended up in Barampur suggested that she was kidnapped as a minor and married off to her husband by someone unknown to her (chapter 2). She had been in Barampur for 17 years (since 1995) and felt that her family in West Bengal probably thought that she was dead and had given up searching for her several years ago. She added,

> I do not know what happened to my mother—whether she is dead or alive. I will die and no one from my natal family will know. In the neighborhood, when I see that a woman's brother has come to visit her, I feel like crying. My son will get married and no one will come from my natal home. It has been so many years yet, even now I cry when I think of my parents. I think about my mother and father a lot . . . I no longer remember where my house is, if I did, I would have left and gone there by now.

The situations of these two women were somewhat different, as Kanchan hoped that resuming contact with her parents would be possible in future (possibly after she had a child), while what emerges in Samita's words is a longing for and loss of a home and relationships that no longer exist.

For cross-regional brides in the first category, the first visit to the *pīhar* took place only after they had had their first child or children, for fear that they might not return (see also Blanchet 2008). For the first visit, their husbands and child or children accompanied them to their *pīhar*. As new brides, cross-regional brides—unlike regional brides—could not avail themselves of frequent visits to their natal homes to ease the process of adjustment. Thus, for them the difficulty of having to adjust in a culturally and linguistically alien context was intensified by isolation from their natal kin. Varsha (CRB, 28, Jat) talked about her experience:

> The first time I went to my natal home was five years after marriage. People in Bengal had started saying to my parents, "You sold her, that is why she does not come to visit, she must have died or they must have killed her." I used to talk to my mother at the phone booth in the village and cry on the phone. She would tell me, "This is what people are saying here, come once so that they believe us." . . . When men go from here to Bengal to marry, they tell the parents that they will bring the daughter to visit twice a year. This is what my husband had said to my parents and he only took me after I had two children. When I go there, my parents cry a lot. They say that they long to see me. My in-laws do not even let me go once in two years.

The first time I met Varsha, she told me that she would visit her natal home next for her younger sister's wedding. Her sister got married ten months later, but she was unable to go, as her in-laws said that they could not afford the train fare. "If they refused to give me the money, where can I get it from?" What emerged in conversations with all cross-regional brides was that both distance and the cost of traveling over long distances made visits difficult. Cross-regional brides said that when they "agreed" to a marriage in UP, they did not fathom how far it was and that they might not be able to return to visit home. As Louisa Schein in her study of interprovincial marriages in China notes, "What they had not comprehended, or bargained for, was the sheer physicality of space that made home so far away" (2005, p. 62). Like Varsha, some other cross-regional brides said that when their husbands went to marry them in their native states, they had assured their parents that they would bring them back to visit twice a year—a promise they did not keep. In fact, when my facilitator Satender (55, Chamar, M) remarked that it was becoming increasingly difficult to bring cross-regional brides and I asked why, he explained that it was for this reason.

Jameela (CRB, 21, Teli) contrasted her situation with regional brides like her *nanad*. "My *nanad* only spends ₹25 when she visits her *pīhar*, while I need ₹2,000–3,000 to go [to Jharkhand]." Mansi (CRB, 33, Chamar) explained that for the poor like her husband, financing a trip to another state was a major expense:

> In so much poverty, how can I spend ₹3,000 to go there? I have been ill for several months. I need to have an ultrasound. I do not have ₹400 for it. Should I spend what my husband earns to feed my children or travel to my *pīhar*?

Mansi shared how she could not visit her *pīhar* as often as she would have liked, yet she felt comforted by the support that she had from her *jethānī*, who took Mansi with her to her own *pīhar* for visits. For cross-regional brides, both money and distance were the reason they could not attend weddings in their natal families. The cost of travel also made it difficult for them to take all their children with them to visit their *pīhar*. It was usually one child or the younger ones who were taken. Some said that their children had never visited their natal homes. Additionally, they outlined reasons, such as widowhood or not being literate, that hampered women from traveling alone. Hemlata (CRB, late 50s, Kumhar), a widow, explained, "I can go if someone takes me there. I cannot even tell if the train goes to Delhi or Guwahati or Mumbai or Meerut. It is not only me who never goes; none of them [other cross-regional brides from Assam] go." Like Hemlata, others, also widows, said that they had not visited their natal families since their husbands died. Even those who were neither widows nor illiterate said that they felt incapable of finding their way independently due to the distance such travel entailed.

Like regional brides, cross-regional brides also explained their inability to visit their native states as being due to the *sās* being ill or elderly and hence unable to work, and having cattle or children that had to be looked after and could not be left in anyone else's care in their absence. Distance, however, created additional difficulties. Jaya (CRB, 45, Jat) explained,

> I cannot leave my *sās*. My *nanad* tells me, "You will go so far and I cannot stay for so many days." Her children are young. If it was near, I could have gone for five days but it will take me five days just to travel to and from Bengal.

Some talked about how they did not learn about the death of a parent (or parents) or siblings until they went back to visit. Even those who did receive news about a death or illness in their natal families either could not go or could go only much later. Additionally, cross-regional brides could not avail themselves of visits to the natal home when they wanted respite from work or fell ill.

As far as visits by the natal kin of cross-regional brides to their *sasurāl* are concerned, most said that someone from their natal family had visited them at least once in Barampur. Of the nine cross-regional brides with married children, only two said that a relative had attended their children's weddings. In such cases, the north Indian prohibition on accepting hospitality at a daughter's in-laws' home could not be followed due to the distances involved, and the brides' natal kin stayed with them when they visited (see also Kaur 2004, p. 2600). During my fieldwork, the widowed mother of one cross-regional bride and the sister of another, both Chamar, were visiting. Of my informants, only one (Jat) cross-regional bride said that her in-laws did not want her parents to visit because they believed that it would reflect poorly on them.

I asked both regional and cross-regional brides about how they got news from and sent news to their natal kin. During my fieldwork, almost every household in Barampur owned a mobile phone. Although it was family or common property, mostly in the control of men rather than a woman's personal communication device (Doron 2012, p. 426), it was highly valued by married women, as it facilitated contacts with the natal home. Regional brides pointed out that even though visits to the natal home became less frequent over time, they used the mobile phone to communicate with their natal families (including their married sisters) at least a few times a month.[2] Even women like Kajri, who had stopped visiting her *pīhar* after her parent's death, said that she talked with her brother using her son's mobile phone. Prior to this, news was communicated through letters. Some non-literate informants said that they relied on others to write letters or often asked an employee at the post office to do so. They also received news when a relative visited on festivals or an in-married woman in Barampur belonging to the same natal village returned from visiting her *pīhar*. If news had to be communicated urgently (such as in case of death), someone was sent from the *pīhar* or *sasurāl*. Elderly informants said that the family *nāi* (barber) was the medium through which news was communicated in the past.

Like regional brides, nine of the 19 cross-regional brides interviewed communicated with their natal families through mobile phones. Some said that they also got news when another cross-regional bride married in Barampur or a neighboring village visited their native states. Some talked about how their husbands sent letters from Barampur and that their fathers or brothers wrote from their natal homes before mobile phones were available. For those like Radha (CRB, early 40s, Chamar), who had been in Barampur for over two decades, visits to the natal home had been the only way to maintain contact before they had mobile phones. Varsha (CRB, 28, Jat) said that when she first moved to Barampur in the early 2000s, the occasional calls she made to her mother from the phone booth in the village had constituted a major expense. This changed dramatically as cheap mobile phones became available and calling charges reduced. Varsha owned a mobile phone that her husband, a truck driver who migrated out for work, had bought for her so she could stay in touch with him. She said that it enabled her to call her mother in Bengal, and she often did so when her *sās* went out and she was able to speak freely with her. For Maya (CRB, mid-40s, Chamar), the mobile phone made her feel as though her kin were closer:

> Earlier we sent letters from here. It took several days to reach them. Yesterday I had a feeling that something had happened there [in Bengal]—maybe my mother died or my father was ill—so I used my son's mobile phone to call my brother. I felt relieved to know that they are all okay.

Other studies similarly note that mobile phones have enabled rural women to be better connected with their natal families (Tenhunen 2014). Radha (CRB, early 40s, Chamar) talked about how she had lost contact with her natal family after her husband died in 2008. She had lost the mobile phone number of her natal family and could not visit them, as there was no one who could accompany her there. There was no other cross-regional bride from her native village married in Barampur and her kin had drifted away. Lakshmi (CRB, late 40s, Kumhar) said that her sons owned mobile phones, but she could not communicate with her natal family because they could not speak Hindi and she could no longer speak Bengali. Likewise, Jaya (CRB, 45, Jat) had no news from her natal family because she had not visited them for over 20 years and could not send or receive letters because her natal kin could not read Hindi. She compared her situation to her *nanad*'s: "She is married in Bijnor [neighboring district] and she has not come to Barampur for two years but she calls and finds out if everything is okay. I cannot even do that." Varsha's (CRB, 28, Jat) older sister was also married in another part of UP (Etah district). She said that she had not seen her sister for 10 years but she spoke to her on the phone. Yet this was becoming increasingly difficult, as her sister now "spoke a different language" (referring to the local dialect of her marital village) and Varsha struggled to understand her.

In sum, visits were highly valued by women whether they married over small or large distances. Visits were crucial for regional brides in the early years, and in the latter, they offered them respite and rest. While visits became less frequent over the life-course, most regional brides maintained some form of contact with their natal kin. As for cross-regional brides, not all were cut off from natal kin contact, yet distance and the cost of travel made visits difficult, and for some, ties with their natal families were eventually severed.

Gift-Giving

As noted by earlier studies, apart from visits, a married woman's ties with her natal kin were sustained through gift-giving. Irawati Karve writes that the giving and receiving of gifts reflects the familial aspect rather than the individual aspect of the transaction—that marriage is very much a relationship between two families rather than between two individuals (1994, p. 63). Given the asymmetrical relationship between wife-givers and wife-takers, gifts move in one direction, with the kin of the bride being "perpetual donors" to the kin of the groom (Vatuk 1975, p. 159) and continues through the course of a woman's married life (Jeffery 1979; Jeffery et al. 1989; Madan 2002; Raheja 1988; Palriwala 1991, 2009). It is for this reason, Patricia Jeffery and Roger Jeffery noted in neighboring Bijnor district, that parents said, "A daughter takes throughout all her life" (1996, p. 188).

Gifts in the early years of marriage are regarded as especially important, as they help to secure a woman's place in her conjugal home (Vatuk 1975). In Barampur, a regional bride received gifts or cash each time she visited her *pīhar* or was visited by her natal kin in her *sasurāl*. A *kothlī* (gifts of clothing and sweets) was given on festive occasions (*Holī*, *Tīj*, and *Bhāī Duj* among Hindus and *Eid* among Muslims). There was *chūchak* (gifts following child-birth) and *bhāt* (given at the marriage of children). This was the practice across both Hindu and Muslim castes. Gift-giving was influenced by a range of factors that included the economic status of the woman's natal family, the years of marriage, and whether a woman's parents were still alive. Women said that in the first year of marriage they received large amounts of gifts, including those for their husband's kin. In the first year, a *kothlī* was sent on all festive occasions, but as the years passed, poor families sent it only once a year.

Status concerns were also significant. Poor Jats, for instance, gave much more to daughters than poor Chamars. Regional brides of different castes said that while women continued to receive gifts on visits even as they grew older and/or were widowed, they stopped receiving a *kothlī* once their mothers died. Also, the pressure to give to daughters was reduced once a woman's *sās* passed away. The amount given also depended on the number of married sisters a woman had, each of whom had to be given a *kothlī*. The amount also depended on what a regional bride's mother received from her own natal family. I was told by several regional brides that they passed on whatever they received from their natal families to their daughters. Birth order and sex of a woman's children were also vital. *Chūchak*, for instance, was usually given for the first two children. If the first two were daughters, then gifts were also given at the birth of a son. In poor families, it was given only at the birth of a boy child. Given the persisting son-preference, the gifts given at the birth of a son far exceeded those given at the birth of a daughter. *Bhāt* was the support extended by a woman's natal kin in the marriage of her children. More was given for a daughter's than a son's wedding to help with the dowry.

Generally, gifts moved in one direction, although there were occasions when this was reversed. When women were married at younger ages, in the period between the wedding and *gaunā*, a woman's marital kin visited her at her *pīhar* on festive occasions with a *kothlī*. This changed once she moved to live in her *sasurāl* with her brother or brothers visiting her with a *kothlī*. On such occasions, she gave them two meters of cloth to reciprocate. Sylvia Vatuk writes, "While recipient status does not entirely rule out the giving of small solicitory prestations to bride-givers (and indeed such are expected on certain occasions), it does mean that the over-whelming balance of presentations should be kept in favor of the bride-taking group" (1975, p. 160), as was the case in Barampur.

With regard to gift-giving in cross-regional marriages, some studies have argued that relations between affines are non-existent in such marriages (Chowdhry 2005) and that "bought brides" do not receive gifts from their natal kin, unlike other brides (Jeffery & Jeffery 1996, p. 231). Ravinder Kaur (2012), in her comparative work on Bengali and Bangladeshi brides, argues that while affinal relationships cannot develop in the case of the latter, for Bengali brides there is sometimes gift-giving and exchange between families. In Barampur, some cross-regional brides said that they received gifts of clothing when they visited their natal homes, but that parents in their native states did not give as much to daughters as parents did in UP. Some, like Varsha (CRB, 28, Jat), dealt with the expectations in a different way. She saved up small amounts from the monthly *kharchā* (expenses) that her husband handed to her and managed to accumulate enough before her visit to her natal home. She told me,

> Here they give a lot to married daughters. The first time I went to my natal home my brother gave me two *dhotīs* [*sārīs*], clothes and shoes for my children, a silver chain for my son, and anklets for my daughter. My parents are very poor. When I went to my *pīhar* the second time, I took ₹2,000 from here and bought a set of clothes each for myself and my children from it. I told my *sās* and husband that my parents gave those gifts.

None of the cross-regional brides, however, had received *chūchak* or a *kothlī* from their natal kin. As far as *bhāt* is concerned, one bride said that she asked her natal kin not to attend her son's wedding, because they would have had to give *bhāt* payments or gifts that they could not afford. Another said that *bhāt* was given by her nephew who came to Barampur from Maharashtra to attend her son's wedding. Faiza (CRB, late 40s, Lohar) talked about how her mother attended her daughter's wedding, but was too poor to give anything. She told me, "My husband bought a few set of clothes to show to the relatives that my mother had given something for the wedding so that no one would say that I am a *Bihārī* [from Bihar] and nothing came from my *pīhar*." As discussed, the gifts a regional bride received from her natal kin depended in part on what her mother received from her own natal family. Faiza explained her inability to provide her daughter with gifts as related both to her husband's poverty but also to not receiving any gifts from her own natal family. She told me,

> When she [daughter] comes to visit she returns *khālī hāth* [empty-handed]. Her *sās* tells her that she has come without anything from her mother's house, but where can we give from? She visits every month and sometimes twice a month. I was forced to give when her son was born because of *sharm*.

Ethnographic studies note that the obligation for parents to provide a married daughter with gifts when she visits often inhibits poor parents from inviting her for frequent visits (Jeffery et al. 1988; Jacobson 1977). Unlike Faiza, other cross-regional brides with married daughters said that they gave gifts to daughters on festive occasions and when they visited. Maya (CRB, mid-40s, Chamar), like some regional brides, pointed out that due to poverty she stopped sending her daughters a *kothli* after the first few years of marriage.

Further, some studies on cross-regional marriage argue that the brides' husbands had not only met the wedding expenses but in some cases continued to extend financial support to the parents of the brides even after the wedding (Chaudhry and Mohan 2011, p. 331; Kaur 2010a, p. 17; Mukherjee 2013, p. 45). In Barampur, cross-regional brides said that neither was the direction of gift-giving reversed (from wife-takers to wife-givers) nor did their husbands extend financial help to their natal families.[3] Varsha (CRB, 28, Jat) said that her brother had asked her husband for money to help with the marriage of her younger sister in Bengal, but that her husband had refused. Similarly, Faiza (CRB, late 40s, Lohar) said that her natal kin had sought her husband's help to rebuild their house in her natal state. She added, "I told them, where can we give from? Even we are poor here." Two cross-regional brides, however, said that after their fathers passed away and their mothers visited them in their *sasural*, their husbands gave their mothers a small sum of money before they returned. In a regional marriage, it would be unthinkable for a woman's natal kin to ask her in-laws for such support. On the contrary, a regional bride's affinal kin often continue to make demands on her natal kin. Urmila (RB, 32, Jat), for instance, told me,

> In my dowry I brought a bed, television, 21 *saris*, 101 utensils, and a gold necklace for my *sas*. I did not bring sets of bedding as is the custom here. My father is poor. He gave whatever he could yet my *sas* said that I did not bring anything. Two years after my wedding my daughter was born. My father sold some of his land and gave whatever my *sas* asked for because her taunts were increasing by the day.

As for Urmila, being taunted for not bringing enough was an experience shared by several regional brides. Likewise, some cross-regional brides too were taunted because their natal kin did not give them anything (a dowry). For regional brides, the expectations were not only with regard to gifts but for meeting other expenses as well. Sarla (RB, 47, Jat) explained, "My in-laws wanted me to rely on my natal kin for everything. They would not even pay for things like my son's school fee or his uniform. They would say, ask your natal kin." Similarly, Kusum (RB, 47, Chamar) said: "When I lived jointly with my in-laws they refused to pay for my treatment when I fell ill. They would say, call your natal kin and ask them to take you."

Thus, in a regional marriage, a woman's natal kin continued to provide her with gifts through the course of her married life. This was not the same for cross-regional brides, although gift-giving was not completely absent. Yet for cross-regional brides, there was some acceptance on the part of their in-laws that their natal kin could not or would not provide. Regional brides, in comparison, were in a more vulnerable position, as the continued demands on their natal kin were based on the expectation that such contributions could enhance the conjugal fund.

Accessing Natal Kin Support

As noted by earlier studies, regional brides could seek the intervention of their natal kin in situations of marital distress. Women described their marital difficulties as related to the husband's infidelity, repeated beating, verbal abuse, dowry-related harassment, the continued demands made by their husbands and/or their affines on their natal kin for goods or cash, and conflicts with the *sās* and/or other affinal women. In such circumstances, regional brides turned to their natal kin for support. Parents, however, had to exercise caution in interfering in a daughter's marital difficulties, as she was now "someone else's property." Women also hesitated in approaching their natal kin, calling them only in crisis situations or, as one informant put it, in *"zyādā pareshānī"* (extreme difficulty) and not for daily conflicts in the *sasurāl*.

In this section, I demonstrate that natal kin relations are an important resource, perhaps the only resource for patrilocally married women, especially in such rural contexts where women's lives are shaped by social dependency and a lack of material or productive property. This context is also devoid of the infrastructure of women's organizations or mediation NGOs (that provide alternative structures of support) described for certain urban contexts (Basu 2015; Grover 2011). Further, women do not have knowledge of the relevant laws (such as the Domestic Violence Act, 2005) and even if they did, it is unlikely that they would have access to state institutions. Thus, as wives, women are likely to find themselves powerless in situations of marital conflict. I argue that natal (mainly male) kin support is then extremely crucial for women to have any bargaining power or agency in situations of marital crisis, and its absence leaves women in an extremely vulnerable position. The agency available to women is an interdependent or relational agency. It is not "individual, purposive and conscious where action reflects choice" (Duncan 2015, p. 3) but rather is one where, as Ian Burkitt argues, "in the exercise of capabilities, capacities and powers we are reliant on others for so much that we ourselves are . . . not able to do." This conceptualization of agency attends to "webs or networks of relations and interdependencies, both interpersonal and impersonal," in which individuals (as interactants) and "their joint actions are embedded" (2016, pp. 323, 335). Further, I show that while cross-regional brides have limited support, even for regional brides natal kin support is not always forthcoming. Through a focus on moments of crisis—marital violence, marital breakdown, and widowhood—I demonstrate both the presence and the absence of support from natal kin.

SEEKING REFUGE: LEAVING TEMPORARILY

In situations of marital conflict, a regional bride's natal kin would first attempt to talk to her husband and in-laws to negotiate better treatment for her. If they failed, the daughter could be taken back to her *pīhar* until her husband or a relative from her *sasurāl* came to collect her and promised better treatment in future. Regional brides pointed out that they could seek refuge at their *pīhar* temporarily but they could not live there permanently. Eventually they had to return to their *sasurāl*. If reconciliation proved impossible, a woman would be remarried; she was highly unlikely to remain at her *pīhar* as an unattached woman due to concerns around her "untied" (hence unregulated) sexuality. Of the 19 regional brides interviewed, nine said that they had sought refuge at their *pīhar* at some stage of their married lives, with the period of refuge varying from two weeks to a year or two, with Sarla (RB, 47, Jat) who spent 16 years at her *pīhar*, being the exception.

When I first met Sarla, she had been married for 32 years. She had been settled in marriage by her parents at the age of 16 to Biram, a farmer, who was 10 years older than her. She described the time she spent at her in-laws' as years of her husband's infidelity, beating, and fighting. She was beaten most often at the provocation of her husband's widowed *chāchī*, with whom her husband had started a sexual relationship shortly after Sarla's wedding. Subsequently, Sarla lived in her *pīhar* for 16 years, returning only for brief durations in that period because she was aware that eventually she would have to return to her *sasurāl*. During my fieldwork, Sarla had been in Barampur for 11 years. When she returned, her brothers negotiated with her in-laws, and her son was given his share of the property. Sarla and her son set up a separate household and she no longer had to live in the extended joint family where she had lived before as a young bride. For the first eight years after returning to Barampur, Sarla had no contact with her husband. She told me that it was possible for her to live at her *sasurāl* without him for so long only because she had the support of an adult son. Her husband started visiting the household that Sarla shared with her adult unmarried son three years prior to my fieldwork. She explained that she resumed contact with her husband and "tolerated" him only because her separated status would hinder her son's marriage prospects.

Likewise, Urmila (RB, 32, Jat) had sought refuge at her *pīhar* on account of "excessive and repeated beatings." She had left her children (two young daughters and an infant son) behind in her *sasurāl* during this period. She explained, "He was having a relationship with another Jat woman . . . so he had a woman and his mother was there to do the housework. Why would he bring me back?" In Barampur, a woman could not return to her *sasurāl* unless she was collected by her husband or someone from the *sasurāl*. Thus, by leaving her children behind, Urmila strategized to ensure her return. She talked about how her husband made several trips to her *pīhar* to collect her, as he needed her to return to care for their children, but her father refused to send her back. She was sent back to her *sasurāl* after six months, on the condition that her husband would reform his behavior. Refuge had enabled both Sarla and Urmila to negotiate a better situation for themselves. This would not have been possible without the support of their natal (especially male) kin and in Sarla's case also an adult son.

Sarla's story would have followed a different trajectory if her only child had been a daughter and not a son. As women's "femaleness and their sexuality is to be controlled by fathers, husbands and sons" (Wadley 1995, p. 4), without a son, Sarla could not have lived in an independent household in her *sasurāl* as a separated woman. The only single-woman households in Barampur were those of elderly sonless widows with married daughters. For Sarla and Urmila, the exercise of agency was made possible through "joint actions" (Burkitt 2016, p. 322) and was "relational with other individuals and collective agents" (Duncan 2015, p. 3). Women like Sarla, and some others, also said that while it was a father or brothers who intervened in a crisis, mothers were particularly valued for the emotional support they provided in trying times.

Refuge was temporary, as the cases above demonstrate, and women like Kripa (75, RB, Jat) explained that a married women had to eventually return to her *sasurāl* for the sake of her parent's *izzat*: "If a woman does not return, people say, look at their daughter *chōr rakhī haī*" (her husband left her), implying that she was responsible for her marital breakdown. Likewise, Sarla talked about feeling shame while living at her *pīhar* because after marriage a woman's rightful place is believed to be her *sasurāl* and not her *pīhar*. She added, "The villagers would ask my mother, 'For how long will she stay here?'" Notions of honor and shame were so deeply ingrained that some women talked about never confiding in their natal kin about their marital troubles. Sakeena (RB, 43, Teli) said that she never considered seeking refuge because it would have resulted in *badnāmī* (a bad reputation) for her parents. She stated, "My mother told me, a woman who cares for her parents' honor does not return to her *pīhar* in a fight. She makes her marriage work through *sabar* [patience, forbearance]."[4] Further, a woman returned and tried to reconcile with her husband because her separated status would affect not only the marriage prospects of her unmarried siblings (Jeffery 2001, p. 18), but also, as Sarla points out, those of her children. Some said that they did not let their parents know about their troubles because they were aware that their parents were too poor to offer refuge for extended periods.

Some regional brides were hesitant to call on their brothers once their parents (especially fathers) passed away. They felt that they would be a "burden" on their brothers due to their economic dependence on them and feared that their brother and his wife would complain about maintaining them. For those like Sarla, who had close bonds with her brothers, this was not a concern, yet she believed that refuge was not sustainable in the long term. She pointed out that as her brothers would age and become dependent on their own children, refuge for her and her son might be called into question. Sarla had sought refuge for over a decade but she said that she was conscious that she and her son had no rights (to parental property) there.

Although post-independence legislation gave a daughter right of inheritance in her parents' property (and from 2005 in the father's share in ancestral property), women do not usually claim their share, for numerous reasons, including avoiding rifts with brothers on whom they may have to rely for support, keeping their natal family prosperous by not claiming their share, and the belief that they were entitled to dowry and gifts rather than house or landed property (Basu 2005, p. 153; Basu 2015; see also Chowdhry 1997). Sarla explained that because she had not disregarded her ties with her brothers by laying claim to what was "theirs," she could continue to draw on their support (material and emotional) even after she returned to Barampur. In her work on a formerly matrilineal caste in the southern state of Kerala, Janaki Abraham (2011) highlights the significance of rights to parental property for a married woman. She shows that a woman's right to inherit property ensured that she could return to her natal home in the event of divorce or separation and even while she was married. Writing on Kerala too, Pradeep Panda and Bina Agarwal (2005) note that property ownership (land or a house) by a woman could both serve as a deterrent to marital violence and provide an exit option. Those like Sarla, who had no such rights, thus, returned to the *sasurāl* as their children (sons) had rights to and could inherit only their fathers' property.

The ability to avail of refuge also changed over the course of a woman's married life. Sarla stressed that not all natal families keep a daughter who returns to them. She talked about her *devrānī* Anita (mid 40s, Jat, F), who, like her, had suffered abuse at the hands of her in-laws and husband. She added, "Anita's mother told her: there are so many corners in the house in your *sasurāl*, no matter what happens, find one corner to die in, but do not come back here." It was not that Anita's mother did not want to support her, for she had previously sought refuge at her *pīhar* for as long as two years. What had changed since was that Anita's father and brother had passed away. Following their death, Anita's widowed mother and sister-in-law were themselves struggling to make ends meet in the absence of a "provider." Her natal home was only 12 kilometers away, yet the death of male kin and financial constraints meant that Anita had "nowhere to go to" in a crisis. Similarly, Kamlesh (RB, late 20s, Kumhar) shared how her brothers were unable to offer her refuge, which she believed would have been available if her father were alive: "My brothers are very poor and have children of their own. My mother is always ill and they spend a lot on her treatment. They cannot say anything to my husband about how he treats me because where will they keep me?" She said that her husband became more violent once he realized that return to her *pīhar* was no longer an option for her. Studies from other parts of India also note that the incidence of both physical and psychological violence is notably less when there is some social support compared with none (Panda & Agarwal 2005, p. 839).

These regional brides found themselves in situations similar to cross-regional brides for whom, while visits were possible, as far as intervention or refuge was concerned, their kin were absent (see Davin 2008, p. 72, on China). As discussed earlier (chapter 5), domestic violence was an experience shared by regional and cross-regional brides alike. It is important to stress here, as Margaret Abraham (2008) does in her work among Indian immigrant women in the US, that abuse is not an experience peculiar to migrant brides but it is heighted by migration distance, as women are cut off from networks of support (see also Mirza 2015; Qureshi 2016 on migrant brides in the UK). Kalawati (CRB, 40, Kumhar) had lost contact with her natal family. She told me,

> He [husband] used to beat me a lot. He would beat me and leave me on the main road and tell me to go away from here. I do not have a *pīhar*, so I cannot go and complain to my brothers. If they were close, even I would go and stay at my *pīhar* for a few days. . . . He [husband] can do whatever he wants. I have nowhere to go to.

The threat of abandonment made cross-regional brides feel particularly vulnerable. As Abraham notes, "frequently the abuser's knowledge that the woman is isolated and that he has no social accountability exacerbates the situation" (2008, p. 315). I heard some regional brides say "There is nowhere to go to," but while for regional brides this suggested the inevitability of return to the *sasurāl*, for cross-regional brides, there was in fact nowhere to go. In her work on domestic violence among cross-regional brides in Haryana, Neerja Ahlawat (2016) found that cross-regional brides who were more educated and geographically closer to their natal homes could leave violent marriages and return to their families. By contrast, my cross-regional bride informants had neither sought refuge nor considered returning permanently to their natal homes. They were clear that it was not an option for them. When parents give daughters in marriage cross-regionally due to compulsions of poverty, keeping a daughter who returns not to visit but to stay was not a possibility.[5] While most regional brides were comparatively better placed, cases such as Anita's and Kamlesh's, described above, suggest that even regional brides could not rely on or assume that natal kin support will be forthcoming.

Leaving Permanently

Jagmati (RB, early 60s, Chamar) remarked, "Even if I could call on them in *pareshānī* [difficulty], for how long can your *pīharwāle* [natal kin] intervene?" Kajri (RB, 35, Jat) described marriage as a "*jāl*" (trap). She added, "Once a woman gets trapped in it, she cannot get out." Both women allude to the limits of natal kin support and the inevitability of return to the marriage and *sasurāl*. As Rajni Palriwala points out, the natal family tends to be a "fall-back," not a source of continuous support (1994, p. 106). Several women stressed that while refuge was available, they could not leave permanently because that would mean a remarriage. What also prevented women from leaving permanently was that it would have meant leaving children (especially sons) behind in the *sasurāl*. Sarla explained, "They [in-laws] would beat him [her son] every day . . . what kind of a life would he have? How could I be happy?" She recalled that she had once sought refuge at her *pīhar* without her son: "For that one and a half years that my son was not with me, I had become really weak . . . I worried and cried all the time . . . I had to return." In fact, some felt that the violence increased after children were born, as husbands felt assured that their wives would feel unable to leave. Even cross-regional brides who were aware that leaving was not an option for them stressed that their difficulties were compounded once children were born. Hemlata (CRB, late 50s, Kumhar) told me, "After children are born, you have to stay. You cannot take someone else's children and live at your *pīhar*."[6] Further, women said that even if they left with their children, it was unlikely that the second husband would accept another man's children or grant them inheritance rights. Thus, women considered their relationships with their children (and also their parents' ability to provide refuge) as vital in making decisions to leave abusive relationships. Agency thus also emerges, as Ian Burkitt argues, "from our emotional relatedness to others" (2016, p. 322).

Kajri did not want to take the risk of finding herself in an even more unfavorable situation. She said, "What if the second one turned out to be worse than my husband. What would I do then?" Similarly, Sarla commented, "If happiness was in my destiny, I would have been happy in this marriage." Women feared that a secondary marriage might mean more peril for them, an observation also made by Shalini Grover (2011) in her work in Delhi. She noted that cautionary discourses about remarriage were widespread. While Sarla had succeed in resisting her parents' attempts to arrange a secondary marriage for her, some like Priti (22, Chamar) could not.

Priti was married in 2009 at the age of 18. During my fieldwork, she was separated from her husband and had been living at her *pīhar* in Barampur for three years. Priti had stayed with her husband, a drug addict, for just over a month following the wedding. Her husband had been in a relationship with his *bhābī*, something Priti learned about soon after she moved to live at her *sasurāl*. For the first year, her in-laws made several attempts at a reconciliation and Priti did return briefly to live at her *sasurāl*. She talked about the violence she experienced and repeatedly told me that she did not want to remarry and would not. Her mother, Kusum (RB, 47, Chamar), asserted that Priti had no choice but to remarry; "After we are dead, her brother will not keep her," she added. Kusum said Priti would be remarried once her court case was settled. In cases of separation and marital breakdown, court intervention was not usually sought.[7] In this instance, though, a case had been filed in court so that the dowry could be retrieved.[8] For Priti's parents, poor brick-kiln workers, arranging a dowry for her first marriage had been an enormous strain and something they could not do again. Kusum was aware that Priti had become a source of gossip among other Chamar families. I heard Chamar informants remark that Priti's parents were "living off her earnings" and hence were "content with keeping her unmarried" (see also Grover 2011). The pressure to remarry her was constant because Priti's two younger sisters were of marriageable age and a dowry had to be arranged for each of them. Her father also talked about investing in house repair and construction so that they could attract a marriage proposal for their son, aged 25, who they believed would soon become "over-age" for marriage. Priti was remarried in October 2014, a year after I completed fieldwork, even though her court case had not been settled. A month later, I learned from her relative that Priti had committed suicide while she was visiting her *pīhar*. I had no further information until a year later. Priti had been married to a much older widower with grown children. This was a dowryless marriage, I was told. She had refused to return to her *sasurāl* when she came to Barampur to visit but was told by her father that they were no longer willing to keep her.

Unlike Sarla, Priti had failed to resist her remarriage because reconciliation with her husband proved impossible. As a young woman without children and at the prime of the sexual and reproductive phase of her life, reputational concerns meant that she could not be left unmarried. While Sarla and most Jat women do not work for a wage, Priti was a Chamar. Following marital breakdown and her return to her *pīhar*, she continued to work in the brick kiln with her natal family as she had as an unmarried woman. Even though she did not have an independent income, she was earning and contributing to the household income. Yet it was not economically viable for separated women like Priti to live independently. As discussed earlier, this was primarily because women (Hindu and Muslim alike) did not according to custom inherit property despite being granted the same rights as men by law. A woman would have to file suit in a court of law to have her inheritance rights upheld. This is something that very few would be able, or even inclined, to do—even if they were aware of the law.

Dowry is believed to be women's share but it cannot provide any long-term economic security. For Muslim women, *mehr* is meant to provide financial security; however, none of my informants had received their *mehr*. Some had forgone it, others were unaware about the amount that had been settled at the time of the *nikāh*, and some others felt uncertain that it could be claimed in the event of marital breakdown (see also Jeffery 2001). Moreover, women have no rights to the marital home after marital breakdown. As Srimati Basu argues, marital breakdown thus exposes the "fundamental economic infrastructure of marriage"—the social and economic constraints related to income and residence (2015, p. 16).

Furthermore, as Sarah Lamb points out, living singly is not "normal," "familiar," or "unremarked" for most in India with living with the family (marital/natal) being key to "normal personhood" (2018, p. 63). Marriage thus becomes the "primary conduit of socio-economic well-being" (Basu 2019, p. 286). What is ideally needed is "spaces outside marriage" as imagined for same-sex relationships (Tellis 2014, p. 346) or for marriage to be an option that is "freely chosen." Basu argues that this would require "broad transformations" that include rethinking women's dependency on marriage, the labor market, and the generational and conjugal transmissions of property and other resources (2015, p. 217).

Natal kin support had made it possible for Priti to leave a violent marriage. Thus, parents did not always insist that daughters remained in or returned to their marital homes when in crisis. Rather, as Kaveri Qureshi notes in her work among British Pakistanis, if the husband was found to be at fault, women were supported to leave. Priti's case illustrates that people who leave marriages do so not as "autonomous individuals, but supported by their kin" (Qureshi 2016, p. 95). Yet at the same time, her case highlights the limits of natal kin support. Even though her family wanted to keep her, they were bound by local normative structures and social pressures (such as gossip that it was her parents' self-interest that delayed her remarriage), and the future marriage of her brother and especially her sisters for whom dowries had to be arranged. In Priti's case, the withdrawal of parental support can be explained by this family's strategies for their other children's futures and their struggle amidst poverty to move forward. Her mother also feared that in future support from her brother may not be forthcoming (as was the case with Kamlesh). When Priti became aware that her parents could no longer keep her or leave her unmarried, the inescapability of her situation made her end her life. Priti's case demonstrates not only that the absence of support can be devastating for a woman but also that natal kin support is at times a *life-and-death matter*.

WIDOWHOOD

A regional bride's natal kin also played a significant role if she was widowed. Widowhood was described as a fate a woman would not wish on anyone, as it meant a life of increased hardship and dependence and for older widows, often neglect, and the loss of power within the household (Lamb 1999, 2000; Wadley 1995). As Martha Alter Chen and Jean Drèze note, the consequences of patrilocal norms are particularly pronounced for widows because the support that a widow receives in her husband's village following his death is extremely limited (1992, p. 4). In Barampur, across the five castes, a widowed woman (particularly young widows) could be given in a *bithānā* (levirate) marriage to her (generally) unmarried *jeth* or *devar* by her natal kin,[9] a common practice in other parts of western UP, Punjab, and Haryana as well (Chowdhry 1994; Kolenda 1992b; Pradhan 1966).[10] She could also be remarried into a different family, although this was less common. In Barampur, widows talked about how they had had to remove all the accessories they wore as married women when widowed but continued to wear one glass bangle if their brother was alive, highlighting the significance of the brother–sister relationship. In her work in a UP village, Susan Wadley found a similar custom—married women wore two sets of toe rings on each foot, "one for the husband and one for the brother." Following the death of either the husband or brother, one set was removed. It was believed that "if the husband's protection, symbolically and economically, is lost, then a brother's protection should replace it" (1995, p. 97).

Generally, a remarriage was arranged for young widows, and not for older widows with grown children. Even for younger widows, considerations such as number of children influenced decisions around remarriage. For poor widows like Kajri (RB, 35, Jat), the experience of widowhood was defined by her struggles of (economic) survival. Her natal home was in a nearby village but contact with her married brother had been minimal after her parents' death. Kajri had expressed fears around remarriage. At the same time, she often mentioned how her life would have been easier if her father were alive or her brother had, after her husband's death, taken the responsibility to give her in marriage to her *devar*. Although Jat women did not usually engage in waged work, poverty and widowhood had forced Kajri to go out to work to feed her eight children. She believed that a marriage to her *devar* would have offered her respite from the hardships of earning a living: "It is only a man who can keep the household running," she told me. Kajri's *devar* had lived in the same household even while her husband was alive. On several occasions, she complained to me, saying "He does not work." I heard several rumors about Kajri's relationship with her *devar*, an oft-repeated one being that he had fathered her youngest child. Over time, Kajri talked more about her situation vis-à-vis her *devar* and she told me, "*usne jabardastī kī*" (he used force/coerced her) on multiple occasions. It became clear that her desire to be tied to him in a socially sanctioned union had less to do with economic dependence and more with marriage conferring social legitimacy and guarding her reputation, despite the violation.[11]

Whether or not a regional bride had one or more sons affected how likely she was to access support from her natal kin. In Barampur, a widow (who was not remarried) usually remained in her *sasurāl* after her husband's death and relied on her son's support. It was considered unacceptable and shameful for a widow to move to live with her married daughter. If she did not have sons, I was told she had the option of returning to live at her *pīhar*. Widows with young children also had the option to return to their natal families, although it was rare for widows to move to live at the *pīhar* permanently, also noted by earlier studies (Chen 2000). This also varied with caste, age, and who was there in their natal families.

For Anita (mid-40s, Jat, F), who only had one married daughter, returning to the natal home was not an option because of her deceased husband's land. She had leased out her (agricultural) land to her *jeth* and was supporting herself with the money she received from it. She believed that she had to remain in her *sasurāl* to ensure that the land remained with her and her daughter would be able to inherit it. Similarly, Jagbiri (RB, 71, Kumhar) was a sonless widow with three married daughters. She had been living alone in Barampur since her husband passed away. She was landless and worked as a helper in a village school. Her brothers had died and there was no one in her *pīhar* she could move to live with. She told me that she was managing on her own but that once she became incapable of caring for herself, she would have no option but to move to live with her oldest daughter in her *sasurāl*. In her opinion, this was acceptable, as her daughter's in-laws were no longer alive. She added that if she had a son, she would have had to remain in her *sasurāl*, irrespective of how he treated her.

Abha (RB, 25, Chamar) was a young widow with four children—two sons and two daughters (all below 10 years). She told me that a *bithānā* marriage was not possible for her, as her husband's brothers were all married and she had a dispute with them. She did not want to be married elsewhere because she felt that a second husband may not accept her children. When I met her, she was living with her elderly widowed *sās* and her unmarried *nanad*. She said that after her *sās* passes away and her *nanad* gets married, she would take her children to live at her *pīhar* until her sons were old enough to support her. Abha's natal kin had played a significant role in safeguarding her interests and those of her minor children by intervening to prevent her deceased husband's brothers from encroaching on her husband's share of parental property. Additionally, after her husband's death, her *nanad* and she could no longer manage brick-kiln work without male support. She was able to rely on her father and her *tāū*'s son, who worked at the brick-kiln with her, and she was thus able to provide for her children.

I met several women who were widowed at young ages because of poverty. Their husbands had died of illnesses that they developed due to work in hard labor occupations. Some cross-regional brides became young widows because they were married to much older men, a concern, some said, that their natal kin had when the men first went to marry them in their native states. Five of my 19 cross-regional bride informants were widowed. Of them, three were living jointly with their married sons. The remaining two, Devanti and Radha, both Chamar and in their early 40s, had married daughters and three sons each (ages 10 years and below). During my fieldwork, Devanti eloped with another Chamar from Barampur and returned a few months later (chapter 5). Following Devanti's elopement, Radha attempted to elope with a Jat (never-married) man from the village but failed and was brought back by her husband's relatives, following which she attempted suicide. Over the course of the year, I saw Radha struggle with extreme poverty, ill health, and trying to provide for her three young children by herself. She talked about not having an alternative to brick-kiln work, but since she no longer had rights to the labor of her married daughters, working in the kilns on her own was not an option. Her brother had visited her twice in Barampur and had stayed for long durations to help with brick-kiln work while her husband was alive, but she had lost contact with her natal family after her husband's death. Her husband's younger brother lived with his family in the adjoining household, but they offered no support. Her situation shed some light on how eloping and arranging a remarriage for herself may, in her perception, have offered some escape from the hardships of earning a livelihood in the absence of support from an adult son, a husband, or natal kin.

OTHER FORMS OF SUPPORT

There were other situations in which regional brides could call on their natal kin. They could, for instance, rely on their natal kin for monetary support for their own or their children's medical treatments or during a husband's unemployment. Khalida (RB, 45, Teli), for instance, talked about the difficulties they faced in paying for her daughter's (cancer) treatment because of poverty and having to turn to her natal family for help: "My in-laws did not even give us a rupee," she remarked angrily. By contrast, most cross-regional brides said that their parents were too poor to offer them any financial support.

Kusum (RB, 47, Chamar) explained how her natal kin came to her aid in the absence of help from people in her *sasurāl*. She said that even though it was shameful for a woman to give birth at her *pīhar*, she returned to deliver her son there, as she had a troubled relationship with her *jethānī* and *sās* and hence had no reliable support in her *sasurāl* post-childbirth. Koyal (RB, 16, Chamar) had called her natal kin when she had to have an abortion (due to complications): "I started bleeding and they [in-laws] told me that they do not have the money to take me to the doctor. I could have died. Then I called my *māmā* and asked him to take me from here. I had the abortion in my *pīhar*." Urmila (RB, 32, Jat) talked about how her husband and *sās* were pressuring her to abort during her third pregnancy for fear that she might give birth to a third girl child. She said that she returned to her *pīhar* to have an ultrasound. She decided to stay at her *pīhar* till her pregnancy was full term and returned to her *sasurāl* to deliver the child, as she had learned that it was a male child. Sarla (RB, 47, Jat) had sought her father's intervention when her husband's younger brother had made sexual advances on her: "My father came to my *sasurāl* and told my in-laws that I was given in marriage only to my husband and that such behavior would not be tolerated." Varsha (CRB, 28, Jat), who found herself in a similar predicament, however, could not call on her natal kin and continued to be harassed by both her (unmarried) *devars*.

Conclusion

For women in this rural context, marriage entailed territorial dislocation and a reconfiguration of their social worlds and social relationships. Their lives came to be located and lived in their affinal villages, where their in-laws, husbands, children, and work were. Yet regional brides were not completely cut off from their natal families, and their ties with their natal kin were sustained through visits and gift-giving. As for cross-regional brides, there was considerable variation with regard to visits, and gift-giving was not completely absent. While the frequency of visits decreased for most regional brides as they advanced in their married lives, generally regional brides were better placed than those cross-regional brides who either had lost contact with their natal kin or had had no contact at all since they got married. Within the context of their day-to-day lives, regional brides did not have contact with their natal kin any more than cross-regional brides did, but natal kin contact was highly significant if we focus on the reasons and situations in which women called on their kin for support. Knowing that they could call on their natal kin gave most regional brides in Barampur assurance and a greater sense of (potential) rescue, particularly in situations of marital violence, breakdown, and widowhood. The significance of natal kin support for a married woman must, thus, not be understated.

A focus on cross-regional marriage has helped to demonstrate how the vulnerabilities experienced by married women are heightened by the distance from their natal homes because they cannot seek intervention or refuge when in crisis. Yet the comparison between regional brides and cross-regional brides has also enabled me to show that natal kin support is complicated even for regional brides, with relative proximity being only one determining factor. I have shown that regional brides and cross-regional brides may be similarly disadvantaged by poverty, as it denies them opportunities for refuge or return in marital difficulty. Further, for cross-regional and regional brides alike, their relationships with their natal families change over the course of their married lives. The circumstances in which natal kin intervened were varied. Family strategies for the future, community norms and pressures, the composition of the natal family, the gender of children, caste, poverty, livelihood concerns, and rights in the natal home influenced the duration and kind of support. Ideologies of honor and shame, the belief that a married woman's rightful place is in her husband's home, and the awareness that parents were too poor to offer support and that the only alternative to leaving permanently was remarriage and leaving children behind prevented some from even seeking the intervention of their kin. These factors combined in complex ways to determine the extent to which support was available. Over time, the death of parents and the marriage of brothers marked a change in women's relations with their natal families. The absence of male kin, especially fathers, left some regional brides without support. For such regional brides, like for cross-regional brides, their natal kin were absent as far as support was concerned. The absence of support intensified women's difficulties.

In the context described here, women inherit neither their husbands' nor their fathers' property. Nor do they have an independent income that provides them with economic independence or the right of abode in the marital home in the event of marital breakdown. A life outside of marriage is not sustainable or an option available to them. They are dependent on the protection of a father, husband, or son for their survival. Women in Barampur do not have access to NGOs, women's courts, or state institutions. It is, then, only the support that a married woman has from her natal kin that can provide her with an option to leave, even if only temporarily. This may enable her either to negotiate a better situation for herself, or simply provide her with the space to recuperate before returning to her marriage. Women's agency thus unfolds within "manifold social relations" (Burkitt 2016, p. 336)—it is highly dependent on their relations to others, both their personal relationships to their families and the caste and economic relations in which they are embedded.

Conclusion

This book has discussed what an ethnography of a rural north Indian context tells us about contemporary marriage and its gendered implications. It has addressed moral panics and widely accepted stereotypes about the "low status" and "plight" of women from "poor areas" who marry far away in bride-deficit culturally distinct contexts. It has done so by problematizing *marriage itself*. By integrating discussions from the global north and global south, this book proceeded as a critique of marriage—an institution "fused with trouble and strife" (Basu 2015), as the words of Jaya and Sarla, in the opening page of the book, captured so succinctly. It adopted a comparative approach to interrogate the lived experiences of women who *moved for marriage*, regionally and cross-regionally, to become brides in patrilineal, patri-virilocal marriages in a context of poverty and inequalities of gender and caste. While recognizing where geographic distance and regional origins make a difference, such an approach made it possible to recognize continuities in the lived experiences of regional brides and cross-regional brides, enabling a more nuanced understanding of the gendering of marital relationships and the lived realities of all in-married women within this rural context.

Carried out in a village in India's most populous state, this study brought back into focus not only the *rural* but also a political economy perspective to highlight the centrality of marriage that remains a compulsory life transition as also an economic necessity for women. I demonstrated that despite changes that have occurred over the last decades of the 20th century and into the 21st century, there have been no fundamental shifts within gender relationships. In this concluding chapter, I draw together the arguments of different chapters in relation to the themes of inequalities, marriage migration, intimacy and relationality, and social change around which this book has been framed.

Inequalities

This ethnography focuses on an adverse context. Within this patrilineal, patri-virilocal context, the long-standing preference for the male child and disfavor of daughters across castes (Hindu and Muslim, although to varying degrees), along with a desire to limit family size, have led to increased attempts at daughter elimination. Even Dalits, among whom gender relations have been more egalitarian compared to upper castes, now display son preference and daughter disfavor. Female infanticide, a practice adopted in the past, may have declined but discrimination through neglect and the use of sex selection to abort female fetuses have continued despite legislation that made sex-selective abortion illegal. Marked imbalances in the sex ratios have been one consequence of such practices and are regarded as contributing to a shortage of brides in India's northern and northwestern states that has made marriages between men in these bride-deficit states and women from the less prosperous eastern and southern parts of the country increasingly common.

I have addressed why, given the long history of masculine sex ratios in western UP, the inability of some men to marry within local contexts is spoken of as a situation peculiar to the contemporary context. I highlighted the limitations of explanations based on demographic factors alone and argued that marriageability needs to be linked to wider changes in political economy (chapter 2). While analysis by demographers has been vital in grasping the extent of the gender imbalance (see Guilmoto 2018), empirical studies, such as this one, have shed light on how communities are responding to demographic shifts. I showed that changing criteria for what qualities make an "eligible" and "desirable" husband have created challenges for growing numbers of men (chapters 1 and 2). Caste differences in livelihoods, education, salaried employment, and individual characteristics have become crucial alongside sex ratios, with some men being more adversely affected than others by bride shortages and being then left out of local marriage markets.

While some failed to marry, others adopted different strategies in response to the difficulties confronted. These included forms of exchange marriage, payment to the parents of the bride (instead of dowry), relaxation in certain "rules" of marriage, and cross-regional marriage. I found that as men and their families had devised ways to marry, there appeared to be little change in attitudes toward the girl child or attempts to correct the abysmal sex ratios, even among those who acknowledged that the impact of this will continue to be felt in the foreseeable future. Indian state and central governments, on their part, have intervened through various policy initiatives and girl child schemes (see Palriwala 2016). Prominent among these is the *Beti Bachao, Beti Padhao Yojana* (Save the Daughter, Educate the Daughter) campaign, launched in 2015 by the Bharatiya Janata Party (BJP)–led government. Some, however, note that campaigns such as these have been inadequate and had little effect (EPW Engage 2019; Kaur 2020). The way forward, as Rajni Palriwala (2016) argues, must involve efforts at addressing the factors that encourage son preference and daughter aversion and the institutional structures that lend support to these practices.

There is now a growing body of literature, mostly on India and China, that focuses on the consequences of a "male surplus." The long-term implications of gender imbalances, especially involuntary bachelorhood, however, remain to be seen and could be an area for future research. The following are some questions that need addressing: in rural contexts such as this, as families move toward nuclearization and in the absence of joint resources keeping brothers together, there might be less incentive to accommodate the unmarried, especially the landless and unemployed. How would this impact the future of care and living arrangements? Unlike in western contexts, the labor intensity of women's work makes solo living difficult in rural contexts such as this. Moreover, it is considered shameful for men to perform what are regarded as "female tasks" (e.g., cooking, cleaning). If families become unwilling to accommodate never-married men, will there be an increase in solo living? How would solo living work for men if women's contribution to paid work is essential to the sustenance of households? How would living alone work for men who need someone, usually women, to take care of domestic tasks? Further, in a cultural context where the elderly are cared for by families, in the absence of alternative or institutionalized care arrangements, who will care for aging bachelors?

This book not only has discussed how sex ratio imbalances (combined with others form of "disadvantage") have affected men's ability to marry but also has contributed to the discussion on the moral panic around the rise in "deviant" behavior as a consequence of this inability to marry (chapter 2). Additionally, I have attended to the implications of demographic imbalances for women and gender inequalities. Contrary to the predictions made by some demographers (Das Gupta & Li 1999), bride shortages have not placed women in a more favorable position. It has not resulted in greater valuation of women and greater choice for them in mate selection. It has led to neither a decline in dowry nor in a rise in dowryless marriages within the regional context. What we find instead is an escalation in dowries in hypergamous marriages, given the scarcity of "eligible" grooms. Even in isogamous marriages, dowry persists across castes, which continues to perpetuate daughter disfavor. There have been some positive changes with more women going into higher education (among some castes) and a rise in the age at marriage, yet this is also feeding into the persistence of dowry. Furthermore, education for women is not aimed at gaining employment or an independent income that may provide them with more bargaining power but rather is seen as a desirable criterion for marriage (chapter 1).

In cross-regional brides' native states too, the practice of dowry disadvantages women. The inability of poor parents to provide a dowry results in marriage in a distant place, which heightens the vulnerabilities experienced by women in patrilocal marriages (chapter 7). Other factors that motivated marriage migration decisions included difficult family situations or insecure dependence on family members and "individual attributes" (e.g., disability, previous marriage). Poverty, however, was dominant in most accounts and draws attention to the issue of wide regional disparities. Yet few cross-regional brides said that the desire for upward mobility ("spatial hypergamy") influenced marriage migration decisions, as some scholars have found for both India and China (chapter 2). Crucially, while a cross-regional marriage enabled brides' families to fulfill their obligation of marrying their daughters and escape dowry, this led to cross-regional brides being perceived as *mol kī* in the receiving community.

This raised the issue of distinguishing between how terms are used in local contexts and how they are defined academically: can cross-regional marriages be categorized as "bride-buying" according to anthropological understandings of marriage payments? Some NGO reports, media accounts, and academic studies have described women in cross-regional marriages as "purchased wives." Likewise, some studies on international cross-border marriages have portrayed all women in such marriages as victims of trafficking and assumed that they have no agency in (marriage) migration decisions. In investigating why women become cross-regional brides, I have challenged these simplistic commentaries by showing that apart from a few cases, there is evidence of the exercise of agency within constraint. I argued that economic circumstances may push women to marry far away, but in the process they may secure a life with less extreme poverty. Family situations may give them little choice but to enter a cross-regional marriage, but it did offer escape from insecure dependence on family members. "Individual characteristics" might make cross-regional marriage the only option, but some did assert their agency in "choosing" that over their other limited options (chapter 2).

The association of such marriages with trafficking also stems from their being commercially mediated. In contrast to regional marriages, mostly arranged through networks of kin (chapter 1), cross-regional marriages were spoken of as involving "go-betweens" and payments made by the groom (instead of receiving a dowry) and were hence construed as the "sale" of women in keeping with textual and Brahmanical understandings, irrespective of what the payments entailed and to whom they were made. The discussion of post-marital experiences of cross-regional brides shows that they were not all forced into "sexual slavery," and, apart from one case, not "sold and resold." They were accorded the status of wives and their children were accepted as legitimate. The brides and the children of such unions were granted the caste status of their husbands and fathers, respectively (chapters 3 and 4).

The "incorporation" of women of unknown caste statuses and their children into their husbands' castes does not indicate the weakening of caste within this regional context, however. Cross-regional alliances suggest that deviation from the endogamy norm is allowed insofar as it does not challenge status hierarchies within the local context and the social order remains intact. The distance between the incoming brides' natal and marital homes helps maintain ambiguity and hence silence regarding their caste statuses. Women of unknown and "differential" caste statuses are thus accommodated into caste-bound rural communities, with such marriages rationalized on grounds of *majbūrī*. This has not been accompanied by an observable rise in inter-caste (arranged) marriages within the regional context. In fact, as Ravinder Kaur (2010b) also notes for Haryana and UP, the import of brides from other states has been accompanied by a tightening of control over local women and punishments for those who self-arrange their marriages. As the bases of caste dominance are challenged, due to factors such as a decline in systems of patronage, fragmentation of land, unemployment, some expansion of education and employment for previously excluded groups (such as Dalits due to reservation), the rise of low castes within politics, and inheritance rights for women (even if they seldom lay claim to parental property), control of marriage should be seen as one form of caste assertion that represents an anxiety around maintaining status (see also Chowdhry 2007 on Haryana). Thus, the enforcement of endogamy through parentally arranged marriages continues to ensure the persistence of caste in rural north India (chapter 1).

Furthermore, while the children of cross-regional couples inherit the caste status of their fathers, the mother's caste status is not entirely irrelevant and did emerge as an issue in the negotiation of their marriages. I have made a case for bringing into focus the class status of fathers that reveals a continuing cycle of poverty and disadvantage that may in part offer insights on the marriage possibilities of sons of cross-regional couples. While the marriage of children of cross-regional couples is an area that I have explored in some detail elsewhere (Chaudhry 2019b), it remains a subject for future research.

Although the cross-regional brides' regional origins are overlooked when the alliance is made, some cross-regional brides *do face* discrimination in receiving communities. Like regional brides, they were at times verbally abused by other women. For them, however, the abuse served as a reminder of where they came from or that a payment had been made for them (e.g., *Bangāl kī* [from Bengal], *mol kī* [bought wife], *pūrabni* [from the east]) (chapters 5 and 6). Some were derided for their darker skin, which served as a proxy of caste, or their linguistic abilities (chapter 4). Some women said that none of this had ever been said to their faces but that they were aware that they were spoken of in this way. While mindful *not to underestimate* the significance of these experiences, I wish to emphasize that in Barampur, cross-regional brides did not face caste discrimination and "othering on a *daily basis*" (emphasis mine) as has been argued for Haryana by Reena Kukreja (2018b: 383). This discrimination did not constitute the major part of their lived experiences. As for most regional brides, cross-regional brides' day-to-day lives were dominated by concerns of poverty and livelihood, illness, conflicts with the *sās* or other affinal women, and domestic violence, as the bulk of my ethnography has demonstrated (chapters 4 to 7). Reflecting on my fieldwork, at times I forget whether I was speaking to a regional bride or a cross-regional bride. Much of the information I collected about discrimination was in response to specific questions I asked.

Indeed, my focus on post-marital experiences reveals that cross-regional brides have much in common with regional brides and that recognizing not only differences but also these similarities better reflects the lived realities of all in-married women within this rural context. When exploring aspects of married women's everyday lives, such as decisions around work, factors other than regional origins were far more significant. For regional and cross-regional brides alike, composition of the household and age and seniority were crucial in decisions around household work. Caste, stage in the life-course, widowhood, and poverty were vital in decisions about women's waged work (chapter 4). The conjugal relationship was highly inegalitarian and marital violence (coerced sex, beating, verbal abuse, and control over childbearing decisions) was an experience shared by many of my regional and cross-regional bride informants alike (chapter 5). Crucially, what was significant with regard to women's ability to exercise agency was not whether they were regional or cross-regional but rather seniority that offered all women the possibility of eventually sharing power within their households (chapter 4). Age and seniority also offered some women, irrespective of regional origins, the possibility to evade violence and access support from other women as their mobility increased (chapters 5 and 6).

Violence within marriage was normalized across castes and needs to be located within broader contextual factors that made all women susceptible to violence to varying degrees. Violence against wives was attributed to factors such as alcohol, suspicion, the intergenerational transmission of violence, provocation by affinal kin, and male insecurities and masculinities continuously threatened by precarious livelihoods for which women had to bear the brunt (chapter 5). Violence within the family was not limited to wives but also extended to young unmarried women who asserted choice in marriage through their inter-caste or inter-religious liaisons (chapter 1).

This enforcement of marital norms through violence in the northern and northwestern states is not a recent development (see Chowdhry 1994, 2007). Additionally, in the contemporary context, the regulation of marriage is being increasingly strengthened since the electoral victory of the Hindu nationalist BJP nationally (in 2014 and again in 2019) and in the UP state assembly elections (in 2017). There have been, for instance, widespread campaigns since 2014 in villages and towns of western UP by Hindutva organizations centering on "love jihad"—allegedly an organized conspiracy, whereby Muslim men trick and aggressively convert vulnerable Hindu women to Islam through marriage. Charu Gupta argues that this "campaign against love" has multiple layers that include concerns around Hindu female purity, attempts at invoking Hindu male prowess while simultaneously demonizing Muslim men, fabricating fears of a declining Hindu population, constructing a homogenous Hindu identity and nation by unifying a society sharply divided along caste-class lines, and reinstating family patriarchies. Furthermore, it reveals "deep-seated anxieties of Hindutva politics regarding female free will, the subversive potential of love, pliable and ambiguous religious identities, and syncretic socio-religious practices, which continue to exist in different forms" (2016, pp. 292–293).

In 2017, Uttar Pradesh's BJP-led government set up "Anti-Romeo Squads" with the aim of keeping a check on "eve-teasing" and harassment to deal with the growing violence against women in the state. These squads, activists argue, have been used instead to police and hound young men and women in public spaces (Wire Staff 2017). "Love jihad," however, pre-dates

BJP's electoral success in 2014 (see Gupta 2016). This alleged conspiracy also came to be used in the dominant narrative to account for the violent attacks on Muslims in neighboring Muzaffarnagar and Shamli districts a few weeks after I completed fieldwork in 2013. Their impact was felt in several western UP districts, including in Baghpat. This deployment of communal politics that placed women's "honor" at its center successfully undid histories of shared living between Hindus and Muslims in the region over centuries (see Mander et al. 2016)

I have also drawn attention to the violence perpetrated by dominant-caste men on lower-caste and Muslim women in the village. Dalit women in particular spoke of this threat of violence as a regular feature of their lives. What appeared to be specific to the present context and to the younger generation of Jat men was the harassment of Jat women by young Jat men linked to their poor marriage prospects. Yet the narratives focusing on this also revealed patriarchal attitudes that shifted the blame onto the women for inviting the violence. This may have to do with more young women becoming increasingly visible in public spaces and the growing anxieties around the control of female sexuality (chapter 2). As with the control over marriage, violence against women in public spaces has to do with public assertions of dominant status as also with assertions of masculinities that are enacted through various hierarchies of generation, caste, class, and gender. Crucially, violence in the public domain feeds into the private and vice versa.

As far as reporting violence is concerned, women in Barampur did not have knowledge of the relevant laws (e.g., The Domestic Violence Act, 2005) or access to the police and courts. Moreover, as Nisha Srivastava has also noted for rural UP, in cases of domestic violence, registering a case with the police is regarded more of an "aberration" than a practice because the police are known to be unsympathetic to women (2002, p. 14). State officials tend to share the widely held beliefs that domestic violence is a "private" matter and justified as a means of disciplining. In cases of rape, lower-caste and Muslim men find themselves helpless in the face of those who wield power and on whom they may be dependent for their survival. Jats also tend to control the (elected) *panchāyats* and have a dominant role in or links with the bureaucracy and police in this part of UP (see also Jeffrey 2010, pp. 53–63). On one occasion, I witnessed the mother of one of the young men accused in a gang rape pleading with the Jat village headman to use his clout to clear her son's name so that he could go ahead with taking the test to join the UP Police! In order to understand why violence against women is so endemic in rural contexts such as this, we thus need to look at the wider structures of patriarchal, caste, and class dominance, communal politics, and norms and attitudes that not only support but also legitimize this violence.

Marriage Migration

I return to the three implications of the rules of patrilineal, patri-virilocal marriage for women's autonomy, outlined by Rajni Palriwala and Patricia Uberoi (2008), in the light of the material presented in the book. I will also highlight the areas of difference between regional and cross-regional brides. First, regarding women's inheritance rights as daughters, in Barampur, Hindu and Muslim regional brides alike did not claim and inherit parental property, despite legislation which has made it possible for them to do so. This meant that in cases of marital breakdown, returning to the natal home permanently was not an option for them, which made it difficult for them to leave their marriages. Even in instances where there was no parental property to lay claim to, as married women had no rights in their natal home, the cost of maintaining them meant that their fathers and/or brothers were either unable or unwilling to sustain them for the long term on return. Dowry was used as a rationale for excluding women from inheritance rights, yet it offered them no long-term economic security. Return to the natal home permanently also meant a remarriage and leaving children behind, which women feared given negative experiences of their (primary) marriages. Moreover, while marriage formalizes the transfer of rights and maintenance from a woman's natal home to her affinal home, women did not claim matrimonial property and had no rights to the matrimonial home in the event of marital breakdown (chapter 7).

Second, as for an in-married woman's unfamiliarity with the local customs and family traditions of her husband's family, marriage marked a critical life transition for regional and cross-regional brides alike as they were all uprooted from their homes and natal families and had to undergo a difficult process of adjustment in a new home among strangers. The move, whether over small or large distances, was "deeply felt" (Qureshi and Rogaly 2018, p. 212). The process of adjustment was far more difficult for cross-regional brides, however. They had to undergo a re-socialization process of sorts—learning a new language and adopting the new food habits, dress, and way of life of a culturally alien context. They had to shed all markers of a pre-marital identity; for some this included a name change. Furthermore, unlike regional brides, they could not benefit from frequent visits to their natal homes in the early years in order to counter their isolation and ease the process of adjustment.

Regional brides continued to feel ambivalent about incorporation and belonging (to either the *pīhar* or *sasurāl*) until they became the mothers (of sons), and this sense of ambiguity reduced as they advanced in their married lives, becoming matriarchs of their households and firmly embedded in their marital villages. As for cross-regional brides, they were incorporated in some senses, yet for them, the question of belonging was more complicated: it was negotiated with an understanding that they were not fully accepted by those in their marital communities. Even though they spoke the language and dressed like UP women, they were perceived as different. These perceptions were shaped less by the fact that they looked different (e.g. because of their facial features) and more by assumptions that they came from "outside" or "faraway"—that they belonged to different (lower) castes and that they had not been "given away" in a "proper" marriage with a dowry (chapters 3 and 4).

Third, in assessing the implications of geographic distance for accessing natal kin support, I have highlighted how the tyranny of distance reduces the amount and type of support that cross-regional brides can access from their natal kin. While natal kin contact is neither obtained nor sought by regional brides on a day-to-day basis, natal kin ties are sustained through visits that offer some respite from work and by gifts that help enhance the conjugal fund and secure a woman's place in her *sasurāl*. Natal kin support becomes particularly crucial in moments of crisis as it alone provides possibilities for intervention and refuge. Cross-regional brides had access to neither. While cross-regional brides did maintain contact with their natal homes through phone calls, letters, and infrequent visits, distance cut them off from networks of support. This intensified their vulnerabilities in situations of marital violence, breakdown, and widowhood, an observation also made for transnational marriages (Abraham 2008; Mand 2008; Mirza 2015; Qureshi 2016). Additionally, those who could no longer speak their first languages found it difficult to sustain communication with their natal families. For some, ties were severed over time due to distance.

Crucially, however, even regional brides could not assume that natal kin support would be forthcoming. Natal kin were not a source of unending support because a married daughter's rightful place was believed to be in her husband's home. Extending the north–south contrast (Dyson & Moore

1983; Trautmann 1981) to regional and cross-regional marriages suggests that (relative) proximity (in regional marriage) did not *guarantee* support. Importantly, it was poverty and changes over the life-course (e.g., death of male kin, particularly fathers), and not geographic distance, that made for the absence of natal kin support for the north India (regional) bride (chapter 7).

Intimacy and Relationality

As earlier writing on South Asia has noted, an understanding of the conjugal relationship cannot be gained without an understanding of its embeddedness within a wider network of kinship relationships because affinal kin attempt to prevent the development of intimacy between husband and wife. Yet I have argued for bringing the conjugal couple into focus through the use of the analytic of intimacy. This has enabled me to provide valuable insights on the texture of the conjugal relationship. Through cross-cultural comparisons, I have shown how intimacy develops in relationships made between strangers, i.e., in arranged marriage contexts, and *can exist even in violent relationships* and remain with a modicum of support (*sāth*) and dependence. The aim here is not to celebrate the small everyday "practices of intimacy" as positive for gender relations overlooking the violence and the inequalities that come to define the relations between spouses. Rather, through my discussion of *sāth denā* (supportive relationships), I argue for recognizing their significance in offering women ways to cope and endure in what are often very difficult circumstances and for which escape routes are practically nonexistent (chapter 5). At the same time, I have also argued for understanding endurance not as passive acceptance but as a particular form of gendered agency distinct from western ideas of women's agency. I have highlighted the necessity of incorporating the specificity of cultural contexts in writing about intimacy, with a view to offering an alternative to Euro-American understandings.

My focus on the conjugal couple has shown that while women desired and yearned to be supported by their husbands, the conjugal relationship was generally not their most intimate relationship. Yet married women were not completely isolated and without support. Through a focus on women's relationships beyond the couple (chapters 6 and 7), I have described a rather different reality from that presented in accounts that have argued that cross-regional brides have no contact with their natal kin and that they are regularly discriminated against and isolated from others in their affinal homes (Blanchet 2008; Chowdhry 2005; Kukreja 2018a, 2018b; Kukreja & Kumar 2013). In everyday contexts, cross-regional and regional brides gradually built relational lives with their children and other women in their marital villages, with stage in the life-course being crucial. Importantly, some cross-regional brides forged the closest ties with regional brides. As for natal kin, regional brides did not and could not call on them on a daily basis, although their natal kin were a vital source of support for them. In a context of material and social dependency, only a woman's natal kin could provide a woman the option to leave marriage, even if only temporarily.

My findings support Lynn Jamieson's (1998) argument that intimacy is multi-dimensional. In women's relationships with their husbands, children, natal kin, and other women, a mix of dimensions—sharing, trust, emotional support, practical care, empathy, affection, and material support—were important in generating and sustaining closeness in the relationships. Jamieson has argued that academic and popular discussions often underplay the performing or receiving of practical care as a "practice of intimacy" (2011, p. 3). In the cultural context described here, where the expression of affection (whether between husband and wife or mother and child) is constrained, acts of practical care become indicative of love and particularly crucial in developing intimacy. Through my ethnography, I have shown that women confide the stresses and strife of conjugality with others—their adult children (mostly daughters), female friends, and natal kin. There is thus an outlet and support for women's grievances that allows them to cope with their marriages. These other relationships thus *enable* conjugality (chapters 6 and 7).

I have tried to unpack certain tropes about what marriage means through my discussion of *sāth denā* and endurance, and I drew on similar discussions in the literature on *sabar* (patience), *bhada* (suffering), adjustment, *sūkh dūkh* (joys and sorrows), and *nibhānā* (as the "doing" of life itself) (chapter 5). In reflecting on why this clutch of ideas keeps recurring in discussions of South Asian marriage, it is useful to think about the social construction of marriage not only in terms of dominant ideas and ideologies (upper-caste, Brahmanical—marriage as the "gift of a virgin," etc.) but also in terms of ideas about the marital relationship itself. In these ideas, we see the coming together of the wider political economy of marriage that women enter unequally—economically, socially and symbolically—and the meanings that women attribute to marriage. Marriage is *zarūrī* (necessary/compulsory), as it is a *majbūrī* (compulsion) with the onus being on women to keep marriage intact ("*nibhānā partā hai*") through endurance, patience, sacrifice and adjustment. Only if they do so will support be forthcoming from their natal kin. If the relationship breaks, it may also jeopardize support from other relationships—children and other women. Thus, ideas of care, affect, and intimacy (reflected in women's talk of *sāth denā*), the desire for the conjugal relationship to be the most significant relationship, the lack of exit options, and the reification of the need to cope with marriage, whether good or bad, all come to shape the gendered experiences of marriage.

Social Change

A spate of recent writings on marriage and intimacies in India has explored aspects of change. These have focused on urban spaces, metropolitan cities, and the educated elite, however, with the existing accounts of rural women's lives mostly published in the 1980s and 1990s. By contrast, this book returns to the *rural* and assesses change. Thinking about how wider social and economic transformations are impacting on families and gender relations in Barampur, social change is visible in improved means of transport and communication, access to higher education, especially for women of some castes, a shift away from agriculture to non-farm employment, rural-urban migration for work, and access to new technologies and consumer goods—ultrasound machines, televisions, the internet, and mobile phones.

While Jat farmers in this part of UP benefited through the Green Revolution, a range of factors that included land fragmentation over time and poor returns from agriculture made dependence on agriculture alone unsustainable for the Jats, who started investing in the education of their children and exploring alternative non-farm employment. Higher education, however, did not result in salaried employment for a large proportion, as liberalization failed to create adequate employment, with UP in particular lagging behind in this regard (Jeffrey 2010; Srivastava & Ranjan 2016). This has resulted in out-migration and daily commuting for work to cities such as Delhi and also in male unemployment. For significant numbers of Muslims, Dalits, and intermediate castes such as Kumhars, a dissociation from traditional caste occupations and the lack of available employment in agriculture for a large part of the year have meant migration for (seasonal) work at the lower end of the informal economy, induced by poverty (e.g., in the brick kilns). This is similar to the observation made for the state as a whole: "Though there has been a substantive shift of workers from agriculture and allied activities, most of such opportunities are casual in nature and fetch low income to a large majority of workers in the state. The incidence of distress-induced migration has increased over the years" (Mamgain 2019, p. 50). These livelihood strategies have a significant bearing on men's ability to marry (chapter 2).

As for technology, the ultrasound technologies that became available in India after the mid-1980s have contributed to the declining sex ratios in the region, as sex selection has been increasingly used to limit family size (chapter 2). Mobile phones have played a significant role in facilitating contact between married women and their natal kin, especially for cross-regional brides, for whom visits had been the primary and only means to maintain contact previously (chapter 7). For regional brides, mobile phones have not only allowed more frequent contact with their natal kin but also enabled them to play a more active role in negotiating marriages by making enquires about potential brides and grooms from their extended networks (chapter 1). Bollywood films and digital access through mobile phones and the internet have provided exposure to knowledge, shaping ideas of romantic love and giving rise to new desires and other ways of being. They have opened up greater opportunities for young people to pursue pre-marital sex, love, and courtship within a gender-segregated context. Young marriageable women articulated ideas of what they desired in a spouse, something that older women thought unimaginable for their generation. Some younger informants also expressed their desire for a "love" or choice marriage even though they were aware that these desires would not be realized. Mobile phones have also made possible courtship-like practices for soon-to-be spouses (chapter 1) and allowed women to keep in touch with migrant husbands (chapter 5). They are also being used by men to access pornography that is believed to be feeding into violence against women (chapters 2).

There has also been a rise in the age at marriage for both men and women, with the earlier practice of marriage at a young age and cohabitation a few years later no longer being maintained. The rise in age at marriage has less to do with more women going into higher education, as suggested by some unmarried Jat women, and is largely related to factors such as parents not being able to afford wedding expenses and arrange a dowry, the search for an "eligible" groom continuing for years, and young men gaining employment to attract a marriage proposal. Crucially, factors such as a delay in marriage, higher education, and/or salaried employment have not led to a greater say in marital decisions for young men and women, whether in primary or secondary marriages. Self-initiated relationships, even when intra-caste, do not culminate in marriage (chapter 1). There has been some weakening in certain social practices of caste in the village with regard to access to common village spaces and entry into upper-caste households, but this has not extended to greater flexibility in marriage. Parentally arranged marriage remains the norm in this rural context, tied to the reproduction of caste and patriarchy. As in urban contexts, marriage bureaus and professional matchmakers have appeared in this rural context, and networks created through labor migration have widened the marriage circle, yet marriages continued to be primarily arranged through kin and caste ties.

Writing on rural UP two decades ago, Nisha Srivastava (2002) concluded that with economic development, violence against women had increased. My observations from Barampur present a bleak picture. Daughter aversion persists, women's work continues to be devalued, the practices of purdah and dowry are still intact, women have limited control over their fertility, and violence remains a day-to-day experience for many, with emotional asymmetries continuing to define the marital relationship. New opportunities and new technologies demonstrate that the rural is not frozen in an unchanging past, yet what this ethnography has shown is that women still do not have opportunities to make "strategic life choices" (Kabeer 1999). Marriage as an institutional relationship has changed minimally. The political economy of work and property has meant continuing dependence for women on men (fathers/brothers, husbands, and sons). Marriage remains compulsory, and alternative structures of support (e.g., living arrangements with non-kin) are unavailable. Spaces outside marriage—for women to remain unmarried, men and women to pursue homoerotic desire, or women to leave marriage and remain as separated or divorced women or live alone—are unrealizable. Sadly, inequalities have not lessened but persist and have taken on new forms.

Appendix 1

Castes in Barampur (Source: Village Survey)

Hindu castes	Muslim castes
Badhai	Dhobi
Bairagi	Faqir
Bania	Lohar
Bharbuja	Neelgarh
Brahmin	Teli
Chamar	
Dakaut	
Darzi	
Dhimar	
Jat	
Jogi	
Julaha	
Kumhar	
Manihar	
Nai	
Sonar	
Valmiki	

Appendix 2

Village Survey Questionnaire

Serial Number:

Date:

1. **Name of Household Head:**

2. **Religion:**

3. **Caste:**

4. ***Gotrā:***

5. **How many members of this HH migrate out of the village for (including daily commuters)?**

Employment		Education		Permanent Migrants	
Male	Female	Male	Female	Male	Female

6. Details of Household Members:

Relation to HH Head	Sex	Age	Education	Occupation (in Words)		Marital Status*	Income								
				At Source	At Migration Destination		From Occupation at Source			From Migration			Rent		
							D	W	M	D	W	M	D	W	M
1. HH Head															
2															
3															
4															
5															
6															
7															
8															
9															
10															

*M: Married; NM: Not/Never Married; D: Divorced; W: Widowed; S-Separated

7. Nature of Household: Joint [   ]   Nuclear [   ]

8. Marriage Details of Couples in the HH and Previously Married:

Relation to HH Head	Age at Marriage		Current Age of Bride	Do bride and groom belong to the same: (Y/N)							Marriage Distance (km)	Are both bride and groom from rural areas? (Y/N)	*Who conducted the marriage?	**Who arranged the marriage?
	Bride	Groom		Caste	Religion	Gotra	Village	District	State					
1														
2														
3														
4														
5														

9. Marriage Details of Out-Married Sisters/Daughters of the HH:

Relation to HH Head	Age at Marriage		Current Age of Bride	Do bride and groom belong to the same: (Y/N)							Marriage Distance (km)	Are both bride and groom from rural areas? (Y/N)	*Who conducted the marriage?	**Who arranged the marriage?
	Bride	Groom		Caste	Religion	Gotra	Village	District	State					
1														
2														
3														
4														
5														

*(A) Brahman priest; (B) Other (specify)
**(A) Parents/siblings/spouse of sibling; (B) Extended family members; (C) caste members; (D) Payment to individual middlemen/women; (E) Marriage bureau; (F) Print/other advertisement; (G) Others (specify)

10. Property/Assets:

(A) House:

Own		Rented		Kuccha		Pucca		Kuccha-Pucca mixed	

(B) Agricultural land		(C) Cattle	(D) Other
Bigha	Acres		

Who Works on the Land?

Family Members					Hired Labor
HH Head	Wife	Son(s)	Daughter(s)	Other Relations	

Cattle work:

Family Members					Hired Labor
HH Head	Wife	Son(s)	Daughter(s)	Other Relations	

Notes:

Appendix 3

Details of Cross-Regional Bride and Regional Bride Informants

I conducted semi-structured interviews with the following 38 key informants:

	RB				CRB		
	Name	Age	Caste (Hindu)		Name	Age	Caste (Hindu)
1	Koyal	16	Chamar	1	Kanchan	21	Chamar
2	Abha	25	Chamar	2	Samita	Early 30s	Chamar
3	Aarti	27	Chamar	3	Renuka	33	Chamar
4	Kusum	47	Chamar	4	Mansi	33	Chamar
5	Jagmati	Early 60s	Chamar	5	Meera	Late 30s	Chamar
				6	Radha	Early 40s	Chamar
				7	Devanti	Early 40s	Chamar
				8	Sheela	Early 40s	Chamar
				9	Maya	Mid-40s	Chamar
6	Ritu	25	Jat	10	Savita	Late 20s	Jat
7	Urmila	32	Jat	11	Varsha	28	Jat
8	Kajri	35	Jat	12	Pushpa	Late 30s	Jat
9	Sarla	47	Jat	13	Jaya	45	Jat
10	Kripa	75	Jat				
11	Shanti	24	Kumhar	14	Kalawati	40	Kumhar
12	Kamlesh	Late 20s	Kumhar	15	Lakshmi	Late 40s	Kumhar
13	Munesh	38	Kumhar	16	Chhaya	55	Kumhar
14	Jagbiri	71	Kumhar	17	Hemlata	Late 50s	Kumhar
			(Muslim)				(Muslim)
15	Sakeena	43	Teli	18	Jameela	21	Teli
16	Khalida	45	Teli				
17	Nasira	26	Lohar	19	Faiza	Late 40s	Lohar
18	Muneera	32	Lohar				
19	Shazia	Early 70s	Lohar				

Appendix 4

Details of Informants for Structured Interviews

I conducted structured interviews with the following 25 informants.

Name	Sex	Age	Caste	Religion	Occupation	Other Information
Amarpal	M	65	Jat	Hindu	Farmer	Never-married man
Ashok	M	39	Jat	Hindu	Life insurance agent	
Brijpal	M	78	Jat	Hindu	Retired college teacher	
Harpal	M	70	Jat	Hindu	Village school teacher	
Kavita	F	41	Jat	Hindu	*Ānganwādī* worker	
Mahipal	M	67	Jat	Hindu	Retired army man	His three sons are government employees
Rampal	M	87	Jat	Hindu	Retired college teacher	Younger brother is a never-married man
Saroj	F	35	Jat	Hindu	*Āshā* worker	
Shakuntala	F	37	Jat	Hindu	Housewife	Postgraduate
Vedpal	M	63	Jat	Hindu	Village school teacher	Daughter-in-law is a CRB
Ajay	M	24	Chamar	Hindu	Brick-kiln worker	Was facing difficulty in finding a wife
Babli	F	19	Chamar	Hindu	Student	Daughter of CRB 8

continued

Continued.

Name	Sex	Age	Caste	Religion	Occupation	Other Information
Dharmo Devi	F	70	Chamar	Hindu	Brick-kin worker	Mother-in-law of CRB
Karampal	M	55	Chamar	Hindu	Farmer	Husband of CRB 9
Ratan	M	22	Chamar	Hindu	Brick-kiln worker	Husband of CRB 1
Satender	M	55	Chamar	Hindu	Brick-kiln worker	His adult son was facing difficulties in finding a wife
Deepa	F	Early 30s	Kumhar	Hindu	CRB	Acted as go-between for several marriages
Ompal	M	55	Kumhar	Hindu	Potter, vegetable seller	Husband of CRB 14
Prakash	M	Early 40s	Kumhar	Hindu	Brick-kiln worker	Husband of NB 13 Was married in exchange for the daughter of CRB 17
Ramesh	M	50	Kumhar	Hindu	Potter, brick-kiln worker	Husband of CRB
Sudeshna	F	23	Kumhar	Hindu	Housewife	Daughter-in-law of CRB 16
Virender	M	52	Kumhar	Hindu	Shopkeeper	Never-married man
Vivek	M	26	Kumhar	Hindu	Journalist	Father's elder brother is a never-married man and his own elder brother is married to a CRB
Abdul	M	30	Lohar	Muslim	Factory worker	His father's brother's son is married to CRB 19
Yusuf	M	77	Lohar	Muslim	Blacksmith	

Glossary

alag: Separate/nuclear

ānganwādī: Government-run center that provides basic healthcare and non-formal pre-school education in villages

badlā: Exchange

bāhar kī: From outside

bahū: Son's wife/daughter-in-law

behanoī: Sister's husband

bhābī: Brother's wife

bicholīa: Matchmaker

bīchwālā: Go-between

būā: Father's sister

caste/khāp panchāyat: Extra-constitutional bodies that function as parallel law-enforcing agencies to the elected panchāyats.

chāchī: Father's younger brother's wife

chālā: Co-habitation (also called gaunā)

chaupāl: Courtyard

dādī: Father's mother

dāī: Traditional birth attendant

dawāt: Feast

devar: Husband's younger brother

devrānī: Husband's younger brother's wife

dūkh: Sadness

gālī: Verbal abuse

gaunā: Co-habitation (also called chālā)

ghūnghat: Veiling

gotrā: Patrilineage or clan

izzat: Honor

jeth: Husband's elder brother
jethānī: Husband's elder brother's wife
kālā/kālī (masculine/feminine): Literally black, but used for dark skin
kām: Work
kāmyāb: Successful
kanyādān: Gift of a virgin
kunbā: Extended family
majbūrī: Compulsion
māmā: Mother's brother
māmī: Mother's brother's wife
māsī: Mother's sister
mazdūr: Casual laborer
mol kī: Bought wife
nanad: Husband's sister
naukrī: Job
nikāh: Muslim marriage ceremony
nirol: Ideal/regular marriage
panchāyat: Local government institution
pardā: Veiling/seclusion
pardesh: Foreign land
phuphā: Mother's sister's or father's sister's husband
pīhar: Natal home
randwā: Never-married man/widower
rotī: Indian bread
sāmān: Goods
sarkārī: Government
sās: Husband's mother/mother-in-law
sasurāl: In-laws'/marital home
sāth denā: Supportive relationship
shādī: Wedding
sharm: Shame
sūkh: Happiness/peace
sūsar: Husband's father/father-in-law
taklīf: Trouble
tāū: Father's elder brother

Notes

Introduction

1. Barampur is a pseudonym and the names of all informants have been changed.

2. See the websites of Empower People (n.d.) and Shakti Vahini (n.d.); see also Kant and Pandey (2003).

3. See Sharada Srinivasan (2017) on the marriage of men from Tamil Nadu with Kerala women. She describes such cross-regional marriages as a recent phenomenon in this part of south India.

4. Danièle Bélanger and Andrea Flynn (2018) make a similar observation for transnational marriages in the wider Asian context. They argue that while the connection between marriage and migration is not "new," what is "new" is the sheer scale on which marriage migration is taking place, in terms of both numbers of marriages and the geographic distances involved (pp. 183–184).

5. Likewise, for China, South Korea, and Vietnam, studies note that son preference combined with declining fertility has resulted in pre-natal sex determination and sex-selective abortions leading to a female deficit (Bélanger & Khuat 2009; Junhong 2001; Kaur 2020; Kim 2004).

6. I do not use "local" marriage (unlike the existing literature), as "local" is rather vague. "Regional" captures the specificity of a marriage arranged within the north Indian region especially, as I found cases where marriages were arranged between families in contiguous states. For instance, some brides had moved to Barampur from their natal villages in Haryana. Although inter-state, these were parentally arranged marriages that conformed to community norms of marriage. Western UP and Haryana are contiguous and are linguistically and culturally similar, although there might be differences in dialect, work patterns, etc., which also exist within UP. I do not use "normative" marriage because I include variants in the category of regional marriage (such as dowryless marriages) that are caste endogamous and arranged within the "acceptable" marriage radius.

7. In this book, I use "cross-border marriage" as a wide term to include all marriages that cross national borders.

8. In India, consensual same-sex sexual relations were criminalized until 2009 under section 377 of the Indian Penal Code (retained from the colonial law, which criminalized "carnal acts against the order of nature"). In 2013, the judgment was reversed by the Supreme Court and same-sex relationships were recriminalized. In 2018, following an appeal against the 2013 judgement, Section 377 was declared "unconstitutional."

9. The Protection of Women from Domestic Violence (2005), by including "relationship in the nature of marriage," is believed to be the first legislation in India to provide recognition to non-marital adult heterosexual relationships. These, however, are distinguished from "live-in-relationships" and exclude relationships with a "keep" (who is maintained financially and used mainly for sexual purposes), "a servant," and a "one-night stand." The Act also excludes adult same-sex relationships. Anuja Agrawal points out that it would be a mistake to see the Act as providing legal status to non-marital relationships. What it does is acknowledge the existence of such relationships and the rights of women in them to protection from domestic violence (Agrawal 2012, p. 53).

10. Jamieson outlines the "dimensions of intimacy" in response to Anthony Giddens's claim that disclosing intimacy is the organizing principle in people's life (1998, pp. 7–10).

11. Anthropologists writing on the West have also challenged this model of Western and non-Western personhood. In her work among British adoptees, for instance, Janet Carsten writes of their search for their birthparents that was motivated by a desire "to know where I came from," "to be complete," or "to find out who I am" (2000, p. 689). She demonstrates the salience of kin relations for persons in the West too.

12. "Scheduled Castes" is the official designation for the ex-untouchable caste groups in the Indian constitution.

13. The Indian Constitution entitles Scheduled Castes, Scheduled Tribes, and Other Backward Classes to reservation in government employment and educational institutions.

14. ASHA workers are community health workers. In 2005, the ASHA program was launched in India as a key component of the National Rural Health Mission (see the website of the Mininstry of Health and Family Welfare, Government of India).

Chapter 1

1. In local usuage, *larkā* (boy) and *larkī* (girl) are used to refer to all unmarried men and women. This reflects the importance of marriage in transition to social adulthood and highlights the significance of the inability to marry.

2. In India, color consciousness becomes prominent in the matchmaking process. The desirability of light or fair skin is gendered: it is much more significant for women to be fair than men, as studies on matrimonial advertisements have noted (Jha & Adelman 2009). In Barampur, fair skin was highly desired in new and potential brides. On one occasion, a Muslim informant asked me to suggest a skin lightening cream for her oldest daughter so that they would be able to attract a marriage proposal for her. Her daughter had been "rejected" by one potential groom's father on grounds of her "dark" skin. There is wide variation in skin tone across India, yet the preference for light skin can be found across the country. In Barampur, a strong association was also made between skin colour and caste status—i.e., upper castes have light skin and lower/Dalit castes have darker skin—even though racially based theories of caste remain unsupported (Chaudhry 2019b; Gorringe & Rafanell 2007, p. 104; Still 2014, p. 69).

3. As elsewhere in India, in Barampur, Indian films have been very influential in determining contemporary "love-scapes" (Orsini 2006, p. 35). Almost every household in the village owned a colour television, which was used mostly for viewing devotional content or Bollywood films. I also observed young men in public spaces hanging around, glued to their mobile phones, on which they downloaded and watched Hindi films or listened to songs from Bollywood films. The mobile phone was also used by young men to access pornographic content, as one disgruntled older informant told me.

4. Geert De Neve (2016) made a similar observation in his work in urban Tamil Nadu. He found that while "love marriages" that transgress caste and religious boundaries have become increasingly popular, parentally arranged marriages are still preferred, as the former result in the withdrawal of vital support structures. Shalini Grover (2011), in her study of a low-income neighbourhood in Delhi, draws attention to how women in self-arranged as opposed to arranged marriages cannot avail of parental refuge in situations of marital distress (see also Ahearn 2001, p. 258, on Nepal).

5. It is not only in rural contexts, but also in urban ones where inter-community relationships struggle to get acceptance. In her work on pre-marital relationships in Delhi, for instance, Parul Bhandari (2017) rarely encountered inter-religious relationships, and the ones that she became aware of broke off, as did upper–lower caste relationships, for fear that they would fail to gain parental approval.

Chapter 2

1. Writing over three decades ago, earlier ethnographers on UP noted that the rules for a good marriage were changing, with education and salaried employment becoming more significant than landholding (Jeffery & Jeffery 1996; Wadley 1994, p. 241).

2. In July 2013, all the leading Indian newspapers ran articles about the entrance examination paper for recruitment of Railway Protection Force constables being leaked in western UP.

3. Such claims must be looked at in the light of economic uncertainty and the threats posed to Jat dominance by the politics of reservation and the rise of Dalits within UP politics (see Jeffrey 2010, p. 46–54).

4. Studies report marriages between Jat men and lower-caste women within the region during the colonial period (Briggs 1920; Chowdhry 2007; Darling [1928] 1977). An increase in inter-caste runaway marriages has in fact been noted for contemporary Punjab (Kaur 2015, p. 66).

5. See also Caren Freeman's account of an ethnic Korean (Chosŏnjok) Chinese bride on her misgivings about the type of Korean men who travel to China to find a bride (2005, p. 89).

6. The earliest account of the *jajmānī* system was provided by William H. Wiser in his book *The Hindu Jajmānī System*, published in 1936 (for more on this, see Gould 1986; Fuller 1989; Kolenda 1963).

7. Due to both time and monetary constraints, it was not possible to trace the families of each of the key cross-regional bride informants in their native states. Given the research focus on women's post-marital experiences, I decided to confine my fieldwork to Barampur. Data on why women migrated over long distances for marriage were collected through interviews with cross-regional brides.

Chapter 3

1. In her work on marriages between Bangladeshi women and men in UP, Thérèse Blanchet noted that "accusations of trafficking were proffered only when it was known that a girl had been sold to a man of another religious group" (2008, p. 314).

Chapter 4

1. A woman's status in her affinal home is not constant and changes with motherhood, especially with the birth of a son. Other factors such as her hold over her husband, his economic contribution to the joint household, her and her husband's state of health, and the life-span of her father-in-law were crucial in determining her power and control within the household (Dube 1997, p. 93).

2. *Bahū* is usually the kinship term used for a daughter-in-law, but in Barampur wives were referred to as so-and-so's *bahū*.

3. The literal translation of *desh* is "country" but what is implied here is that the place she married into was foreign—strange and unfamiliar (see also Blanchet 2008, pp. 162–163).

4. On the relationship between caste and vegetarianism, Pauline Kolenda writes, "a vegetarian diet characterizes the purer castes. There are, furthermore, degrees of non-vegetarianism. It is especially defiling to eat the meat of the sacred cow. The next worst is eating pork, then mutton, then chicken, then fish, then eggs" (1992a, p. 80). For more on attitudes around cross-regional brides consuming non-vegetarian foods in their native states, see Chaudhry (2019b).

5. For brick-kiln work, workers are mobilized through contractors, with advances given well before actual migration. This often leads to forms of "debt bondage." Migrant workers are recruited in pairs (male–female) or family units, and direct piece-rates are paid for the output of collective units of labor (Mazumdar and Agnihotri 2014, pp. 128, 146).

6. In contrast to the sentiment of "*jī nahī lagtā*" (I did not like it) that defined the early months, "*jī lag gayā* after children were born" was what several women told me. *Jī* is difficult to translate into English; the sentiment that is being conveyed is that it started feeling like home/familiar.

7. Several scholars have discussed the question of the placement of children of inter-caste unions (Davis 1941; Dube 2003; Tambiah 1973; Yalman 1963). In Barampur, there was a "patrilineal bias" (Parry 1979, p. 131) in the attribution of caste status to the children of inter-caste unions. Children of cross-regional couples were granted their fathers' caste, with the "differential" caste of their cross-regional mothers having no bearing on this.

Chapter 5

1. Helen E. Ullrich's study (2010) in Karnataka, south India, which explores change over four generations among the upper-caste Havik Brahmins, is the only study I found on a rural context that notes a shift from marriage as "a relationship of respect" for the husband to one based on companionate ideals. Unlike the urban studies, it does not discuss the question of equality in relationships.

2. I heard several rumors of extramarital relationships that included those between a woman and her *sūsar*, *jeth*, or *devar* but also between married women and unmarried (unrelated) men. There was always a motive attributed to these relationships, and the possibility of a woman exploring pleasure outside marriage through such relationships was never considered.

3. Most of my key informants had delivered at home in their husband's village relying on the village *dāī*. Hospital deliveries took place only in cases of complications. During my fieldwork, however, young brides said that they had been or would be taken by the ASHA (accredited social health activist) for delivering at the government hospital. Some from wealthier families had delivered at private hospitals. For some women, the decision about where the delivery would take place was made by the *sās*. Women like Jameela (CRB, 21, Teli) also shared their reluctance to deliver at a hospital because of *sharm* at giving birth in the presence

of strange men (see Jeffery & Jeffery 2010 for a detailed discussion on the barriers that women and families face in accessing government health care services).

4. In her discussion of Rajasthani folk songs, Gloria Goodwin Raheja notes the association between fertility and adultery. She writes that men, being desperate for progeny, may allow themselves to be deceived if it results in the birth of a male child. She adds that at times, the "adulterous progenitor" is identified as the husband's brother, and the wife's infidelity thus "serves the approved end of perpetuating the groom's patrilineage" (Raheja & Gold 1994: 59).

5. Shalini Grover points out that her interest in interrogating marriage, love, and relationships in the Delhi neighbourhood where she worked was reinterpreted in the vernacular idiom as "*sukh aur dukh ki kahanian*"—people's journeys or stories through happy, sorrowful, and difficult times (2011, p. 17).

6. Bapna writes: "The Hindi term nibhaana, a very evocative term in its multiple usages, does not lend itself to easy translation and therefore, I will continue using the term without substituting it with a translated English word. Some of the English terms that capture its meaning would be 'to keep' (as in to keep a promise), 'to perform,' 'to maintain,' 'to stand by,' 'to fulfil.' Two terms that come close, to my mind, are the noun 'observance' (fulfilling the requirements of law, morality or ritual) and the verb 'to abide' (acting in accordance with a rule or decision)" (2021, p. 117).

Chapter 6

1. T.N. Madan reported that among the Kashmiri Pandits, a daughter-in-law was called a "parrot of the pillow" because it was believed that she had the power to exert influence over her husband when they both retired to bed (2011, p. 121).

2. In her study of close-kin (intra-*khāndān*) marriages among a Muslim community in South India, Sylvia Vatuk (1989) noted the recognition of close bonds between married daughters and their parents. A married daughter was not required to transfer her allegiance away from her natal family and could even reside with her aged parents if they required care. Further, her rights in parental property were upheld. Principles of patri-virilocal residence did not operate strictly in this community as in most north Indian contexts.

3. Even in south India, where the north Indian norms of deference do not apply and widowed women can move to live with a married daughter, they may find themselves in a precarious position. In her work in low-income settlements in Chennai, Penny Vera-Sanso noted that when widowed or deserted women joined a married daughter's household, they did so either as "paying guests" or as "temporary, self-supporting additions" to their daughter's family. They had rights neither to be housed nor to use household resources and had to rely on maintaining good relations with their son-in-law, as he had the authority to ask them to leave (1999, p. 586).

4. Women used the terms *saheli* (female friend) and *dosti* (from *dost*, i.e., male friend) to speak about friendship.

5. All three had been "deceived" and brought to Barampur and married off (see chapter 2).

Chapter 7

1. Uxorilocally resident son-in-law. Uxorilocality is the rule of residence in or near the wife's home after marriage.

2. Here again, stage in the life-course becomes crucial. As Assa Doron notes, for young brides, mobile phone usage may be highly regulated by the husband and in-laws, but a woman comes to have increased access as she advances in her married life and rises in the household hierarchy (2012, p. 430).

3. This is quite different for the situation described for some cross-border international marriages. For instance, brides from Vietnam who became wives in East Asia were a vital source of financial support for their parents because of the remittances they sent back to their natal homes (Bélanger & Flynn 2018). Likewise, for Vietnamese women who marry Singaporean men, Brenda S.A. Yeoh et al. (2014) note that such marriages were motivated in part by women's desire to be able to remit money to their natal families.

4. Kaveri Qureshi was told by her Pakistani informants in Britain that when a daughter leaves her parents' home on her wedding palanquin, the parents say, "this is your dead body leaving the house," so that she never thinks to return (2016, p. 126).

5. Several informants told me about Suresh (a Chamar), who was previously married to a cross-regional bride. I was told that she had left with her parents, who had come to Barampur to get her. No one had any information on whether she had returned to her natal home or her parents had arranged another marriage for her.

6. Writing on international marriages also notes that children become a key consideration in women's decisions to end marriages. In such marriages, there is the additional issue of residency status that is dependent on remaining married. In situations of abuse, having children complicates women's situation, with them having to endure abuse for fear of losing access to and custody of their children (Ito 2005; Raj & Silverman 2002).

7. In the settlement of marital disputes, the intervention of caste *panchāyats* was not sought. Such disputes were mediated by family and caste elders and at times by an influential member of the village community. In the course of my fieldwork, not once did I witness a caste *panchāyat* being called upon to settle a familial or inter-caste dispute.

8. Divorce is under civil law, requiring a direct petition before the court. Retrieval of dowry is undertaken by invoking Section 498A (cruelty by husband

or his relatives) CrPC (Criminal Procedure Code) and/or 406 Indian Penal Code (punishment for criminal breach of trust), both of which move through FIRs (First Information Report) with the police, and reach the courts thereafter. In the popular imagination, there seemed to be no distinction between civil and criminal law or between police-run prosecutions and independent civil petitions.

9. For the Jats of Haryana, Prem Chowdhry (1994) noted that such marriages were considered the most effective way to control a widow's right of inheritance and thereby retain property within the family.

10. A clear distinction is made between primary and secondary marriages. Secondary unions are not thought to be as sacrosanct as the first marriage and may involve a very simple ceremony or no ceremony at all. Among Hindus, a woman can be married with full rites only once (Dube 1997; Dumont 1970).

11. See Srimati Basu on Indian laws around rape and marriage, where she critiques rape laws for seeing rape not as violation—"a specific transgression of consent and bodily integrity"—but through the lens of sexual victimization and vulnerability (2015, p. 77). She discusses rape prosecutions where marriage is evoked as a solution to rape—that rape can be erased through marriage between the raped woman and the rapist. She writes, "such cases underlie the stature of rape as sex rather than violence; but they also depict rape as a violation of property, to be made whole by restoring the woman to marriedness." She argues that "marriage itself is a form of property at stake in rape" because rape threatens access to the benefits of marriage (p. 87).

Bibliography

Abeyasekera, A.L. (2016). "Narratives of choice: marriage, choosing right and the responsibility of agency in urban middle-class Sri Lanka," *Feminist Review*, 113, no. 1, pp. 1–16.

Abraham, J. (2011). "Why did you send me like this? Marriage, matriliny and the providing husband in north Kerala, India," *Asian Journal of Women's Studies*, 17, pp. 32–65.

Abraham, J. (2014). "Contingent caste endogamy and patriarchy: Lessons for our understanding of caste," *Economic and Political Weekly*, 49, no. 2, pp. 56–65.

Abraham, M. (2008). "Domestic violence and the Indian diaspora in the United States," in Palriwala, R., & Uberoi, P. (eds.), *Marriage, Migration and Gender*, Sage, New Delhi, pp. 303–325.

Abu-Lughod, L. (1991). "Writing against culture," in Fox, R. (ed.), *Recapturing Anthropology*, School of American Research Press, Santa Fe, NM, pp. 137–162.

Adams, R.G., & Allan, G. (1998). "Contextualising friendship," in *Placing Friendship in Context*, Cambridge University Press, Cambridge, pp. 1–17.

Agal, R. (2006). "India's 'bride buying' country," BBC News, 5 April, viewed 9 September 2019, http://news.bbc.co.uk/1/hi/world/south_asia/4862434.stm

Agarwal, B. (1994). *A field of one's own: Gender and land rights in South Asia*, Cambridge University Press, Cambridge.

Agarwal, S., & Unisa, S. (2007). "Discrimination from conception to childhood: A study of girl children in rural Haryana, India," in Attane, I., & Guilmoto, G.Z. (eds.), *Watering the neighbour's garden: The growing demographic female deficit in Asia*, Committee for International Cooperation in National Research in Demography, Paris, pp. 247–266.

Agnihotri, S.B. (2001). "Rising sons and setting daughters: Provisional results from the 2001 census," in Mazumdar, V., & Krishnaji, N. (eds.), *Enduring conundrum: India's sex ratio: Essays in honour of Asok Mitra*, Rainbow Publishers, Delhi, pp. 199–201.

Agnihotri, S.B. (2003). "Survival of the girl child: Tunnelling out of the chakravyuha," *Economic and Political Weekly*, 38, no. 41, pp. 4351–4360.

259

Agrawal, A. (2012). "Law and live-in relationships in India," *Economic and Political Weekly*, 47, no. 39, pp. 50–56.

Ahearn, L. (2001). *Invitations to love: Literacy, love letters, and social change in Nepal*, University of Michigan Press, Ann Arbor.

Ahlawat, N. (2009). "Missing brides in rural Haryana: A study of adverse sex ratio, poverty and addiction," *Social Change*, 39, no. 1, pp. 46–63.

Ahlawat, N. (2016). "The dark side of the marriage squeeze: Violence against cross-region brides in Haryana," in Kaur, R. (ed.), *Too many men, too few women: Social consequences of gender imbalance in India and China*, Orient BlackSwan, New Delhi, pp. 197–219.

AIDWA (2003). *Expanding dimensions of dowry*, Progressive Printers, Delhi.

Alagarajan, M., & Kulkarni, P.M. (2008). "Religious differentials in fertility in India: Is there a convergence?" *Economic and Political Weekly*, 43, no. 48, pp. 44–53.

Allan, G. (1989). *Friendship: Developing a sociological perspective*. Westview Press, Boulder, CO.

Allan, G. (2010). "Friendship and ageing," in Dannefer, D., & Phillipson, C (eds.), *The SAGE handbook of Social Gerontology*, SAGE Publications, London, pp. 239–247.

Allan, G., & Adams, R.G. (2007). "The Sociology of friendship," in Bryant, C.D., & Peck, D.L. (eds.), *21st century sociology*, vol. 2, SAGE Publications, Thousand Oaks, CA, pp. 123–131.

Arnold, F., Choe, M.K., & Roy, T.K. (1998). "Son preference, the family building process and child mortality in India," *Population Studies*, 52, no. 2, pp. 301–315.

Aziz, A. (1983). No title, *Economic and Political Weekly*, 18, no. 15, pp. 603–604.

Bajwa, H. (2019). "Not a minor problem! Bride trafficking remains a booming business in Haryana," *The New Indian Express*, 7 January, viewed 14 March 2019, http://www.newindianexpress.com/nation/2019/jan/07/not-a-minor-problem-bride-trafficking-remains-a-booming-business-in-haryana-1921519.html

Bapna, G. (2012). "Marriage, language and time: Toward an ethnography of nibhaana," *Economic and Political Weekly*, 47, no. 43, pp. 109–117.

Barrett, M., & McIntosh, M. (1982). *The anti-social family*, Verso/NLB, London.

Basu, S. (2005). "*Haklenewali*: Indian women's negotiations of discourses of inheritance," in Basu, S. (ed.), *Dowry and Inheritance*, Women Unlimited, New Delhi, pp. 151–170.

Basu, S. (2015). *The trouble with marriage: Feminists confront law and violence in India*, Orient BlackSwan, New Delhi.

Basu, S. (2019). "Gender and Law," in Srivastava, S., Arif, Y. and Abraham, J. (eds.), *Critical Themes in Indian Sociology*, Sage, New Delhi, pp. 282–297.

Basu, S., & Ramberg, L. (eds.) (2015). *Conjugality unbound: Sexual economies, state regulation and the marital form in India*, Women Unlimited, New Delhi.

Bedi, R. (2003). "India's Craving for Boy Babies Leads to Bride Shortage," *Telegraph*, 7 March, viewed 9 September 2019, https://www.telegraph.co.uk/education/3308893/Indias-craving-for-boy-babies-leads-to-bride-shortage.html

Bélanger, D., & Flynn, A. (2018). "Gender and migration: Evidence from transnational marriage migration," in Riley, N.E., & Brunson, J. (eds.), *International handbook on gender and demographic processes*, Springer, Dordrecht, pp. 183–201.

Bélanger, D., & Khuat, T.H.O. (2009). "Second trimester abortions and sex selection of children in northern urban Vietnam," *Population Studies*, 63, no. 2, pp. 163–171.

Bell, S., & Coleman, S. (1999). *The anthropology of friendship*, Berg, Oxford.

Berreman, G.D. (1972). *Hindus of the Himalayas: Ethnography and change*, University of California Press, Berkeley.

Berreman, G.D. (2012). "Behind many masks: ethnography and impression management," in Antonius C., Robben, G.M., & Sluka, J.A. (eds.), *Ethnographic fieldwork: An anthropological reader*, 2nd edn, Wiley-Blackwell, pp. 153–174.

Bhandari, P. (2017). "Pre-marital relationships and the family in modern India," *South Asia Multidisciplinary Academic Journal*, 16, https://doi.org/10.4000/samaj.4379

Bhat, P.N.M., & Zavier, A.J.F. (2007). "Factors influencing the use of prenatal diagnostic techniques and sex ratio at birth in India," in Attané, I., & Guilmoto, C.Z. (eds.), *Watering the neighbour's garden: The growing demographic female deficit in Asia*, Committee for International Cooperation in National Research in Demography (CICRED), Paris, pp. 131–160.

Bhat, R.L., & Sharma, N. (2006). "Missing girls: Evidence from some north Indian states," *Indian Journal of Gender Studies*, 13, no. 3, pp. 351–374.

Bianchi, S.M., et al. (2012). "Housework: Who did, does or will do it, and how much does it matter?" *Social Forces*, 91, no. 1, pp. 55–63.

Biswas, R. (2011). "Of love, marriage and kinship: Queering the family," Sen, S., Biswas, R., & Dhawan, N. (eds.), *Intimate others: Marriage and sexualities in India*, Stree, Kolkata, pp. 414–435.

Blanchet, T. (2008). "Bangladeshi girls sold as wives in north India," in Palriwala, R., & Uberoi, P. (eds.), *Marriage, Migration and Gender*, Sage, New Delhi, pp. 152–179.

Blanchet, T., et al. (2003). *Bangladeshi girls sold as wives in north India*, Drishti Research Centre, Dhaka.

Borneman, J. (1996). "Until death do us part: Marriage/death in Anthropological discourse," *American Ethnologist*, 23, no. 2, pp. 215–235.

Bossen, L. (2007). "Village to distant village: The opportunities and risks of long-distance marriage migration in rural China," *Journal of Contemporary China*, 16, no. 50, pp. 97–116.

Bourdieu, P. (1976). "Marriage strategies as strategies of social reproduction," in Forster, R., & Ranum, O. (eds.), *Family and society: Selections from the Annales, Economies, Societies, Civilisations*, Johns Hopkins University Press, Baltimore, pp. 117–144.

Bourdieu, P. (1977). *Outline of a theory of practice*, Cambridge University Press, Cambridge.

Bourdieu, P. (1986). "The forms of capital," in Richardson, J.G. (ed.), *Handbook of theory and research for the sociology of education*, Greenwood Press, Westport, CT, pp. 241–258.

Brettell, C.B. (2017). "Marriage and migration," *Annual Review of Anthropology*, 46, pp. 81–97.

Briggs, G.W. (1920). *The religious life of India: The Chamārs*, Association Press, London.

Burkitt, I. (2016). "Relational agency: Relational sociology. Agency and interaction," *European Journal of Social Theory*, 19, no. 3, pp. 322–339.

Carsten, J. (2000). "Knowing where you've come from: Ruptures and continuities of time and kinship in narratives of adoption reunions," *Journal of the Royal Anthropological Institute* 6, pp. 687–703.

Carter, J. (2012). "What Is commitment? Women's accounts of intimate attachment," *Families, Relationships and Societies*, 2, no. 1, pp. 137–153.

Census of India. (1933). *United Provinces of Agra and Oudh: Imperial and provincial tables*, 1931, vol. XVIII, part I, United Provinces, Allahabad.

Census of India. (1951). *District census handbook, Meerut*, Office of the Registrar General, Government of India, New Delhi.

Census of India. (1961). *District census handbook, Meerut*, Office of the Registrar General, Government of India, New Delhi.

Census of India. (1971). *District census handbook, Meerut*, Office of the Registrar General, Government of India, New Delhi.

Census of India. (1981). *District census handbook, Meerut*, Office of the Registrar General, Government of India, New Delhi.

Census of India. (1991a). *District census handbook, Meerut*, Office of the Registrar General, Government of India, New Delhi.

Census of India. (1991b). *C-series: Socio-cultural tables, Uttar Pradesh*, Office of the Registrar General, Government of India, New Delhi.

Census of India. (2001a). *C-Series: Socio-Cultural Tables, Baghpat*, Office of the Registrar General, Government of India, New Delhi.

Census of India. (2001b). *District census handbook, Baghpat*, Office of the Registrar General, Government of India, New Delhi.

Census of India. (2011a). *District census handbook, Baghpat*, Office of the Registrar General, Government of India, New Delhi.

Census of India. (2011b). *Primary census abstract, Baghpat*, Office of the Registrar General, Government of India, New Delhi.

Chakraborty, K. (2012). "Virtual mate-seeking in the urban slums of Kolkata, India," *South Asian Popular Culture*, 10, no. 2, pp. 197–216.

Chakravarti, U. (2003). *Gendering caste through a feminist lens*, Stree, Kolkata.

Chakravarti, U. (2005). "From fathers to husbands: Of love, death and marriage in north India," in Welchman, L., & Hossain, S. (eds.), *Honour crimes, paradigms and violence against women*, Zed, London, pp. 308–331.

Chao, E. (2005). "Cautionary tales: Marriage stategies, state discourse and women's agency in a Naxi village in southwestern China," in Constable, N. (ed.),

Cross-border marriages: Gender and mobility in transnational Asia, University of Pennsylvania Press, Philadelphia, pp. 34–52.

Charsley, K. (2008). "Vulnerable brides and transnational *ghar damads*: Gender, risk and adjustment among Pakistani marriage migrants to Britain," in Palriwala, R., & Uberoi, P. (eds.). *Marriage, migration and gender*, Sage, New Delhi, pp. 152–179.

Chaudhry, S. (2018). "'Now it is difficult to get married': Contextualising cross-regional marriage and bachelorhood in a north Indian village," in Srinivasan, S., & Li, S. (eds.), *Scarce women and surplus men in China and India: Macro demographics versus local dynamics*, Springer, Cham, pp. 86–104.

Chaudhry, S. (2019a). "'For how long can your *piharwale* intervene?' Accessing natal kin support in rural north India," *Modern Asian Studies*, 53, no. 5, pp. 1613–1645.

Chaudhry, S. (2019b). "'Flexible' caste boundaries: Cross-regional marriage as 'mixed' marriage in rural north India," *Contemporary South Asia*, 27, no. 2, pp. 214–228.

Chaudhry, S., & Mohan, T.D. (2011). "Of marriage and migration: Bengali and Bihari brides in a UP village," *Indian Journal of Gender Studies*, 18, no. 3, pp. 311–340.

Chauhan, R. (2007). "Seeking a suitable match: Economic development, gender and matrimonial advertisements in India," in Misra, K.K., & Lowry, J.H. (eds.), *Recent studies on Indian women: Empirical work of social scientists*, Rawat Publications, Jaipur, pp. 152–170.

Chen, M.A. (2000). *Perpetual mourning: Widowhood in rural India*, Oxford University Press, New York.

Chen, M.A., & Drèze, J. (1992). *Widows and well-being in rural North India*, Development Economics Research Programme, Suntory-Toyota International Centre for Economics and Related Disciplines, London.

Chopra, R. (2004). "Encountering masculinity: An ethnographer's dilemma," in Chopra, R., Osella, C., & Osella, F. (eds.), *South Asian masculinities: Context of change, sites of continuity*, Women Unlimited, New Delhi, pp. 36–59.

Chowdhry, P. (1994). *The veiled women: Shifting gender equations in rural Haryana, 1880–1990*, Oxford University Press, Delhi.

Chowdhry, P. (1997). "A matter of two shares: A daughter's claim to patrilineal property in rural north India," *Indian Economic & Social History Review*, 34, no. 3, pp. 289–320.

Chowdhry, P. (2005). "Crisis of masculinity in Haryana: The unmarried, the unemployed and the aged," *Economic and Political Weekly*, 40, no. 49, pp. 5189–5198.

Chowdhry, P. (2007). *Contentious marriages, eloping couples: Gender, caste and patriarchy in northern India*, Oxford University Press, New Delhi.

Chowdhry, P. (2011). "Men, marriage and sexuality in northern India," in Sen, S., Biswas, R., & Dhawan, N. (eds.), *Intimate others: Marriage and sexualities in India*, Stree, Kolkata, pp. 241–262.

Chowdhry, P. (2012). "Infliction, acceptance and resistance: Containing violence on women in rural Haryana," *Economic and Political Weekly*, 47, no. 37, pp. 43–59.

Committee on the Status of Women in India (CSWI) (1974). *Towards equality*, Department of Social Welfare, Government of India, New Delhi.

Connell, R.W. (1995). *Masculinities*, Polity Press, Cambridge.

Constable, N. (2005). "Introduction: Cross-border marriages, gendered mobility and global hypergamy," in Constable, N. (ed.), *Cross-border marriages: Gender and mobility in transnational Asia*, University of Pennsylvania Press, Philadelphia, pp. 1–16.

Constable, N. (2009). "The commodification of intimacy: Marriage, sex, and reproductive labour," *Annual Review of Anthropology*, 38, pp. 49–64.

Corbridge, S., Harriss, J., & Jeffrey, C. (2013). "Does caste still matter in India?" in *India today: Economy, politics and society*, Polity Press, Cambridge, pp. 239–257.

Cornwall, A. and Lindisfarne, N. (1994). "Introduction," in Cornwall, A., & Lindisfarne, N. (eds.), *Dislocating masculinity: Comparative ethnographies*, Routledge, London, pp. 1–10.

Croll, E.J. (2006). "The intergenerational contract in the changing Asian family," *Oxford Development Studies*, 34, no. 4, pp. 473–491.

Darling, M.L. [1928] (1977). *The Punjab peasant in prosperity and debt*, Manohar, Delhi.

Das, V. (1975). "Marriage among the Hindus," in Jain, D. (ed.), *Indian Women*, Publications Division Ministry of Information and Broadcasting, Government of India, New Delhi, pp. 76–86.

Das, V. (1976). "Masks and faces: An essay on Punjabi kinship," *Contributions to Indian Sociology*, 10, no. 1, pp. 1–30.

Das Gupta, M. (1987). "Selective discrimination against female children in rural Punjab, India," *Population and Development Review*, 13, no. 1, pp. 77–100.

Das Gupta, M., & Li, S. (1999). "Gender bias in China, South Korea and India, 1920–1990: Effects of war, famine and fertility decline," *Development and Change*, 30, no. 3, pp. 619–652.

Davies, K. (2011). "Friendship and personal life," in Vaneesa, M. (ed.), *Sociology of personal life*, Palgrave Macmillan, Houndmills, Basingstoke, pp. 72–84.

Davin, D. (2008). "Marriage migration in China: The enlargement of marriage markets in the era of market reforms," in Palriwala, R., & Uberoi, P. (eds.), *Marriage, migration and gender*, Sage, New Delhi, pp. 63–77.

Davis, K. (1941). "Intermarriage in caste societies," *American Anthropologist*, 43, pp. 376–395.

del Estal, E. (2018). " 'I was bought for 50,000 rupees': India's trafficked brides—in pictures," *The Guardian*, 7 March, viewed 11 January 2019, https://www.theguardian.com/global development/2018/mar/07/india-girls-women-trafficked-brides-sexual-domestic-slavery del Franco, N. (2012). *Negotiating adolescence in rural Bangladesh: A journey through schools, love and marriage*, Zubaan, New Delhi.

Del Rosario, T. (2008). "Bridal diaspora: Migration and marriage among Filipino women," in Palriwala, R., & Uberoi, P. (eds.), *Marriage, migration and gender*, Sage, New Delhi, pp. 78–97.

Delphy, C., & Leonard, D. (1992). *Familiar exploitation: a new analysis of marriage in contemporary western societies*, Polity, Cambridge.

De Neve, G. (2016). "The economies of love: love marriage, kin support and aspiration in a South Indian garment city," *Modern Asian Studies*, 50, no. 4, pp. 1220–1249.

Desai, A. (2010). "A matter of affection: Ritual friendship in central India," in Killick, E., & Desai, A. (eds.), *The ways of friendship: Anthropological perspectives*, Berghahn Books, New York, pp. 114–132.

Desai, A., & Killick, E. (2010). *The ways of friendship: anthropological perspectives*, Berghahn Books, New York.

Deshpande, A., & Newman, K. (2007). "Where the path leads: The role of caste in post-university employment expectations," *Economic and Political Weekly*, 42, no. 41, pp. 4133–4140.

DHNS (2019). "Bride trafficking must stop now," *Deccan Herald*, 27 February, viewed 14 March 2019, https://www.deccanherald.com/opinion/second-edit/bride-trafficking-must-stop-720547.html

Dobash, R.E., & Dobash, R. (1980). *Violence against wives: a case against the patriarchy*, Open Books, London.

Dobash, R.E., & Dobash, R.P. (1998). *Rethinking violence against women*, Sage, London.

Donnan, H. (1988). *Marriage among Muslims: Preference and choice in northern Pakistan*, Hindustan Publishing, Delhi.

Donner, H. (2008). *Domestic goddesses: Maternity, globalisation and middle-class identity in contemporary India*, Ashgate, Burlington, VT.

Donner, H. (2016). "Doing it our way: Love and marriage in Kolkata middle-class families," *Modern Asian Studies*, 50, no. 4, pp. 1147–1189.

Doron, A. (2012). "Mobile persons: Cell phones, gender and the self in north India," *The Asia Pacific Journal of Anthropology*, 13, no. 5, pp. 414–433.

Dube, L. (1988). "On the construction of gender: Hindu girls in patrilineal India," *Economic and Political Weekly*, 23, no. 18, pp. WS11–WS19.

Dube, L. (1997). *Women and kinship: Comparative perspectives on gender in South and South-East Asia*, United Nations University Press, Tokyo.

Dube, L. (2003). "Caste and women," in Rao, A. (ed.), *Gender and caste*, Women Unlimited, New Delhi, pp. 223–248.

Dumont, L. (1970). *Homo hierarchicus: The caste system and its implication*, University of Chicago Press, Chicago.

Duncan, S. (2015). "Women's agency in living apart together: Constraint, strategy and vulnerability," *The Sociological Review*, 63, no. 3, pp. 589–607.

Duncombe, J. and Marsden, D. (1993). "Love and intimacy: The gender division of emotion and 'emotion work': A neglected aspect of sociological discussion of heterosexual relationships," *Sociology*, 27, no. 2, pp. 221–241.

Dyson, J. (2010). "Friendship in practice: Girls' work in the Indian Himalayas," *American Ethnologist*, 37, no. 3, pp. 482–498.

Dyson, T., & Moore, M. (1983). "Kinship structure, female autonomy and demographic behaviour in India," *Population and Development Review*, 9, no. 1, pp. 35–60.

Empower People. (n.d.) "Focusing on empowerment of trafficking survivors," visited 26 November 2019, http://www.empowerpeople.org.in/bride-trafficking.html

EPW (Economic and Political Weekly) Engage (2019). "*Beti Bachao*: Government's Efforts to Eradicate Female Infanticide and Sex-Selective Abortion are Inadequate," visited 5 September 2020, https://www.epw.in/engage/article/beti-bachao-eradicate-female-infanticide-violence-against-women-girls-abortion

Fan, C.C., & Huang, Y. (1998). "Waves of rural brides: Female marriage migration in China," *Annals of the Association of American Geographers*, 88, no. 2, pp. 227–251.

Fan, C.C., & Li, L. (2002). "Marriage and migration in transnational China," *Environment and Planning A*, 34, no. 4, pp. 619–638.

Feld, S., & Carter, W.C. (1998). "Foci of activity as changing contexts for friendship," in Adams, R.G., & Allan, G. (eds.), *Placing friendship in context*, Cambridge University Press, Cambridge, pp. 136–152.

Freeman, C. (2005). "Marrying up and marrying down: The paradoxes of marital mobility for Chosonjok brides in South Korea," in Constable, N. (ed.), *Cross-border marriages: Gender and mobility in transnational Asia*, University of Pennsylvania Press, Philadelphia, pp. 80–100.

Froerer, P. (2010). "Close friends: The importance of proximity in children's peer relations in Chhattisgarh, central India," in Killick, E., & Desai, A. (eds.), *The ways of friendship: Anthropological perspectives*, Berghahn Books, New York, pp. 133–153.

Fuller, C.J. (1989). "Misconceiving the grain heap: a critique of the concept of the Indian jajmani system," in Parry, J., & Bloch, M. (eds.), *Money and the morality of exchange*, Cambridge University Press, Cambridge, pp. 33–63.

Fuller, C.J. (1996). "Introduction: Caste today," in Fuller, C.J. (ed.), *Caste today*, Oxford University Press, Oxford, pp. 1–31.

Fuller, C.J., & Narasimhan, H. (2008). "Companionate marriage in India: The changing marriage system in a middle-class Brahman subcaste," *Journal of the Royal Anthropological Institute*, 14, pp. 736–754.

Gabb, J., & Fink, J. (2015). *Couple relationships in the 21st century*, Palgrave Macmillan, Basingstoke, Hampshire.

George, S.M. (2002). "Sex selection/determination in India: Contemporary developments," *Reproductive Health Matters*, 10, no. 19, pp. 190–192.

Gershuny, J., & Sullivan, O. (2014). "Household structures and housework: Assessing the contributions of all household members with a focus on children and youths," *Review of Economics of the Household*, 12, no. 1, pp. 7–27.

Giddens, A. (1992). *The Transformation of intimacy: Sexuality, love and eroticism in modern societies*, Stanford University Press, Stanford, CA.

Gilbertson, A. (2014). "From respect to friendship? Companionate marriage and conjugal power negotiation in middle-class Hyderabad," *South Asia: Journal of South Asian Studies*, 37, no. 2, pp. 225–238.

Gilmartin, C., & Tan, L. (2002). "Fleeing poverty: Rural women, expanding marriage markets, and strategies for social mobility in contemporary China," in Chow, E N. (ed.), *Transforming gender and development in East Asia*, Routledge, New York, pp. 203–216.

Goffman, E. (1963). "Stigma and social identity," in *Stigma: Notes on the management of spoiled identity*, Prentice-Hall, Englewood Cliffs, NJ, pp. 1–40.

Gold, A.G. (2006). "Love's cup, love's thorn, love's end: The language of *prem* in Ghatiyali," in Orsini, F. (ed.), *Love in South Asia: A cultural history*, Cambridge University Press, Cambridge, pp. 303–330.

Gooch, L., & Jolley, M.A. (2016). "Sold like cows and goats': India's slave brides," Aljazeera, 14 November, viewed 2 December 2019, https://www.aljazeera.com/indepth/features/2016/11/cows-goats-india-slave-brides-161114084933017.html

Goody, J. (1973). "Bridewealth and dowry in Africa and Eurasia," in Goody, J., & Tambiah, S.J., *Bridewealth and dowry*, Cambridge University Press, Cambridge, pp. 1–58.

Gorringe, H., & Rafanell, I. (2007). "The embodiment of caste: Oppression, protest and change," *Sociology*, 41, no. 1, pp. 97–114.

Gould, H.A. (1960). "The micro-demography of marriages in a north Indian area," *Southwestern Journal of Anthropology*, 16, no. 4, pp. 476–491.

Gould, H. (1986). "The Hindu jajmani system: A case of economic particularism," *Journal of Anthropological Research*, 42, no. 3, pp. 269–278.

Graham, H. (1983). "Caring: A labour of love," in Finch, J., & Groves, D. (eds.), *A labour of love: Women, work and caring*, Routledge and Kegan Paul, London, pp. 13–30.

Grover, S. (2011). *Marriage, love, caste and kinship support: Lived experiences of the urban poor in India*, Social Science Press, New Delhi.

Grover, S. (2014). "'*Purani aur nai shaadi*': Separation, divorce and remarriage in the lives of the urban poor in New Delhi," in Kaur, R. and Palriwala, R. (eds.). *Marrying in South Asia: Shifting concepts, changing practices in a globalising world*, Orient BlackSwan, New Delhi, pp. 311–332.

Guilmoto, C.Z. (2008). "Economic, social and spatial dimensions of India's excess child masculinity," *Population-E* (English), 63, no. 1, pp. 91–118.

Guilmoto, C.Z. (2012). "Skewed sex ratios at birth and future marriage squeeze in China and India, 2005–2100," *Demography*, 49, no. 1, pp. 77–100.

Guilmoto, C.Z. (2018). "Sex ratio imbalances in Asia: An ongoing conversation between Anthropologists and demographers," in Srinivasan, S., & Li, S. (eds.), *Scarce women and surplus men in China and India: Macro demographics versus local dynamics*, Springer, Cham, pp. 145–161.

Guilmoto, C.Z., & Attané, I. (2007). "The geography of deteriorating child sex ratio in China and India," in Attané, I., & Guilmoto, C.Z. (eds.), *Watering the neighbour's garden: The growing demographic female deficit in Asia*, Committee for International Cooperation in National Research in Demography (CICRED), Paris, pp. 109–129.

Guilmoto, C.Z., & Rajan, I. (2013). "Fertility at the district level in India lessons from the 2011 Census," *Economic and Political Weekly*, 47, no. 23, pp. 59–70.

Gupta, C. (2016). "Allegories of "Love Jihad" and ghar vāpasī: Interlocking the socio-religious with the political," *Archív Orientální*, 84, no. 2, pp. 291–316.

Gupta, D. (1997). *Rivalry and brotherhood: Politics in the life of farmers in northern India*, Oxford University Press, New Delhi.

Hammersley, M., & Atkinson, P. (1983). *Ethnography: Principles in practice*, Tavistock, London.

Harwin, N., & Barron, J. (2000). "Domestic violence and social policy: Perspectives from women's aid," in Hanmer, J., & Itzin, C. (eds.), *Home truths about domestic violence: Feminist influences on policy and practice a reader*, Routledge, London pp. 205–227.

Hershman, P. (1977). "Virgin and mother," in Lewis, I. (ed.), *Symbols and sentiments: Cross-cultural studies in symbolism*, Academic Press, London, pp. 269–292.

Hershman, P. (1981). *Punjabi kinship and marriage*, Hindustan Publishing Corporation, Delhi.

Hirsch, J.S., & Wardlow, H. (2006). *Modern loves: The anthropology of romantic courtship and companionate marriage*, University of Michigan Press, Ann Arbor.

Holmes, M. (2014). *Distance relationships: intimacy and emotions amongst academics and their partners in dual-locations*, Palgrave Macmillan, London.

Huggler, J. (2009). "The price of being a woman: Slavery in modern India," Independent, 1 April, viewed 9 September 2019, https://www.independent.co.uk/news/world/asia/the-price-of-being-a-woman-slavery-in-modern-iindia-6104766.html

Ibrahim, F. (2018). "Cross-border intimacies: Marriage, migration, and citizenship in western India," *Modern Asian Studies* 52, no. 5, pp. 1664–1691.

International Centre for Research on Women (ICRW). (2014). *Masculinity, intimate partner violence and son preference in India*. New Delhi.

Ishii, S.K. (2016). *Marriage migration in Asia: Emerging minorities at the frontiers of nation-states*, NUS Press in association Kyoto University Press, Singapore.

Ito, R. (2005). "Crafting migrant women's citizenship in Japan: Taking family as a vantage point," *International Journal of Japanese Sociology*, 14, pp. 52–69.

Jackson, C. (1999). "Men's work, masculinities and gender divisions of labour," *Journal of Development Studies*, 36, no. 1, pp. 89–108.

Jacobson, D. (1977). "Flexibility in north Indian kinship and residence," in David, K. (ed.), *The new wind: Changing identities in South Asia*, Mouton, The Hague, pp. 263–283.

Jacobson, D. (1982). "Purdah and the Hindu family in central India," in Minault, G., & Papanek, H. (eds.), *Separate worlds: Studies of purdah in South Asia*, Chanakya, Delhi, pp. 81–109.

Jamieson, L. (1998). *Intimacy: Personal relationships in modern societies*, Polity Press, Cambridge.

Jamieson, L. (1999). "Intimacy transformed? A critical look at the pure relationship," *Sociology*, 33, no. 3, pp. 477–494.

Jamieson, L. (2011). "Intimacy as a concept: Explaining social change in the context of globalisation or another form of ethnocentrism?" *Sociological Research Online*, 16, no. 4.

Jamieson, L., et al. (2006). "Friends, neighbours and distant partners: Extending or decentring family relationships?" *Sociological Research Online*, 11, no. 3.

Jejeebhoy, S.J. (1998). "Wife-beating in rural India: A husband's right? Evidence from survey data," *Economic and Political Weekly*, 33, no. 15, pp. 855–862.

Jeffery, P. (1979). *Frogs in a well: Indian women in purdah*, Zed, London.

Jeffery, P. (2001). "A uniform customary code? Marital breakdown and women's economic entitlements in rural Bijnor," *Contributions to Indian Sociology*, 35, no. 1, pp. 1–32.

Jeffery, P. (2014). "Supply-and-demand demographics: Dowry, daughter aversion and marriage markets in contemporary north India," *Contemporary South Asia*, 22, no. 2, pp. 171–188.

Jeffery, P., & Jeffery, R. (1993). "A woman belongs to her husband: Female autonomy, women's work and childbearing in Bijnor," in Clark, A.W. (ed.), *Gender and political economy: Explorations of South Asian systems*, Oxford University Press, Oxford, pp. 66–114.

Jeffery, P., & Jeffery, R. (1996). *Don't marry me to a plowman! Women's everyday life in rural north India*, Westview Press, Oxford.

Jeffery, P., & Jeffery, R. (1997). *Population, gender and politics: Demographic change in rural north India*, Cambridge University Press, Cambridge.

Jeffery, P., & Jeffery, R. (2010). "Only when the boat has started sinking: A maternal death in rural north India," *Social Science and Medicine*, 71, no. 10, pp. 1711–1718.

Jeffery, P., Jeffery, R., & Jeffrey, C. (2008). "Disputing contraception: Muslim reform, secular change and fertility," *Modern Asian Studies*, 42, no. 2/3, pp. 519–548.

Jeffery, P., Jeffery, R., & Lyon, A. (1988). "When did you last see your mother? Aspects of female autonomy in rural north India," in Caldwell, J., Hill, A.G.,

& Hull, V.J. (eds.), *Micro-approaches to demographic research*, Kegan Paul, London, pp. 321–333.

Jeffery, P., Jeffery, R., & Lyon, A. (1989). *Labour pains and labour power: Women and childbearing in India*, Zed, London.

Jeffrey, C. (2010). *Timepass: Youth, class, and the politics of waiting in India.*, Stanford University Press, Stanford, CA.

Jeffrey, C., Jeffery, P., & Jeffery, R. (2008). *Degrees without freedom? Education, masculinities and unemployment in north India*, Stanford University Press, Stanford, CA.

Jha, S., & Adelman, M. (2009). "Looking for love in all the white places: A study of skin color preferences on Indian matrimonial and mate-seeking websites," *Studies in South Asian Film and Media*, 1, no. 1, pp. 65–83.

John, M., et al. (2009). "Dispensing with daughters: Technology, society, economy in north India," *Economic and Political Weekly*, 44, no. 15, pp. 16–19.

Joshi, V. (2010). "Economic resurgence, lopsided reform and jobless growth," in Heath, A., & Jeffery, R. (eds.), *Diversity and change in modern India: Economic, social and political approaches*, Oxford University Press, Oxford, pp. 73–106.

Junhong, C. (2001). "Prenatal sex determination and sex-selective abortion in rural Central China," *Population and Development Review*, 27, no. 2, pp. 259–281.

Harrison, K. (1998). "Rich friendships, affluent friends: middle-class practices of friendship," in Adams, R.G., & Allan, G. (eds.), *Placing friendship in context*, Cambridge University Press, Cambridge, pp. 92–116.

Kabeer, N. (1999). "Resources, agency, achievements: Reflections on the measurement of women's empowerment," *Development and Change*, 30, pp. 435–464.

Kalmijn, M. (1998). "Intermarriage and homogamy: Causes, patterns, trends," *Annual Review of Sociology*, 24, pp. 395–421.

Kalmuss, D. (1984). "The intergenerational transmission of marital aggression," *Journal of Marriage and Family*, 46, no. 1, pp. 11–19.

Kandiyoti, D. (1988). "Bargaining with patriarchy," *Gender and Society*, 2, no. 3, pp. 274–290.

Kandiyoti, D. (1998). "Gender, power and contestation: Rethinking bargaining with patriarchy," Jackson, C., & Pearson, R. (eds.), *Feminist visions of development*, Routledge, London, pp. 135–151.

Kannabiran, K., & Kannabiran, V. (1991). "Caste and gender: Understanding dynamics of power and violence," *Economic and political weekly*, 26, no. 37, pp. 2130–2133.

Kant, R., & Pandey, K.K. (2003). *Female foeticide, coerced marriage and bonded labour in Haryana and Punjab: A situational report*, Shakti Vahini, Haryana.

Kapadia, K. (1991). *Siva and her sisters: Gender, caste and class in rural south India*, Westview Press, Boulder, CO.

Kapur, P. (1970). *Marriage and the working woman in India*, Vikas Publications, Delhi.

Karve, I. (1994). "The kinship map of India," in Uberoi, P. (ed.), *Family, kinship and marriage in India*, Oxford University Press, New Delhi, pp. 50–73.

Kaur, R. (2004). "Across-region marriages: Poverty, female migration and the sex ratio," *Economic and Political Weekly*, 39, no. 25, pp. 2595–2603.

Kaur, R. (2008). "Dispensable daughters and bachelor sons: Sex discrimination in north India," *Economic and Political Weekly*, 43, no. 30, pp. 109–114.

Kaur, R. (2010a). "Bengali bridal diaspora: Marriage as a livelihood strategy," *Economic and Political Weekly*, 45, no. 5, pp. 16–18.

Kaur, R. (2010b). "Khap panchayats, sex ratio and female agency," *Economic and Political Weekly* 45, no. 23, pp. 14–16.

Kaur, R. (2012). "Marriage and migration: Citizenship and marital experience in cross-border marriages between Uttar Pradesh, West Bengal and Bangladesh," *Economic and Political Weekly*, 47, no. 43, pp. 78–84.

Kaur, R. (2014). "Sex ratios, khaps and marriage reform," *Economic and Political Weekly*, 49, no. 31, pp. 18–20.

Kaur, R. (2015). "Tackling India's 'bare branches,'" *Seminar* 665, pp. 63–67.

Kaur, R. (2016). "Introduction: Mapping the consequences of sex selection and gender imbalance in India and China," Kaur, R. (ed.), *Too many men, too few women: Social consequences of gender imbalance in India and China*, Orient BlackSwan, New Delhi, pp. 1–32.

Kaur, R. (2020). "Gender and demography in Asia (India and China)," in Ludden, D. (ed.), *The Oxford research encyclopedia of Asian history*, Oxford University Press, New York, viewed 8 October 2020, https://oxfordre.com/asianhistory/view/10.1093/acrefore/9780190277727.001.0001/acrefore-9780190277727-e-345

Kaur, R., & Dhanda, P. (2014). "Surfing for spouses: Marriage websites and the new Indian marriage?" in Kaur, R., & Palriwala, R. (eds.), *Marrying in South Asia: Shifting concepts, changing practices in a globalising world*, Orient BlackSwan, New Delhi, pp. 271–292.

Kaur, R., & Palriwala, P. (2014). *Marrying in South Asia: Shifting concepts, changing practices in a globalising world*, Orient BlackSwan, New Delhi.

Khandelwal, M. (2009). "Arranging love: Interrogating the vantage point in cross border feminism," *Signs: Journal of Women in Culture and Society*, 34, no. 3, pp. 583–609.

Khare, R.S. (1960). "The Kanya-Kubja Brahmans and their caste organisation," *Southwestern Journal of Anthropology*, 16, pp. 348–367.

Killick, E., & Desai, A. (2010). "Introduction: Valuing friendship," in *The ways of friendship: Anthropological perspectives*, Berghahn Books, New York, pp. 1–19.

Kim, D.S. (2004). "Missing girls in South Korea: Trends, levels and regional variations," *Population* (English edition), 59, no. 6, pp. 865–878.

Kim, D.S. (2010). "The rise of cross-border marriage marriage and divorce in contemporary Korea," in Yang, W.-S., & Lu, M.C.-W. (eds.), *Asian cross-border marriage—demographic patterns and social issues*, Amsterdam University Press, Amsterdam, pp. 127–156.

Kodoth, P. (2008). "Gender, caste and matchmaking in Kerala: A rationale for dowry," *Development and Change*, 39, no. 2, pp. 263–283.

Kolenda, P. (1963). "Toward a model of the Hindu jajmani system," *Human Organization*, 22, no. 1, pp. 11–31.

Kolenda, P. (1967). "Regional differences in Indian family structure," in Crane, R.I. (ed.), *Regions and regionalism in South Asian studies: An exploratory study*, Duke University, Program in Comparative Studies in South Asia, Monograph and Occasional Paper Series, Monograph No. 5, Durham, NC.

Kolenda, P. (1984). "Woman as tribute, woman as flower: Images of 'woman' in weddings in north and south India," *American Ethnologist*, 11, no. 1, pp. 98–117.

Kolenda, P. (1992a). "Purity and pollution," in Madan, T.N. (ed.), *Religion in India*, Oxford University Press, New Delhi, pp. 78–94.

Kolenda, P. (1992b). "Widowhood among untouchable Chuhras," in Ostor, A., Fruzzetti, L., & Barnett, S. (eds.), *Concepts of person: Kinship, caste and marriage in India*, Harvard University Press, Cambridge, MA, pp. 172–220.

Krishnan, S. (2015). "Agency, intimacy, and rape jokes: an ethnographic study of young women and sexual risk in Chennai," *Journal of the Royal Anthropological Institute* (n.s.), 22, pp. 67–83.

Krishnan, V.B. (2019). "What is the biggest reason for migration in India?" *The Hindu*, 22 July, viewed 2 February 2020, https://www.thehindu.com/data/india-migration-patterns-2011-census/article28620772.ece

Kukreja, R. (2018a). "Caste and cross-region marriage in Haryana, India: Experience of Dalit cross-region brides in Jat households," *Modern Asian Studies*, 52, no. 2, pp. 492–531.

Kukreja, R. (2018b). "An unwanted weed: Children of cross-region unions confront intergenerational stigma of caste, ethnicity and religion," *Journal of Intercultural Studies*, 39, no. 4, pp. 382–398.

Kukreja, R., & Kumar, P. (2013). *Tied in a knot: Cross-region marriages in Haryana and Rajasthan: Implications for gender rights and gender relations*, Tamarind Tree Films, New Delhi.

Kumar, S. (2016). "Agrarian transformation and new sociality in western Uttar Pradesh," *Economic & Political Weekly*, 51, no. 26–27, pp. 61–71.

Lamb, S. (1997). "The making and unmaking of persons: Notes on aging and gender in north India," *Ethos*, 25, no. 3, pp. 279–302.

Lamb, S. (1999). "Aging, gender and widowhood: Perspectives from rural West Bengal," *Contributions to Indian Sociology* (n.s.), 33, no. 3, pp. 541–570.

Lamb, S. (2000). *White saris and sweet mangoes: Aging, gender and the body in north India*, University of California Press, Berkeley.

Lamb, S. (2018). "Being single in India: Gendered identities, class mobilities, and personhoods in flux," *Ethos*, 46, no. 1, pp. 49–69.

Lambert, H. (1996). "Caste, gender and locality in rural Rajasthan," in Fuller, C.J. (ed.), *Caste today*, Oxford University Press, Oxford, pp. 93–123.

Larsen, M., & Kaur, R. (2013). "Signs of change? Sex ratio imbalance and shifting social practices in northern India," *Economic and Political Weekly*, 48, no. 35, pp. 45–52.

Lauser, A. (2008). "Philippine women on the move: Marriage across borders," *International Migration*, 46, no. 4, pp. 85–110.

Lavely, W. (1991). "Marriage and mobility under rural collectivism," in Watson, R.S., & Ebrey, P.B. (eds.), *Marriage and inequality in Chinese society*, University of California Press, Berkeley, pp. 286–312.

Lee, H. (2012). "Political economy of cross-border marriage: Economic development and social reproduction in Korea," *Feminist Economics*, 18, no. 2, pp. 177–200.

Libbee, M. (1980). "Territorial endogamy and the spatial structure of marriage in rural India," in Sopher, D.E. (ed.), *An exploration of India: Geographical perspectives on society and culture*, Cornell University Press, Ithaca, NY, pp. 65–104.

Lietchy, M. (2003). *Suitably modern: Making new middle class culture in a new consumer society*, Princeton University Press, Princeton, NJ.

Liu, L., et al. (2014). "Male marriage squeeze and inter-provincial marriage in central China—evidence from Anhui," *Journal of Contemporary China*, 23, no. 86, pp. 351–371.

Lu, M.C. (2008). "Commercially arranged marriage migration: Case studies of cross-border marriages in Taiwan," in Palriwala, R., & Uberoi, P. (eds.), *Marriage, migration and gender*, Sage, New Delhi, pp. 125–151.

Lyon, A. (1988). One or two sons: Class, gender and fertility in north India, doctoral thesis, University of Edinburgh.

Mamgain, R.P. (2019). "Employment, its quality and inequality," in Mamgain, R.P. (ed.), *Growth, disparities and inclusive development in India perspectives from the Indian state of Uttar Pradesh*, Springer, Singapore, pp. 49–73.

Mand, K. (2006). "Social relations beyond the family?" *Community, Work and Family*, 9, no. 3, pp. 309–323.

Mand, K. (2008). "Marriage and migration through the life course: Experiences of widowhood, separation and divorce among transnational Sikh women," in Palriwala, R., & Uberoi, P. (eds.), *Marriage, migration and gender*, Sage, New Delhi, pp. 286–302.

Madan, T.N. (2002). *Family and kinship: A study of the Pandits of rural Kashmir*, Oxford University Press, New Delhi.

Madan, T.N. (2011). *The Hindu householder: The T.N. Madan omnibus*. Oxford University Press, Oxford.

Mander, H., et al. (2016). "Wages of communal violence in Muzaffarnagar and Shamli," *Economic and Political Weekly*, 51, no. 43, pp. 39–45.

Madsen, S.T. (1991). "Clan, kinship and panchayat justice among the Jats of western Uttar Pradesh," *Anthropos*, 86 (H.4/6), pp. 351–365.

Mahmood, S. (2001). "Feminist theory, embodiment, and the docile agent: Some reflections on the Egyptian Islamic revival," *Cultural Anthropology*, 16, no. 2, pp. 202–236.

Majumdar, R. (2004). "Looking for brides and grooms: *Ghataks*, matrimonials and the marriage market in colonial Calcutta, circa 1875–1940," *The Journal of Asian Studies*, 63, no. 4, pp. 911–935.

Manayath, N. (2015). "The shameless marriage: Thinking through same-sex erotics and the question of gay marriage in India," in Basu, S., & Ramberg, L. (eds.), *Conjugality unbound: sexual economies, state regulation and the marital form in India*, Women Unlimited, New Delhi, pp. 251–280.

Marriott, M. (1955). "Little communities in an indigenous civilisation," in *Village India*, University of Chicago Press, Chicago, pp. 171–222.

Marriott, M. (1976). "Hindu transactions: Diversity without dualism," in Kapferer, B. (ed.), *Transaction and meanings: Directions in the Anthropology of exchange and symbolic behavior*, Institute for the Study of Human Issues (ISHI), Philadelphia, pp. 109–142.

Masoodi, A. (2014). "Human trafficking caters to demand for brides," Mint, 5 September, viewed 9 September 2019, https://www.livemint.com/Politics/7cSn-08nD9gvIEAbZcQrP7I/Human-trafficking-caters-to-demand-for-brides.html

Mayer, A. (1960). *Caste and kinship in central India: A village and its region*, Routledge and Kegan Paul, London.

Mayer, A. (1996). "Caste in an Indian village: Change and continuity 1954–1992," in Fuller, C.J. (ed.), *Caste today*, Oxford University Press, Delhi, pp. 32–64.

Mazumdar, I., & Agnihotri, I. (2014). "Traversing myriad trails: Tracking gender and labour migration across India," in Truong, T.D., et al. (eds.), *Migration, gender and social justice, perspectives on human insecurity*, Springer, London, pp. 123–151.

Mazumdar, I., Agnihotri, I., & Neetha, N. (2013). "Migration and gender in India," *Economic and Political Weekly*, 48, no. 10, pp. 54–64.

McGee, M. (2004). "Samskara," in Mittal, S., & Thursby, G. (eds.), *The Hindu world*, Routledge, London, pp. 332–356.

Miller, B.D. (1981). *The endangered sex: Neglect of female children in rural north India*, Cornell University Press, Ithaca, NY.

Miller, B.D. (1997). "Female infanticide and child neglect in rural north India," in Brettell, C.B., & Sargent, C.F. (eds.), *Gender in cross-cultural perspectiveI*, 2nd edn, Prentice-Hall, Upper Saddle River, NJ, pp. 453–465.

Milner, M. Jr. (1988). "Status relations in South Asian marriage alliances: Toward a general theory," *Contributions to Indian Sociology*, 22, pp. 145–169.

Min, H., & Eades, J.S. (1995). "Brides, bachelors and brokers: The marriage market in rural Anhui in an era of economic reforms," *Modern Asian Studies*, 29, no. 4, pp. 841–869.

Ministry of Health and Family Welfare, Government of India (n.d.). National Health Mission, viewed 20 June 2020, https://nhm.gov.in/index1.php?lang=1&level=1& sublinkid=150&lid=226

Minturn, L. (1993). *Sita's daughters coming out of purdah: The Rajput women of Khalapur revisited*, Oxford University Press, Oxford.

Mirza, N. (2015). "South Asian women's experience of abuse by female affinal kin: A critique of mainstream conceptualisations of domestic abuse," *Families, Relationships and Societies*, 10, no. 10, pp. 1–17.

Mishra, P. (2016). "Imbalanced sex-ratio and cross-region marriages: The challenges of transcending caste boundaries," in Kaur, R. (ed.), *Too many men, too few women: Social consequences of gender imbalance in India and China*, Orient BlackSwan, New Delhi, pp. 220–244.

Mishra, P. (2018). "Being 'bare branches': Demographic imbalance, marriage exclusion and masculinity in north India," in Srinivasan, S., & Li, S. (eds.), *Scarce women and surplus men in China and India: Macro demographics versus local dynamics*, Springer, Cham, pp. 25–46.

Mody, P. (2008). *The intimate state: Love-marriage and the law in Delhi*, Routledge, New Delhi.

Mody, P. (2019). "Contemporary intimacies," in Srivastava, S., Arif, Y., & Abraham, J. (eds.), *Critical themes in Indian Sociology*, Sage, New Delhi, pp. 257–266.

Morgan, D. (1996). *Family connections: An introduction to family studies*, Polity Press, Cambridge.

Mukherjee, S. (2013). "Skewed sex ratio and migrant brides in Haryana: Reflections from the field," *Social Change*, 43, no. 1, pp. 37–52.

Mukhopadhyay, M. (2011). "Choice and agency in marital decisions: A study among Hindu Bengalis across class in Kolkata," Sen, S., Biswas, R., & Dhawan, N. (eds.). *Intimate others: Marriage and sexualities in India*, Stree, Kolkata, pp. 121–148.

Nakamatsu, T. (2003). "International marriage through introduction agencies: Social and legal realities of 'Asian' wives of Japanese men," in Piper, N., & Roces, M. (eds.), *Wife or worker? Asian women and migration*, Rowman and Littlefield, Langham, pp. 181–201.

Narayan, K. (1986). "Birds on a branch: Girlfriends and wedding songs in Kangra," *Ethos*, 14, no. 1, pp. 47–75.

Narayan, K. (2004). "Honor is honor, after all: Silence and speech in the life stories of women in Kangra, north-west India," in Arnold, D., & Blackburn, S. (eds.), *Telling lives in India: biography, autobiography and life history*, Indiana University Press, Bloomington, pp. 227–251.

Narayan, K. (2016). *Everyday creativity: Singing goddessess in the Himalayan foothills*, University of Chicago Press, Chicago.

Nisbett, N. (2006). "The internet, cybercafés and the new social spaces of Bangalorean youth," in Coleman, S., & Collins, P. (eds.), *Locating the field: Space, place and context in Anthropology*, Bloomsbury Academic, London, pp. 129–148.

Nisbett, N. (2007). "Friendship, consumption, morality: Practising identity, negotiating hierarchy in middle class Bangalore," *Journal of the Royal Anthropological Institute*, 13, no. 4, pp. 935–950.

Okin, S.M. (1989). *Justice, gender and the family*. Basic Books, New York.

Oldenburg, V.T. (2002). *Dowry murder: The imperial origins of a cultural crime*, Oxford University Press, New York.

Orsini, F. (2006). "Introduction," in Orsini, F. (ed.), *Love in South Asia: A cultural history*, Cambridge University Press, Cambridge, pp. 1–39.

Osella, C. (2012). "Desire under reform: Contemporary reconfigurations of family, marriage, love and gendering in a transnational south Indian matrilineal Muslim community," *Culture and Religion*, 13, no. 2, pp. 241–264.

Osella, C., & Osella, F. (1998). "Friendship and flirting: Micro-politics in Kerala, south India," *Journal of the Royal Anthropological Institute*, 4, no. 2, pp. 189–206.

Pache, V. (1998). "Marriage fairs among Maheshwaris: A new matrimonial strategy," *Economic and Political Weekly*, 33, no. 17, pp. 970–975.

Pahl, R., & Spencer, L. (2004). "Personal communities: Not simply families of 'fate' or 'choice,'" *Current Sociology*, 52, no. 2, pp. 199–221.

Palriwala, R. (1989). "Reaffirming the anti-dowry struggle." *Economic and Political Weekly*, 24, no. 17, pp. 942–944.

Palriwala, R. (1991). "Transitory residence and invisible work: A case study of a Rajasthan village," *Economic and Political Weekly*, 26, no. 48, pp. 2763–2772.

Palriwala, R. (1994). *Changing kinship, family, and gender relations in South Asia: Processes, trends, and issues*, Women and Autonomy Centre (VENA), Leiden University.

Palriwala, R. (2000). "Family: Power relations and power structures," in Kramarae, C., & Spender, D. (eds.), *Routledge international encyclopedia of women: Global women's issues and knowledge*, vol. 2, Routledge, New York, 669–674.

Palriwala, R. (2009). "The spider's web: Seeing dowry, fighting dowry," in Bradley, T., Tomalin, E., & Subramaniam, M. (eds.), *Dowry: Bridging the gap between theory and practice*, Women Unlimited, New Delhi, pp. 144–176.

Palriwala, R. (2016). "Acts of omission and acts of commission: The adverse juvenile sex ratio and the Indian state," in Kaur, R. (ed.), *Too many men, too few women: Social consequences of gender imbalance in India and China*, Orient BlackSwan, New Delhi, pp. 275–301.

Palriwala, R., & Kaur, R. (2014). "Introduction: Marriage in South Asia, continuities and transformations," in Kaur, R. and Palriwala, P. (eds.)., *Marrying in South Asia: Shifting concepts, changing practices in a globalising world*, Orient Black Swan, New Delhi, pp. 1–48.

Palriwala, R., & Uberoi, P. (2008). "Exploring the links: Gender issues in marriage and migration," in Palriwala, R., & Uberoi, P. (eds.), *Marriage, migration and gender*, Sage, New Delhi, pp. 23–60.

Pananakhonsab, W. (2016). *Love and intimacy in online cross-cultural relationships.* Palgrave Macmillan, London.

Panda, P., & Agarwal, B. (2005). "Marital violence, human development and women's property status in India," *World Development*, 33, no. 5, pp. 823–850.

Papanek, H. (1982). "Purdah: Separate worlds and symbolic shelter," in Minault, G., & Papanek, H. (eds.), *Separate worlds: Studies of purdah in South Asia*, Chanakya, Delhi, pp. 3–53.

Pappu, R. (2011). "Reconsidering romance and intimacy: The case of the single unmarried woman," in Sen, S., Biswas, R., & Dhawan, N. (eds.). *Intimate others: Marriage and sexualities in India*, Stree, Kolkata, pp. 370–390.

Parry, J. (1979). *Caste and kinship in Kangra*, Routledge and Kegan Paul, London.

Parry, J. (2001). "Ankalu's errant wife: Sex, marriage and industry in contemporary Chhatisgarh," *Modern Asian Studies*, 35, pp. 783–820.

Partners for Law in Development (PLD). (2010). *Rights in intimate relationships: Towards an inclusive and just framework of women's rights and the family.* New Delhi.

Patel, T. (2007). *Sex-selective abortion in India: Gender, society and new reproductive technologies*, Sage Publications, New Delhi.

Patel, V. (2017). "Parents, permission, and possibility: Young women, college, and imagined futures in Gujarat, India," *Geoforum* 80, pp. 39–48.

Pateman, C. (1988). *The sexual contract*, Polity in Association with Basil Blackwell, Cambridge.

Pettigrew, J. (1975). *Robber noblemen: A study of the political system of the Sikh Jats*, Routledge and Kegan Paul, London.

Plunkett, F.T. (1973). "Royal marriages in Rajasthan," *Contributions to Indian Sociology*, 7, no. 1, pp. 64–80.

Pocock, D.F. (1972). *Kanbi and Patidar: A study of the Patidar community of Gujarat.* Clarendon Press, Oxford.

Pradhan, M.C. (1966). *The political system of the Jats of northern India*, Oxford University Press, London.

Qureshi, K. (2016). *Marital breakdown among British Asians: Conjugality, legal pluralism and new kinship*, Palgrave Macmillan, London.

Qureshi, K. (2019). *Chronic illness in a Pakistani labour diaspora*, Carolina Academic Press, Durham, NC.

Qureshi, K., & Rogaly, B. (2018). "Womanhood implies travel: Punjabi marriage migration between India and Britain," in Riley, N.E., & Brunson, J. (eds.), *International handbook on gender and demographic processes*, Springer, Dordrecht, pp. 203–214.

Raghavan, S. (2015). "There's a shortage of brides in India, and it's a problem," *Washington Post*, 10 September, viewed 14 March 2019, https://www.washington post.com/news/worldviews/wp/2015/09/10/theres-a-shortage-of-brides-in-india-and-its-a-problem/

Raj, A., & Silverman, J. (2002). "Violence against immigrant women: The roles of culture, context, and legal immigrant status on intimate partner," *Violence against Women*, 8, no. 3, pp. 367–398.

Raheja, G.G. (1988). *The poison in the gift: Ritual, prestation and the dominant caste in a North Indian Village*, University of Chicago Press, Chicago.

Raheja, G.G. (1995). "Crying when she's born, and crying when she goes away: Marriage and the idiom of the gift in Pahansu song performance," in Harlan, L., & Courtright, P.B. (eds.), *From the margins of Hindu marriage: Essays on gender, religion, and culture*, Oxford University Press, New York, pp. 19–59.

Raheja, G.G., & Gold, A.G. (1994). *Listen to the heron's words: Reimagining gender and kinship in north India*, University of California Press, Berkeley.

Rao, N. (2015). "Marriage, violence and choice: Understanding Dalit women's agency in rural Tamil Nadu," *Gender and Society*, 29, no. 3, pp. 410–433.

Rao, V. (1993). "The rising price of husbands: A hedonic analysis of dowry increases in rural India," *Journal of Political Economy*, 101, no. 4, pp. 666–677.

Reader, S. (2007). "The other side of agency," *Philosophy*, 4, pp. 579–604.

Reddy, G. (2006). "The bonds of love—companionate marriage and the desire for intimacy among hijras in Hyderabad, India," in Hirsch, J.S. & Wardlow, H. (eds.), *Modern loves: The anthropology of romantic courtship and companionate marriage*, University of Michigan Press, Ann Arbor, pp. 174–192.

Rege, S. (2003). "A Dalit feminist standpoint," in Rao, A. (ed.), *Gender and caste*, Women Unlimited, New Delhi, pp. 90–101.

Robitaille, M.C., & Chatterjee, I. (2017). "Mothers-in-law and son preference in India," *Economic and Political Weekly*, 52, no. 6, pp. 42–50.

Rogers, M. (2008). "Modernity, 'authenticity,' and ambivalence: Subaltern masculinities on a south Indian college campus," *Journal of the Royal Anthropological Institute* (n.s.), 14, pp. 79–95.

Roseneil, S., & Budgeon, S. (2004). "Cultures of intimacy and care beyond 'the family': personal life and social change in the early 21st century," *Current Sociology*, 52, no. 2, pp. 135–159.

Roy, R. (2007). *A little book on men*. Yoda Press, New Delhi.

Sahay, G.R. (2015). "Dominance of Jats is unabated: Caste and dominance in the villages of western Uttar Pradesh," *Contributions to Indian Sociology*, 49, no. 2, pp. 216–249.

Sambrani, R., & Sambrani, S. (1983). "Economics of brideprice and dowry," *Economic and Political Weekly*, 18, no. 15, pp. 601–603.

Sangari, K. (1993). "Consent, agency and rhetorics of incitement," *Economic and Political Weekly*, 28, no. 18, pp. 867–882.

Sassatelli, R. (2010). "A serial ethnographer: An interview with Gary Alan Fine," *Qualitative Sociology*, 33, pp. 79–96.

Schein, L. (2005). "Marrying out of place: Hmong/Miao women across and beyond China," in Constable, N. (ed), *Cross-border marriages: Gender and mobility in transnational Asia*, University of Pennsylvania Press, Philadelpia, pp. 53–79.

Scheper-Hughes, N. (2014). "Family life as *bricolage*: Reflections on intimacy and attachment in death without weeping," in Otto, H., & Keller, H. (eds.), *Different faces of attachment: Cultural variations on a universal human need*, Cambridge University Press, Cambridge, pp. 230–261.

Schensul, S.L., et al. (2018). "Sexual intimacy and marital relationships in a low-income urban community in India," *Culture, Health and Sexuality*, 20, no. 10, pp. 1087–1101.

Sen, S., Biswas, R., & Dhawan, N. (eds.) (2011). *Intimate others: Marriage and sexualities in India*, Stree, Kolkata.

Seymour, S. (1999). *Women, family, and child care in India: A world in transition*, Cambridge University Press, Cambridge.

Shakti Vahini. (n.d.) Viewed 26 November 2019, https://shaktivahini.org/

Sharangpani, M. (2010). "Browsing for bridegrooms: Matchmaking and modernity in Mumbai," *Indian Journal of Gender Studies*, 17, no. 2, pp. 249–276.

Sharma, U. (1978a). "Women and their affines: The veil as a symbol of separation," *Man* (n.s.), 13, no. 2, pp. 218–233.

Sharma, U. (1978b). "Segregation and its consequences in India," in Caplan, P., & Bujra, J.M. (eds.), *Women united, women divided: Cross-cultural perspectives on female solidarity*, Tavistock, London, pp. 259–282.

Sharma, U. (1980). *Women, work and property in north-west India*, Tavistock, London.

Sharma, U. (1989). "Studying the household: Individuation and values," in Gray, J.N., & Mearns, D.J. (eds.), *Society from the inside out: Anthropological perspectives on the South Asian household*, Sage, London, pp. 35–55.

Sharma, U. (2005). "Dowry in north India: Its consequences for women," in Basu, S. (ed.), *Dowry and inheritance*, Women Unlimited, New Delhi, pp. 15–26.

Sheel, R. (1997). "Institutionalisation and expansion of dowry system in Colonial north India," *Economic and Political Weekly*, 32, no. 28, pp. 1709–1718.

Siddhanta, S., Agnihotri, S.B., & Nandy, D. (2009). "Sex ratio patterns among the scheduled castes in India 1981–2001," paper presented at *World Congress of the International Union for the Scientific Study of Population*, 27 September–2 October, Marrakech, Morocco.

Shukla, S., & Kapadia, S. (2007). "Transition in marriage partner selection process: Are matrimonial advertisements an indication?" *Psychology and Developing Societies*, 19, no. 1, pp. 37–54.

Singh, M. (2009). "Cross-border marriages in the Mewat region of Haryana: A report," paper presented at *Gender and Migration: Negotiating Rights, A Women's Movement Perspective*, 24 September, New Delhi.

Sirriyeh, A. (2013). *Inhabiting borders, routes home: Youth, gender, asylum*. Ashgate, Farnham.

Siwach, S. (2010). "In Haryana, get a bride for Rs 1000 from Bihar," *Times of India*, 28 November, viewed 14 March 2014, http://timesofindia.indiatimes.com/city/chandigarh/In-Haryana-get-a-bride-for-Rs-1000-from-Bihar/articleshow/7003264.cms

Smart, C. (2007). *Personal life: New directions in sociological thinking*, Polity, Cambridge.

Smith, D.J. (2006). "Love and the risk of HIV: Courtship, marriage and infidelity in southeastern Nigeria," in Hirsch, J.S., & Wardlow, H. (eds.), *Modern loves: The anthropology of romantic courtship and companionate marriage*, University of Michigan Press, Ann Arbor, pp. 135–153.

Srinivas, M.N. (1984). "Some reflections on dowry," Oxford University Press, New Delhi, published for the Centre for Women's Development Studies, New Delhi.

Srinivasan, S. (2005). "Daughters or dowries? The changing nature of dowry practices in south India," *World Development*, 33, no. 4, pp. 593–615.

Srinivasan, S. (2017). "Cross-region migration of brides and gender relations in a daughter deficit context," *Migration and Development* 6, no. 1, pp. 123–143.

Srinivasan, S., & Bedi, A.S. (2007). "Domestic violence and dowry: Evidence from a south Indian village," *World Development*, 35, no. 5, pp. 857–880.

Srinivasan, S., & Li, S. (2018). "Unifying perspectives: Understanding scarce women and surplus men in China and India," in *Scarce women and surplus men in China and India macro demographics versus local dynamics*, Springer, Cham, pp. 1–23.

South, S.J., Trent, K., & Bose, S. (2014). "Skewed sex ratios and criminal victimization in India," *Demography*, 51, no. 3, pp. 1019–1040.

Srivastava, N. (2002). "Multiple dimensions of violence against rural women in Uttar Pradesh: Macro and micro realities," in Kapadia, K. (ed.), *The violence of development*, Kali for Women, New Delhi, pp. 235–291.

Srivastava, S. (2012). "Masculinity and its role in gender based violence in public places," in Pilot, S., & Prabhu, L. (eds.), *Fear that stalks: Gender based violence in public spaces*, Zubaan, Delhi, pp. 13–50.

Srivastava, R., & Ranjan, R. (2016). "Deciphering growth and development past and present," *Economic and Political Weekly*, 2, no. 53, pp. 32–43.

Still, C. (2014). *Dalit women: Honour and patriarchy in South India*, Social Science Press, New Delhi.

Suzuki, N. (2005). "Tripartite desires: Filipina-Japanese marriages and fantasies of transnational traversal," in Constable, N. (ed.), *Cross-border marriages: Gender and mobility in transnational Asia*, University of Pennsylvania Press, Philadelphia, pp. 124–144.

Tambiah, S.J. (1973). "From varna to caste through mixed unions," in Goody, J. (ed.), *The Character of Kinship*, Cambridge University Press, London, pp. 191–230.

Tellis, A. (2014). "Multiple ironies: Notes on same-sex marriage for South Asians at home and abroad," in Kaur, R., & Palriwala, R. (eds.), *Marrying in South Asia: Shifting concepts, changing practices in a globalising world*, Orient Black-Swan, New Delhi, pp. 333–350.

Tenhunen, S. (2014). "Mobile telephony, mediation, and gender in rural India," *Contemporary South Asia*, 22, no. 2, pp. 157–170.

Thorat, S., & Newman, K.S. (2007). "Caste and economic discrimination: Causes, consequences and remedies," *Economic and Political Weekly*, 42, no. 41, pp. 4121–4124.

Titzmann, F.M. (2011). "Matchmaking 2.0: The representation of women and female agency in the Indian online matrimonial market," *Internationales Asienforum: International Quarterly for Asian Studies*, 42, no. 3–4, pp. 239–256.

Tilche, A. (2016). "Migration, bachelorhood and discontent among the Patidars," *Economic and Political Weekly*, 51, no. 26 & 27, pp. 17–24.

Trautmann, T. (1981). *Dravidian kinship*, University of California Press, Berkeley.

Trawick, M. (1990). *Notes on love in a Tamil family*, University of California Press, Berkeley.

Twamley, K. (2012). "Gender relations among Indian couples in the UK and India: Ideals of equality and realities of inequality," *Sociological Research Online*, 17, no. 4, pp. 103–113.

Twamley, K. (2014). *Love, marriage and intimacy among Gujarati Indians: A suitable match*, Palgrave Macmillan, Basingstoke.

Twamley, K., & Faircloth, C. (2015). "Introduction to special section: Gender, intimacy, equality: (Un)comfortable bedfellows?," *Sociological Research Online*, 20, no. 4.

Tyagi, A., & Uberoi, P. (1994). "Learning to adjust: Conjugal relations in Indian popular fiction," *Indian Journal of Gender Studies*, 1, no. 1, pp. 93–120.

Uberoi, P. (1994). "Marriage, alliance and affinal transactions," in Uberoi, P. (ed.), *Family, kinship and marriage in India*, Oxford University Press, New Delhi, pp. 225–236.

Ullrich, H.E. (2010). "Marital intimacy: A four-generation study of change among Havik Brahmins," in Leonard, K.I., Reddy, G., & Gold, A.G. (eds.), *Histories of intimacy and situated ethnography*, Manohar, Delhi, pp. 103–134.

Unnithan, M. (1992). "The politics of marriage payments in South Rajasthan," *South Asia Research*, 12, no. 1, pp. 60–73.

Van Der Veen, K.W. (1973). "Marriage and hierarchy among the Anavil Brahmans of south Gujarat," *Contributions to Indian Sociology*, 7, no. 1, pp. 36–52.

Varma, S., & Kumar, M. (2006). *From leather artisans to brick-kiln workers: Narratives of weary travellers*, V.V. Giri National Labour Institute, Noida.

Vatuk, S. (1971). "Trends in north Indian urban kinship: The 'matrilateral asymmetry' hypothesis," *Southwestern Journal of Anthropology*, 27, no. 3, pp. 287–307.

Vatuk, S. (1972). *Kinship and urbanization: White collar migrants in North India*, University of California Press, Berkeley.

Vatuk, S. (1975). "Gifts and affines in north India," *Contributions to Indian Sociology* (n.s.), 9, no. 2, pp. 155–196.

Vatuk, S. (1982). "Purdah revisited: A comparison of Hindu and Muslim interpretations of the cultural meaning of purdah in South Asia," in Minault, G., & Papanek, H. (eds.), *Separate worlds: Studies of purdah in South Asia*, Chanakya, Delhi, pp. 54–78.

Vatuk, S. (1989). "Household form and formation: Variability and social change among South Indian Muslims," in Gray, J.N., & Mearns, D.J. (eds.), *Society from the inside out: Anthropological perspectives on the South Asian household*, Sage, London, pp. 107–139.

Vatuk, S. (1990). "To be a burden to others': dependency anxiety among the elderly in India," in Lynch, O.M. (ed.), *Divine passions: The social construction of emotion in India*, University of California Press, Berkeley, pp. 64–88.

Vatuk, S. (1993). "Women, property and marriage transactions among Indian Muslims," paper presented at the *Annual Meetings of the Association for Asian Studies*, March, Los Angeles.

Vatuk, S. (2007). "The cancer of dowry in Indian Muslim Marriages: Themes in popular rhetoric from the south Indian Muslim Press," in Hasan, M. (ed.), *Living with secularism: The destiny of India's Muslims*, Manohar, New Delhi, pp. 155–175.

Vatuk, S. (2014). "Change and continuity in marital alliance patterns: Muslims in south India, 1800–2012," in Kaur, R., & Palriwala, R. (eds.). *Marrying in South Asia: Shifting concepts, changing practices in a globalising world*, Orient BlackSwan, New Delhi, pp. 28–48.

Vatuk, S. (2015). "What can divorce stories tell us about Muslim Marriage in India?" in Basu, S., & Ramberg, L. (eds.), *Conjugality unbound: Sexual economies, state regulation and the marital form in India*, Women Unlimited, New Delhi, pp. 190–216.

Vera-Sanso, P. (1999). "Dominant daughters-in-law and submissive mothers-in-law? cooperation and conflict in south India," *Journal of the Royal Anthropological Institute*, 5, no. 4, pp. 577–593.

Vishwanath, L.S. (2004). "Female infanticide: The colonial experience," *Economic and Political Weekly*, 39, no. 22, pp. 2313–2318.

Wadley, S. (1994). *Struggling with destiny in Karimpur, 1925–1984*, University of California Press, Berkeley.

Wadley, S. (1995). "No longer a wife: Widows in rural north India," in Harlan, L., & Courtright, P. (eds.), *From the margins of Hindu marriage: Essays on gender, religion and culture*, Oxford University Press, Oxford, pp. 92–118.

Wardlow, H. and Hirsch, J.S. (2006). "Introduction," in Hirsch, J.S., & Wardlow, H. (eds.), *Modern loves: The anthropology of romantic courtship and companionate marriage*, University of Michigan Press, Ann Arbor, pp. 1–31.

Westcott, H. (2012). "Imaginary friends: migrants' emotional accounts about friends outside Australia," *Australian Journal of Social Issues*, 47, no. 1, pp. 87–103.

Williams, L. (2010). *Global marriage: Cross-border marriage migration in global context*, Palgrave Macmillan, New York.

Wire Staff. (2017). "Disband anti-Romeo squads immediately, say women's rights activists," *The Wire*, 4 April, viewed 28 September 2020, https://thewire.in/rights/anti-romeo-squads-activists

Wiser, W.H. (1936). *The Hindu jajmani system*. Lucknow Publishing House, Lucknow.

Yalman, N. (1963). "On the purity of women in the castes of Ceylon and Malabar," *The Journal of the Royal Anthropological institute of Great Britain and Ireland*, 93, no. 1, pp. 25–58.

Yeoh, B.S.A, Chee, H.L., & Dung Vu, T.K. (2014). "Global householding and the negotiation of intimate labour in commercially-matched international marriages between Vietnamese women and Singaporean men," *Geoforum* 51, pp. 284–293.

Index